Race and Social Analysis

Caroline Knowles

SAGE Publications

London • Thousand Oaks • New Delhi

SAGE Publications Ltd
6 Bonhill Street
London EC2A 4PU

SAGE Publications Inc
2455 Teller Road
Thousand Oaks, California 91320

SAGE Publications India Pvt Ltd
B-42 Panchsheel Enclave
Post Box 4109
New Delhi 100 017

British Library Cataloguing in Publication data

A catalogue record for this book is available from the British Library

ISBN 0 7619 6125 9
ISBN 0 7619 6126 7

Library of Congress control number available

Typeset by C&M Digitals (P) Ltd, Chennai, India
Printed and bound in Great Britain by Athenaeum Press, Gateshead

For David

Contents

Preface

This book is about race-making and forms of social dislocation. These are things that have preoccupied me, personally and intellectually, over many years as a teacher, as a researcher, and as a person trying to make sense of the perplexing world in which we live. Part intellectual/personal autobiography this volume inevitably looks at things from a particular standpoint. White and British with rural roots, the journeys and routes composing my own life have taken me to places where disturbing versions of what it means to be British are in operation. In Nigeria and in various parts of Canada, and most recently in Quebec, I have been firmly reminded of the significance of my national identity on what are postcolonial landscapes. Having to negotiate others' definitions of your identity is a humbling and important experience. Being white British involves a reckoning with a brutal military history of colonial conquest, a connection with postcolonial landscapes, and a present of inequitable multiracialism which does not respect the rights of citizens equally.

Being white British requires a reckoning with the past and a personal politics of the present. It demands a reckoning with forms of social injustice and brutality organised by race and ethnicity: some of the most pressing problems of our time. These autobiographical connections leaked into my research agendas and courses. The key themes of this book are also some of the things I have 'tried out' with students in Nigeria, in Canada and in Britain because I think they are important to the ways in which we think about the world and conduct ourselves in it. This is how this book came to be written.

In writing authors inevitably incur many debts. I would like to mention in this context my former colleagues at the Department of Sociology and Anthropology at Concordia University in Montreal; my present colleagues in the Department of Sociology and Social Policy at the University of Southampton; students at both universities; Stephan Feuchtwang who taught me about race, but who bears no responsibility for the many shortcomings of this book; Alrick Cambridge for many significant discussions on these issues; Douglas Harper who sometimes hung around American bus stops and diners with me discussing race; Wendy Bottero for her careful reading of this book when I was on the point of giving up on it; John Solomos and Claire Alexander for intellectual support of various kinds; Pauline Leonard with whom I have done fieldwork and had a chance to discuss some of the concerns that surface in this book; Susan Halford, Derek McGee, Paul Sweetman, Traute Meyer, Graham Crow and Bernard Harris for those incidental 'in the corridor' discussions that make such a difference to daily life; June and Eric Litton for emotional and practical support of various kinds; Chris Rojek and the team at SAGE; Catherine Hann; and David Mofford, Jessica, Will and Sophia Knowles-Mofford who, in their different ways, shared the dislocations which produced this. The resulting text with all of its imperfections, of course, remains my sole responsibility.

Caroline Knowles
University of Southampton, October 2002

Introduction

Race is all around us

Race and ethnicity[1] operate on the surface and in the deep structures of our world. Intricately woven into the social landscapes in which we live, race is all around us; a part of who we are and how we operate. It is *outside* on our streets and *inside* ourselves. It is part of the way the world operates. It couldn't be closer to home or further away. Let me begin by telling you what is outside my window in Southampton: the departure point for our journey.

An ordinary South of England provincial city, Southampton was once, in the hay days when shipping was a major mode of transport, one of the key arrival and departure points in Britain. Still reinventing itself as a dock in the light of containerisation, and sidelined by air travel, it is now an arrival point of a different sort. Southampton is a designated centre for the dispersal and resettlement of asylum seekers from London and the ports of Southern Britain. Let me briefly introduce you to some of the *people* described by the category 'asylum seeker' whom I met in the local centre offering practical help with resettlement. One of *the* key race issues in Britain and elsewhere, the politics of asylum sits on the British race landscape with hardy perennials such as community/police relations and racial violence and harassment. Asylum dogs our relationship with our French neighbours, and poses uncomfortable questions about the narrowness of the scope of national social policy. Outside of my window and yet out of sight are people I hadn't previously noticed. They come from the Sudan, from Somalia, from Afghanistan, from Turkey and elsewhere. They have escaped from a scale of difficulties that include civil war, political persecution, summary execution of family members and being placed in the army by the Taliban who would 'like to take me (the Afghan refugee I met) for war'. They have come to Britain at great expense and considerable personal danger, leaving their families at home. They have paid large amounts of money in American dollars to smugglers or other middlemen who broker transport, plane tickets and passports. Many of them entered Britain illegally, for there are no other avenues through which they can enter. Understandably they look depressed and anxious. They don't want me to look at them and they don't want me to know their names. These people are tough but their sense of struggle and dislocation is palpable. Sometimes they get upset or even violent when they run up against bureaucratic frustration; they have risked their lives to get here in the first place and are used to overcoming all kinds of obstacles. I sit and listen to some of these obstacles.

Whatever the horrors from which they have fled, their current difficulties are about living in a new country with scant understanding of English and local custom with no money and few support networks. They might need a Home Office travel warrant to get from Southampton to Liverpool for their asylum interview, which will determine whether they can stay in Britain. These take time to process. They may have to pay the train fare and then wait 2–3 months to be reimbursed (in vouchers)[2]. They may live with friends, family or other contacts when they first arrive. They will be staying in a tiny room, and soon they will be under each other's feet and need to find other places to stay. This may involve switching to another part of Britain and another contact or friend. They need to let the Home Office know whenever they move: it is their responsibility to stay in touch and not doing so can jeopardise their asylum claim. Their vouchers, used to buy food, are issued in one place and not easily transferred to another. If they move they will have to wait several months for their voucher supply to resume. They need emergency accommodation and can be sent to a bed and breakfast hotel in a small town outside of Southampton in a taxi. This is additionally difficult if they don't speak much English. After two or three weeks in emergency accommodation they will be dispersed – Southampton can only take 400 single people, Portsmouth 900, Glasgow takes thousands, but families – to any part of Britain. There is no right of refusal. They must take whatever they are offered. Southampton accommodation is in private hands and dotted around the city: old rental properties once used by students are recycled as housing for refugees. Many have severe medical problems. They have only the clothes they are wearing. Where can they get more? Where can they get some canned food until their vouchers start arriving? How will they find the Home Office interview venue in Liverpool from the train station? Will the train get them there in time? Will they be given leave to remain? Or will they find themselves right back where they started?

Outside of my window, and yours too, are matters of global significance. As the tectonic plates composing the global order[3] shift ever so slightly – a regime in one place makes life intolerable for its citizens through famine, war or political persecution – people pick up and move, hoping to make new lives in new places. This is an inevitable consequence of the global order within which we live and of the vast social, economic and political differences, which produce radically different kinds of lives and deaths between places, and sometimes in the same place. The wealth, security and comfort of those of us who live in the G8 countries need not be taken for granted, and we have been served notice that this is so. The inequalities from which we benefit are deeply resented by the kinds of globally organised terrorists who bombed New York and Washington in 2001 and who live unmarked among us. Those who live intimately with the prospect of death and hunger are at our gates seeking asylum, making claims upon what we regard as 'our' resources and challenging the comfort zones we have come to take for granted as 'our' right. These are some of the tangible signs that the implicit pact between rich and poor nations – and rich and poor people within nations – has dramatically broken down.

In the future the security of the global order will need more than a few aid handouts and the cancelling of one or two debts. Barber's (2001) *Jihad vs. McWorld* explores some of these arguments about the new polarities of the global order. We are all part of this system and we need to bear this in mind while we ruminate on our (global) responsibilities to asylum seekers. These are matters of collective culpability and moral responsibility, which reach well beyond the confines of our own society and address its place in the global order of things: matters of global social policy in which there currently seems little interest. Race, ethnicity and national belonging have long operated as ways of thinking about who can come to Britain and on what terms. But these frameworks and their calculations of belonging and entitlement are not up to the tasks confronting us. We need to be able to rethink them in ways that incorporate the effects of the global order that now exists in our neighbour-hoods. That the local is global is by now taken for granted in social analysis. But the precise nature of the mechanisms that connect us and our immediate environment with the global order of things is not much explored. These are matters urgently needing attention; and they are not trivial, but matters of life and death.

Race is mundane

My second set of (two) stories about race operate at a distance from Southampton. We might be tempted to consider them more global, at least from the vantage point of Southampton, but they are, in fact, even more localised in being about personal behaviour. These stories involve people travelling around Los Angeles – a city built for the car – by bus. These different forms of travel – car and bus – correspond with different forms and spheres of social relationships: one privatised, the other inevitably invoking sometimes uneasy forms of human community. We – my travelling companion and I – are sat on a seat shared with a middle aged Hispanic man and a younger woman we took to be his daughter at a bus stop. A young white woman arrives and sits between us and the Hispanic man and daughter. The young white woman is wearing a very short skirt, fishnet stockings and a red scarf. The man and his daughter shift uneasily in their seats and then hastily depart as the young white woman says to them 'if looks could kill'. And then, almost as an after-thought, 'illegal aliens' as she strikes up a conversation with us about why she is, unusually, travelling by bus as if it was this, and not her dealing with the Hispanic man and his daughter, that needed explanation. Its sequel occurred on a bus on the return journey the same day. A young, white, working-class woman gets on the bus with three small children. They tussle with each other for a place on their mother's lap. Sitting facing her are an elderly Chinese couple who are instantly absorbed in the charm of these small children. The young woman, seeing the old man's evident interest, unloads one of the children on to his lap. He beams, the child is thrilled. The other children tus-sle with each other for a place on *his* lap. A moment of racial harmony. This story points to the positives of ethnic, racial and cultural difference. Six people share a warm and humorous moment about being human across lan-guage and cultural boundaries and in which happy noises and beaming smiles stand in for words.

These kinds of boundaries between people are both highly significant and inconsequential at the same time. In the first story, dress styles and versions of womanhood grate against and disturb each other. And, most significantly, the white woman's way of being at ease in the world involved her making the Hispanic man and daughter feel unwelcome in it. A situation with no neces-sary connection between ethnicity, race or dress cultures – the same conflict could quite conceivably have occurred between people who were not marked as different from each other – was readily turned into one as an apparently automatic reflex action. Race is never far beneath the surface of ordinary routine encounters in societies like the US and Britain. It is about who we are and how we operate. Both stories tell us that race is ingrained in the mundane interactions composing the world. The second tells us that it doesn't have to be ingrained in a negative, abusive way. Race is about people, lives and circumstances.

Race shapes the global order in which we live

I suggested earlier that race touched on some fundamental matters of life and death. What I meant was that these themes are ordinary, everyday matters and very near the surface of events and processes that draw the contours of our time. I am suggesting that race – and ethnicity, for these two things com-monly operate in tandem – occupy a central position in the social morphology[4] of our time. The last decade of the twentieth century saw the disintegration of the former Soviet Union and the former Yugoslavia and the establishment of smaller political units around claims of common ethnicity. Ethnic cleans-ing, as part of the establishment of ethnic claims in these territories (and in Rwanda) pursued by military means, has produced dramatic and continuous incidences of genocide and the large scale relocation of people into new, usually equally poor, neighbouring states. There was an outburst of genocide in Borneo in the summer of 2001, Nigeria totters on the brink of murderous ethnic conflict as Sharia law is introduced in Northern states, the Israeli/Palestine conflict descends into new levels of barbarity, and Afghan refugees, like the one in Southampton, pour into Pakistan. These, of course, are precisely the kinds of mechanisms that bring asylum seekers to our neighbourhoods. Matters of life and death.

The traffic in human cargo these landscapes of death have produced has serious consequences. Iraqi Kurds are walked through Greece by traffickers, take trains, trucks and leaky boats often with tragic consequences for some, and profitable consequences for others (*Guardian* 27 March 2000). The summer of 2000 revealed 60 Chinese asylum seekers in the back of a truck; 58 of them already dead when they arrived in Dover. And this tragedy has been repeated since, on a smaller scale. Bodies and borders: distinctions between political regimes and calculations of safety and danger; life and death emerge as political landscapes shift regimes and allegiances. I am not suggesting that these situations are caused by the things we refer to as race and ethnicity, but I am suggesting that race and ethnicity play a significant part in their operation. Race and ethnicity, in other words, play a pivotal role in the political contours of the global order in which we live; in its regimes, in the balancing of tolerance and terror, and in the connections drawn between places by human bodies searching for less terrible lives. These kinds of situations reveal the centrality of race in forming the social morphology, the shape, of our time.

Ethnicity is about a series of connections

This book does not tackle those important issues of genocide and ethnic cleansing, others do this more effectively, but I do want to flag them as important issues composing the global ethnic landscape that this book describes and to underscore the salience of ethnicity. The way people cope in the face of death are matters of great importance. The relationship between ethnicity and violence and the operation of ethnicity in ethnic cleansing are serious and perplexing issues. I want to raise them as a significant part of the current political landscape, even though I have nothing to add to what others have said about them. In reviewing what others have written we can learn something about ethnicity, and in the process shift this introductory discussion from establishing the central significance of race and ethnicity in the world in which we live, to considering the relationship between race and ethnicity and social analysis.

One of the difficulties with understanding the relationship between ethnicity and violence, and which surfaces in a different way not directly connected with violence in this volume, is the difficulty of disentangling ethnicity (and race) from the many other circumstances in which they interact. This is a recurring concern in this book, and the inevitable practical and analytic difficulties this causes are noted. So for this reason, as well as for a more general political significance, it is worth exploring a little further how ethnicity operates in the context of ethnic cleansing.

Box's (2000) discussion of Bosnia Herzegovina gives a flavour of some of what is involved in this. His description is set in 1992 in the South Western part of war-ravaged Bosnia Herzegovina in an area that the Croat army and Bosnian Croat militias had recently purged of Serbs. Box's paper is about the pilgrimage centre of Medjugorje. The centre had a difficult relationship with the local church, which itself had a problematic history of relations with the Vatican. Across the street from this pilgrimage enterprise was the leader of the local division of Territorial Defence, an organisation founded as part of the old regime of Tito. In one house, writes Box, there was a world of peace, unity and tolerance propagated by Mary, the mother of God, by way of the Croat Catholic seers and led by the local Catholic priests, the Franciscan Friars. In the other house there was a world of absolute intolerance, cruel and heinous violence, genocide and ethnic cleansing. The two worlds of 'faith' and violence are closely linked. The people were part of the same age-old and tightly knit regional network of Catholic Croat religious nationalists and local violence formations. This was the network responsible for 'cleansing' the Muslim population in South West Bosnia Herzegovinia [A mixture of] 'old resentment and new opportunities' (Box, 2000: 18). This offers the briefest of views of the (uneven) connections of which ethnicity, faith and regimes of violence are capable. Ethnicity clearly activates all sorts of other factors which are not to do with ethnicity, but become connected with it in certain situations. Ethnicity (like race) is a host of some sort: it is activated by, and in turn activates, other things. It is not inherently significant, only contextually so. This example, of course, raises all sorts of questions about the interactions between ethnicity and violence in which the violence part is even more poorly understood than the complicated operation of ethnicity.

Modernity, ethnicity and violence

Elwert, Feuchtwang and Neubert (1999: 9) take matters a little further. They point out that the violence of ethnic cleansing is not a regression to atavistic instincts but a strategic, if limited, choice. They argue that violence always has social channels, a set of dynamics and a broader social context in which it is understood:

> the political arrangements we are used to are not fixed. Insides are broken and turned inside out. New insides are created, often with extreme violations of physical boundaries. The re-inscriptions of territory and the violations of the bodies of residents of the former Yugoslavian federal state, the zones of terror and counter terror in Sri Lanka, the weak frontiers of central Francophone Africa (Burundi, Rwanda, and Congo/Zaire) and of Liberia and Sierra Leone are some of the recent reminders ... Political differences and social exclusions, as well as regional differences, make fragmentation and the remaking of totality and continuity an issue and a condition of the body politic. (1999: 25)

They conclude that modernity goes together with an increase in collective violence (1999: 26); a connection Bauman (1999) also makes in the context of the holocaust. The uncomfortable message is that genocide and ethnic cleansing – the systematic annihilation of lives marked by race and ethnicity – is not the aberration of modernity, but its logical, horrific, accomplishment. If ethnicity was once considered a safe and politically more neutral term than race with its association with racism, then ethnic cleansing reasserts ethnicity's terrible power. Herzfeld (1992: 184) locates this problem more broadly, in *The Social Production of Indifference*. It is not just violence but the destructive routinised inaction, the other side of violence, which for Herzfeld is the real problem (1992: 33). We will return to indifference in discussing the relationship between people and racialised regimes in Chapter 1, at this point it is enough to signal some connection between genocide, ethnic cleansing and indifference.

Death and indifference, both of which settle on ethnicity and race as important human differences (as forms of classification) are key problems of our time. This points to the centrality of race and ethnicity in present political landscapes and their implication in its more lethal and inhuman consequences. In modernity's combination of 'benefits and disaster', race and ethnicity have become a major force: a cause of conflict and a reason for celebration (Riggs, 1998: 269–70). The anthropologist Edmund Leach pointed out that killing is an act of classification (Herzfeld, 1992: 174). Race and ethnicity, matters of life and death, are central in understanding the configuration of current events and the contours of the global order. But these things cannot be accessed, as the discussions held by Elwert, Feuchtwang, Neubert, Bauman and Herzfeld indicate, without social analysis. My LA and Southampton stories also underscore this point. They were told in a way that made connections and looked beneath the surface of things; and these are some of the features of social analysis I want to explore a little further.

Social analysis – the connections between things

Because social analysis can mean many things it is important to specify how it is defined in this particular volume. Social analysis is about what people do. It is about the social processes or mechanisms composing lives. It is about how people comport themselves in the world in relation to each other and in relation to the things composing material cultures. Social analysis is *not* these things – these things are life – but a narrative, a way of speaking, about them. A whole range of people are interested in these things. Those with a professional concern include cultural theorists, social geographers, modern historians, social anthropologists, social policy analysts and sociologists. Thankfully, concern with the human condition is not limited to those with a professional interest. One of the problems this poses, as Giddens (1987: vii) points out, is that social analysis is parasitic on common sense, on what everyone already knows. So is what everybody already knows social analysis? Giddens says no. What everyone already knows is received wisdom. And received wisdom may or may not be a reasonable interpretation of events or situations. That we live in a 'global society' is a piece of social analysis that has dropped into popular thought. So things may not be as clear-cut as Giddens implies in saying that received wisdom is not social analysis.

Let's put it another way; what is it about what people do and the social processes composing lives that we call social analysis? Is the description of these things, for example, social analysis? It rather depends on the extent of arrangement and rearrangement of the world embedded in description. All descriptions involve the arrangement of things. But are they descriptions that extend our understanding of the world? Do they reveal what is not apparent or already known? Do they show things that were not apparent or visible? Social analysis then, as it is used in this volume, involves discovery, it reveals the connections between things. In this scheme of things social analysis is a systematic approach to the understanding of social life (Giddens, 1987: 109–10). Goffman is, in this respect, a major social theorist for his ability to take the routine and the mundane (the fabric of social analysis) and reveal its inner mechanisms (Giddens, 1987: 110). It is in this broad sense that I use the term social analysis in this volume.

Social analysis – lives and landscapes

There is more to it than this. The kind of social analysis I am concerned with is about the connections between things of different scope and scale. It is concerned with how the smallest of things and individual people are connected with the bigger social landscapes in which their lives are set. Capturing the particular in social processes and seeing the connections with bigger social landscapes is what C. Wright Mills referred to as the 'sociological imagination' Wright Mills, 1970: 12). He meant this in a non-disciplinary sense to refer from the 'most impersonal and remote transformations' to the 'most intimate features of the human self' and to the relations between the two (Wright Mills, 1970: 14). Social analysis then, in the sense in which this term is activated in this volume is used as C. Wright Mills (1970: 14) intended it, to situate 'the personal troubles of the milieu' in the 'public issues of social structure'. These, of course, are some of the compositional mechanisms of the (raced) social fabric itself.

Social analysis, as I have already suggested in my opening stories, is about what happens in our neighbourhoods: or, rather, it is an attempt to think systematically about what happens in our neighbourhoods. Most, although not all, of what happens, should be amenable to social analysis as I have just described it. An uncovering of the connections between things of different scope and scale. In Mill's terms the conduits connecting small things with bigger things, the particular and specific with the general, and our place as individual people in the world order, are at the centre of social analysis. Here, in thinking about the asylum seekers in Southampton we have an opportunity to consider the private troubles of individuals and the broader social and historical processes of which they are a part: social analysis. Social analysis must be about what is happening around us or what is its use? Social analysis leads from your neighbourhood to the global order of things. It concerns the women on the Los Angeles bus, and people from afar who have trodden a path to your area. It is about world distribution, the neighbourhood and individual human reactions. Social analysis is about all of these different levels of scope and scale. This book suggests ways of doing social analysis that will work on the buses and in the neighbourhoods of the global order; that has something to say about the Southampton asylum seekers and the racial politics of the Los Angeles bus. It is grounded in what people *do* and in the ways in which the world *works*.

Social analysis is spatial

Buses and neighbourhoods, Los Angeles, Southampton and the global order of things suggest another key aspect of social analysis and another form of *grounding* in the spatial. This book is about people and places and the conduits connecting people and places. How we move around and make ourselves at home in the world are central issues in the lives of asylum seekers, in the lives of the Hispanic Americans and the white woman at the bus stop. We cannot understand these people without understanding their routes and the nature of their journeys: the ways in which they occupy and move through space. These things are fundamental to who they are in the world. The work of Lefebvre and Massey is helpful in pinpointing the social texture of local and global space, as we will see in later chapters. Social analysis then, is not just about people and human action, but the places in which people live their lives, or pass through on their journeys to somewhere else. Space matters: it is, as this book will reveal, indispensable in comprehending the way things *are* and the way things *work*.

Materialism

Contemporary social analysis is heavily bound up with narrative – with what people say and with the way things are presented. This has resulted in a sense of scepticism as people recognise the emptiness of impression management and acknowledge, especially in politics, that it is as important to look at what actually happens in *practice* as well as at what is said about things. Social analysis in this volume is heavily materialist. It is about what *people do* and the social and political implications of that. People's lives are bound up with social relationships, activities and with the objects of our material culture. Objects exceed the classificatory systems in which they originate and have an existence, a 'thingness', of their own (Pinney, 2001). Objects, argues Pinney have agency, they are cultural agency objectified, compressed performativity. The *things* of everyday life are a part of who we are and how we operate in the world at large. So this is a kind of social analysis that insists on the significance of the everyday world of objects for themselves and not as part of a bigger system of signification, although they are undoubtedly also that, just as they also have symbolic properties. My insistence on the materiality of things extends also to concepts which are, by definition, not material, but which none the less have *material* dimensions – practices and implications – in people's lives, like race and ethnicity.

Here we need to think a little bit about theories of race and ethnicity and what my claims about materialism actually mean. I am not suggesting that race is an objective condition of existence: that races are 'real' divisions of human kind. This kind of view – put to rest by the UNESCO statement of 1948 – has repeatedly reared its ugly head in the shape of race and IQ debates, which assert that intelligence and sexuality are distributed across distinguishable gene pools that we can refer to as 'races'. This kind of argument has led to the counter assertion that race is a social myth, an ideological or discursive construct underwriting forms of racial exclusion and disadvantage. As Winant (2000: 183–84) helpfully suggests, race is neither an illusion nor a biological fact. It has a salience and a social reality in everyday lives, in the ways in which people think about themselves and others, in social relationships and social processes, in the operation of global and local space and in the ways in which societies are organised.

These are some of the terms of a materialist social analysis. We will encounter them again later. This book is concerned with the concrete universe of things and places and people, and with the concrete aspects of the abstract, arranged as social categories. These form part of what I mean by materialist: a concern with how things are made – not just how they are represented or narrated. By materialist analysis I mean that I am concerned with the elements composing race and ethnicity. I am also concerned with the ways in which race and ethnicity operate in fabricating social positions. I am concerned with how race and ethnicity *work*, their grammar, the social practices to which race and ethnicity give rise. It is not that discourse, narrative, symbolism and representation are unimportant. Quite the contrary, it is often only through these things that we can access the material. It is race's narratives that alert us to its social practices. But a materialist analysis is one in which narrative, discourse, symbolism and representation *are interrogated for their material substance*. I said earlier that this book was about race-making and forms of dislocation. These are concepts made from material things: bodies moving between places, concrete activities that play a part in the making of people and their interface with social systems. Shotter (1997) helps us with the materialist approach by conceptualising the making of personhood (see Chapter 1) in relational, rather than representational, terms. In the dialogues of social interaction selves are made as ongoing acts of invention. And selves are made in racial and ethnic terms.

Social analysis and race

Despite its centrality in the calibration of the world in which we live, social analysis is rarely approached through the prism of race, which, like gender, has developed as a separate domain of understanding in standard university courses on social studies and on publishers' lists. This book is an attempt to nudge it into the mainstream; to insist that race is a central, not peripheral part of the way things work. I have insisted that a central feature of social analysis is its ability to explain the world in which we live. Race is, as I suggested earlier, central to understanding the world in which we live, the troubles of our time and the individual lives composing it, and this qualifies it as a central object of social analysis. Allow me to expand on this theme of the centrality of race in the making of our time, and develop my earlier point about the asylum seekers in Southampton and the interactions on the Los Angeles bus. Exploring the meaning, significance and operation of race (and ethnicity) in the shaping of the modern world is one of the key themes of this book. The point of examining race and social analysis is precisely this kind of understanding that will, hopefully, unfold as we progress on our journey. At this point it is important to point out that race and ethnicity are often used together in this book and sometimes they are used interchangeably. Sometimes one of these concepts takes centre stage and the other a back seat depending on the context. These concepts are not synonymous (Goldberg, 1993: 79), they have separate intellectual histories and (sometimes) spheres of application, but they are closely identified and often operate in tandem. What I have to say about the centrality of race in the modern world applies also to ethnicity. So, unless I want to make a point specifically about ethnicity I will just say race for the sake of the simplicity of the sentence. If, in the mix of things I am discussing ethnicity plays a central part, then I will use the term ethnicity. These are matters of balance and simplicity in sentence construction.

Race lends itself ideally to the kind of analytic framework outlined earlier. If we want to understand race then we need an analytic framework that addresses divergent levels of scope and scale, for race is simultaneously very personal and built into the structures of societies and the global order of things. Winant (1994a: 37) argues that race is 'engraved on our beings, and perceptions, upon our identities' while simultaneously constructing the broader social landscape of the racial order in which they are cast. Broader patterns of racialisation create new racial subjects and transform existing ones (Winant, 1994a: 58). Race is a way of life and a way of being in the poetics of the racial order[5]. By extension the (micro) racial orders of locales and (macro) racial orders of nation states and the connections between them, are set within the broader geographies of globalisation, and Winant (1994a: 18) insists that we grapple with these racial dynamics of globalisation although he doesn't suggest how we might go about this. He does, nevertheless, point the way to a raced version of globalisation (as does Hesse, 1999); and in this volume we will walk a little further down this path and see where it leads:

> The battle for racial justice is fought not only in the open political arena of the state and social movements, not only in the struggle for adequate social representation, significations and consciousness of difference; it is also fought on the interior terrain of the individual – his/her intra psychic world and immediate relationships. (Winant, 1994a: 168)

Winant proposes that the analysis of race has a personal as well as a global dimension. I very much agree with Winant on this too, although, as with globalisation, he does not suggest how this might be pursued. People are at the centre of the analytic frame I put forward in this book, albeit in a limited way. I do not deal with the unconscious or with emotions, both highly significant in people-centred conceptualisations of race and which need much more investigation. Race and ethnicity are evidently about the unconscious and about emotions. Gunaratnam and Lewis' (2001) analysis of race in social work points to the feelings of anger and fear surrounding race, and yet which never enter into what we write about it. How can emotion – fear and hatred – not be involved in the corporeal violation of some versions of ethnic cleansing, in Rwanda for example, where ethnic bodies were not just extinguished but mutilated. Race is about people, their emotions, their routine activities and the manner in which they experience the world. As Winant (1994a: 164) says of Brazil, 'the significance of race combines with constant, daily practical reminders that race is as crucial a factor as ever in shaping life chances and experience'; a way of knowing and interpreting the social world that it is emblematic of human difference; that stands for more than it is.

I have insisted that social analysis addresses practical things that are happening around us. But as soon as we start to comment on these things we are inevitably in the business of words. This is how academics ply their trade: words on words. In writing this book I select and explore the words other people have written and which have a bearing on the themes composing the general approach to social analysis I have set out. Sometimes other people's words are used as stepping-stones and sometimes more critically displaced as a way of moving things in a different direction. But the selected writing of others helps, one way or another, to reach the ultimate goal, which is to extend our understanding of how things work in relation to race and ethnicity, with the refugees in our neighbourhoods and the social relationships of the LA bus in the centre of things. So, while my words are words on word too, they are words that hold people and things at the centre of the research frame – a materialist analysis. This could not have been written without the writing of others, an indispensable part of the struggle for understanding, and a precursor to social change.

This book suggests more practical ways of seeing things and contains alternative research agendas, which are inevitably, unexecuted, for this is the nature of this kind of book. The themes chosen have practical relevance in exploring the world around us. They are also central concerns in contemporary social theory and have something to teach us about the racial grammar of the world in which we live. By grammar I do not mean the underlying principles by which race works – there is no such thing – but the social practices to which race gives rise; or the things race makes happen. Racial grammar is practical and embodied: a set of outcomes furnishing our selves and our landscapes. It is talked and walked by human bodies with skin operating in space and time. It operates in the way white people strut around Budleigh Salterton in Devon and the illegal transit of asylum seekers. It is burnt into the built environment of grand heritage buildings and ethnic ghettos. The overall aim of this book is to piece some of these things together as a way of understanding how the world works through race: its racial grammar. What I have just said about race is also good for ethnicity. Ethnicity sometimes has its own grammar and sometimes contributes to the grammar of race. These, then, are the basic principles of a materialist analysis on which this volume was constructed. Now we will take a closer look at some of its content.

Content of this volume

Chapter 1 places people at the centre of the analytic frame and makes a case for understanding individual difference, social agency and the existential dimensions of lives. It contains a discussion of the contemporary meaning of subjectivity, of what it means to be a person in the world today. It is about what makes the racial and ethnic texture of people and about their place in the bigger scheme of things. It examines the interface between people and racialised regimes by looking at the people part of race and ethnicity-making. This compositional approach to race is, of course, quite different from essentialist positions that hold that race is about the distribution of traits through distinguishable gene pools. In fact this chapter focuses on anthropological work on ethnicity, on performance and clothes as part of the weaving of the social fabric. Too subtle for race-making, these things have found a place in the literature on ethnicity and so they form the focus and race takes a back seat in this chapter. Chapter 2 extends the work of Chapter 1, placing raced subjectivity in the context of auto/biography as stories of lives and deaths. This chapter explores what can be learned about the landscapes of race from individual lives. It examines the ways in which race inflects lives and the relationship between lives and histories. It traces the conduits connecting lives with bigger social units from local communities and nations, reflecting on the social templates revealed in auto/biographical work concerned with race. The material for this chapter is drawn from the auto/biographies of African Americans, as this is a genre of race writing that is more developed in America than in Britain. Unlike Chapter 1, this chapter is focused on race with ethnicity playing a subsidiary part. These, of course, are matters of political processes and their discourses. The purpose of these first two chapters is to pin down some of the aspects of racial grammar that centre on people, forms of human agency and volition, in the making of selves and the regimes of which selves are composed.

Chapters 3, 4 and 5 discuss *key mechanisms in race-making* – in space, globalisation and migration. These are also important themes in contemporary social analysis. Chapter 3 sets out some of the spatial contours of race and ethnicity – which are given equal importance in this chapter – and shows how space contains important clues about social morphology and racial grammar. Urban segregation, turf wars, nation, belonging, entitlement, commemoration and memory are some of the ways race and ethnicity feature in the arrangement and social relationships of space. Further possibilities for understanding racial grammar through space are explored here: the architectural politics of the built environment, embodied performance, pathways and movement and social relationships and practices. Space, I argue, operates as an archive and as a log of raced and ethnicised human agency. Space forms an indispensable part of a materialist analysis of race.

Chapter 4 pursues the spatial contours of race and ethnicity which, again, have equal status in this chapter, in examining the racial and ethnic grammar of globalisation. This chapter establishes what a number of writers have suspected but not fully demonstrated: the ways in which globalisation is a story of race and ethnicity. Taking globalisation theory to task for its levels of abstraction and inattention to social processes, this chapter suggests that we can make an analysis of race in any circumstances that have a global resonance. It traces some of the grammar of race in the context of the global adoption of babies, the trade in human organs, the Thai sex industry and the activities of Central West African traders. It argues that we can trace the racial grammar of globalisation through colonial connections, through understanding migration and in the local setting of urban life.

Chapter 5 pursues the 'people movement' side of globalisation in more detail, in an examination of routines of movement and dwelling, belonging and displacement. This chapter separates different kinds of movement and displacement through an examination of circumstances of arrival and departure in individual migration stories, contrasting asylum seekers with lifestyle migrants in Hong Kong. Both Chapters 4 and 5 contribute to conceptualising the geographies of global migration and the place of individual stories within them. Understanding the global calibration of race and ethnicity is indispensable to a materialist analysis.

Chapter 6 examines the social mechanisms of race-making involved in the production of whiteness. Why whiteness? White race-making is highly significant given the privileged position of whiteness in the racial grammar of globalisation. It is as important to understand the composition of racial privilege, as it is to understand the composition of race through disadvantage. Critical white studies uncover whiteness, but not in the ways I suggest in Chapter 6. How whiteness operates in postcolonial landscapes is an important political question that has ramifications in the operation of global politics and the local politics of multi-racialism. Drawing on the lessons of subjectivity and space aired earlier in the book, this chapter examines the contributions of boundaries and performance, everyday experience, consciousness and subjectivity and the significance of empire in the making of white Britishness. But this occurs in the broader landscapes of empire and draws on American, Canadian and Australian versions of whiteness, which have a force in their respective nation-building projects. This chapter brings together some of the themes developed in earlier chapters, and applies them to understanding whiteness. It asks critical questions about culpability, which arise from the emphasis placed on the social agency of people. What is the culpability of white people in the operation of racialised regimes? Problematising whiteness draws the analysis away from problematising blackness and other forms of racialised/ethnicised otherness and places the culpability for racial and ethnic distinctions back where it belongs.

Like all attempts at social analysis *Race and Social Analysis* struggles to keep up with events on a rapidly moving social landscape. Social scientists are always trying to catch up with events, trying to make sense of the things others just get on with. A profession driven by angst! I am, for example, acutely aware that like others, I am trying to make sense of human agency and subjectivity at a time when what it means to be a person is being rewritten by developments in cloning and the decoding of DNA. We have finally discovered the blueprint for how people are made, and we have discovered new ways of replicating ourselves which allow us to produce children as a source of organs and tissue for others. This raises serious questions about what it means to be human and to participate in forms of association that come with this. All of this has implications for race. As does the shift to non-face to face forms of communication and association made possible in cyber technology. In the future will race matter less or simply matter in new ways?

Overall, this project is about the conceptualisation of things by examining how they actually work. As I said earlier, it is a materialist analysis grounded in the practical actions and accomplishments of people in time and place. Its themes: subjectivity, space, migration and globalisation are part of the familiar repertoire of late modernist and postmodernist analysis. Many of the architects of these analyses claim or admit that these things are to do with race. But often they are not able to say *how* in concrete terms and so these connections remain rather nebulous. This is not just because the connection of these themes with race and ethnicity is not properly thought through – although often it is not – but rather because of a more general problem, which is to do with the abstract character of much contemporary social analysis. Enormously evocative, much writing on migration, globalisation, space and subjectivity omits a proper encounter with concrete, material, social processes, as the idea of 'flow', divorced from its mechanisms of operation in the literature on globalisation demonstrates. These themes are often abstract in the first place, and then race is run across their surface without breaking it; without penetrating the surface of the concept and trying to piece together its contribution to race-making. The result is that race, with a couple of notable exceptions, has had only a rhetorical relationship with contemporary social theory. This state of affairs was one of the catalysts for this book. As I suggested earlier, race works through social processes and is embedded in the social fabric of most societies and it is, given its place in the social arrangement of life, death and inequality, important that we understand how it operates. Like ethnicity, race is a concept with a body count. It cannot have a rhetorical relationship with social analysis because it does not have a rhetorical relationship with the world social analysis purports to understand; rather, it has a material relationship to it. Race composition and racial grammar are the keys to a more concrete and thorough analysis of race and suggesting what this understanding might look like is the overall objective of this book.

Social contexts

One last piece of framing. Because this book is centrally concerned with spatial aspects of social analysis it is important to say something about the places that are drawn on to provide examples and demonstrations of the argument. Places are, of course, particular and always indicated in the text. The places I draw on are Britain, the United States, Canada and, sometimes, Australia. There are important differences between these places in terms of the ways in which race works in them. The political landscapes of race are quite particular. This is not just a matter of looking at national differences, although this is relevant. There are significant microclimates in some places. There are important differences across Canada, for example, in terms of migrant populations, individual and collective histories of migration and settlement, and the relationship between migration and nation building. Vancouver looks to the West and the Pacific rim for its arrivals and historic exclusions. Its current migrants are wealthy. Toronto traditionally leans towards the Caribbean and the less affluent, but now has a substantial Chinese population in the suburb of Markham hedging its bets on the long-term effects of government in Beijing on Hong Kong. Quebec with its own forms of nationalism is quite different again. Often in *Race and Social Analysis* I bring together material and examples from Britain and the United States and so it is important to underscore the differences between these race-political landscapes when they are wielded in this fragmented form to make a point. Even though they are historically linked (as are Canada and Australia) through empire and migration, Britain and America had quite different relationships to empire business and to the (Black) Atlantic slave trade. Each made and sustained whiteness by different routes: even if the migrants of one provided nation building material for the other.

The United States instituted and sustained formal juridical means of racial separation of white citizens and black sub-citizens. Britain never had to do this on home soil, where the mechanisms of racial segregation were less formalised and historically more recent. But Britain had legally encoded systems of racial differentiation in the territories of the empire effecting more formal means of racial classification than were ever practised in Britain. The East African empire, particularly in Kenya, operated a system of practical racial apartheid. The United States industrialised on a racially complex landscape from the vestiges of slavery. Britain industrialised in a less evidently racialised way. Or perhaps it is more accurate to say that the racialised aspects of British industrialisation operated across the distance of empire rather than at home. The political landscape of the United States was much later marked by large-scale, black-led social movements (Civil Rights) and it had more highly developed forms of affirmative action. The ripples of these movements hit British shores: only partly a case of living vicariously, Black Power took specifically British forms providing impetus and inspiration in the forays of the Black Power's leaders such as Stokely Carmichael and Malcolm X, across the Atlantic to Britain. There was an important and powerful global circulation of ideas and political tactics and forms linking Britain and America around the black leadership offered in the Black

Power Movements of the 60s and its precursors in the Harlem renaissance in the 1940s[6]. America offered mentors and leadership in black struggles on which parallel movements in Britain drew. Britain operated at the fulcrum of empire and later the post-empire landscape of the commonwealth and its late twentieth century migration flows. Canada and Australia are part of the British Commonwealth; the graduate class of empire. They were connected with Britain and other parts of the empire by various means including migrations around the empire that are poorly documented and understood. Like the US, Canada and Australia had complicated racialised nation-building projects through which they aimed to maintain themselves as white nations, a situation which persisted until well into the postcolonial period of the 1960s.

Having advanced my scheme for race and social analysis and stressed the importance of practical understanding I will end this introduction on a humble and uncertain note considering the place of understanding – and by implication social analysis – in the overall scheme of things. The ethnic cleansing exercises of the twentieth century serve as a stark reminder that the mobilisation of understanding is no simple business. Understanding something and effectively dealing with it politically are two quite different enterprises. For those of us who research race and ethnicity in the liberal belief that to crack something open and critically examine its composition leads to understanding as a first step in addressing social injustice; there is a disconcerting lack of progress when it comes to race and ethnicity. The mobilisation of knowledge in political projects is one of the most challenging problems of our time, and disconcertingly few academics struggle with it. As the volumes of academic research on race and ethnicity accumulate; as declarations of racialised human rights become more extensively incorporated into the machinery of governance and commercial practice; so the acts of human barbarity executed on its behalf mount just as fast. The accumulated mountain of narrative confronts the equally large accumulated and ghastly mountain of bodies and forms of mutilation piled up in the ethnic cleansing operations that dogged the twentieth century and show no signs of abating in the twenty first. Does understanding race and ethnicity make no difference at all in terms of practical and political outcomes? Does it actually make things worse? I am sustained here by two thoughts. Lefebvre (1994: 5) says that all interpretation is transformative. It is difficult in the circumstances to see the wisdom of this, and hard not to become despondent. And, second, Winant (1994a: 18) stresses the importance of contemporary political relationships. How do we activate what we learn in the service of more enlightened forms of human community? We may not be doing any good in writing about race and ethnicity, but we have no option in the circumstances but to plod on. But it is futile to hope that at some point it will make a difference. We have to find imaginative ways of mobilising what we know in the service of making a difference and it is not at all obvious how to do this. The alternative is to do nothing; and doing nothing is collusion with the way things are.

Being white British, once a source of automatic pride, is now a source of shame and embarrassment. How difficult it is to be British! Social analysis has auto/biographical supports. For me, as for other whites who write about race, race is more than an exercise in self-understanding and angst. For many of us the issue is to find a way to be who we are that does not sustain, but actively challenges, the racial order in which our nation and its people are cast. We receive daily reminders of this racial order and our own comfortable position within it and in the racial harassment and attacks, which show no sign of diminishing in various parts of Britain and in the highly qualified reception given to asylum seekers. So while our efforts might be ineffectual in the larger scheme of things, we have no option but to pursue the path of understanding and social change through political engagement because of who we are, and because the world demands it.

Summary

- Race and ethnicity work on a number of levels in organising the social world. They operate at the level of the personal, the structural, the global and are engrained in who we are and what we do in the world in our routine activities. They are inextricably bound up with the texture of social life.
- Social analysis is about the connections between things which are not apparent on the surface. A materialist social analysis is concerned with the connections – at different levels of scope and scale – between people and places and things.

Racial/ethnic grammar: the social practices to which race/ethnicity give rise.

Social morphology: refers to the ways in which the values and priorities of a society are built into the arrangement and use of space. Space can, in this case, be interpreted as an archive of society's values.

Race and ethnicity: Concepts, ideas, referring to social and political (but not biological) distinctions made between people. Race and ethnicity are arbitrary social inventions, which form part of the broader social context in which they have meaning and a force in practice. Their power lies in the force they have in people's thinking, actions and practices, and in their effect on the way things are organised. This volume emphasises these things as part of a materialist analysis. Referring to the arbitrary character of race Mason (1994) says that there are no races but there is race. The same is true for ethnicity: there are no ethnic groups but there is ethnicity. Mason continues that it is racism that establishes the social character of race. And, by extension it is the nature of the forms of meaning, differentiation, exclusion and annihilation that establish the social character of ethnicity. Ethnicity is often used to carve finer social distinctions than are referred to by race. And for this reason it is more closely aligned with individual notions of identity. Anyone interested in following these things up should read Miles (1989, 1996), Back and Solomos (2000), Goldberg (1993) and Hall (1991a).

Notes

1. To write 'race and ethnicity' every time is clumsy to read. Race and ethnicity are not the same but often operate together. I use race when I am talking about both in a circumstance in which race is the dominant concept in operation. When I use ethnicity race may also be in operation but in a subordinate position. On occasions when I refer to race and ethnicity, it is to draw particular attention to their combination. Race and ethnicity have different, and circumstantially generated, meanings. They have separate intellectual histories and political commitments. These things will be clear by the end of this book as part of what is embedded in it is the gradual unravelling of these concepts, their intellectual frameworks and their analytical possibilities. Consequently I don't want to give pen-sketch definitions at this point, not least because their complexity works against it.

2. The British government announced the phasing out of the voucher scheme as a way of providing material support for asylum seekers in November 2001. Cash is to replace vouchers as part of an overhaul of the asylum scheme that includes 'smart' ID cards but still gives asylum seekers a living standard 30 per cent below the official poverty line drawn in income support. The controversial dispersal policy remains. The legislative framework for this is the 1999 Immigration and Asylum Act under which Britain attempts to balance its moral obligations under the 1951 UN Convention on the Status of Refugees with a speeded up decision-making process on asylum applications at the same time as assuaging popular opinion that Britain is a 'soft touch'.

3. What is meant by the term global order is explored in Chapter 3.

4. Social morphology is a term used by Lefebvre (1996: 89–95) to refer to the ways in which the arrangement and use of space reveals the texture of a society, showing the contours of its values, its moral geography. The social practices of society create society's space and are revealed analytically in its examination (Lefebvre, 1996: 38).

5. Poetics is used in this context in a way that is inspired by Bachelard (1994: xv–xvi) to invoke the actuality, the novelty and the dynamism of things as poetic images with no causality or archetypal features. Poetics refers to a kind of ontology, a philosophical study of the nature of being but which does not look for laws or regular features but accepts the particularity of things. The racial order is a term used by Winant (1994a: 267) to refer to the racial structuration of societies and the global connections between them in various and flexible forms as the exterior side in social policy and political organisation where it takes certain forms in the organisation of inclusion and exclusion. Winant contrasts this to the interior side of race, which is about the marking of personal identity by the racial order in which one lives. It may be useful to identify these two different aspects but clearly, as *Race and Social Analysis* will show, they are closely connected. Winant (1994a: 270) argues for racial formation theory, the context for racial order. In racial formation theory race is not the product of some other, more significant, social distinction but is itself a fundamental organising principle of contemporary social life. In this context, says Winant, 'race can be defined as a concept which signifies and symbolises sociopolitical conflicts and interests in reference to different types of human bodies'. I agree with his project, if not the forms of its execution. So, in the poetics of racial orders, I refer to the ways in which race works, situationally, as a people-centred social enterprise in shaping the contours of our time.

6. Transatlantic dimensions to Black politics in the era of civil rights consisted of theoretical/educational aspects, organisational and political aspects and mentoring. In all of these aspects America provided forms of leadership for what was happening in Britain. African American thinkers and academics provided role models and intellectual impetus in Black liberation politics. There was a Black Panther Party in Britain and a branch of the Universal Coloured People's Association. The British Journal *Black Liberator* provided a third world view of race in social movements influenced by Cuba and China as well as by the US, discussing black struggles from which important lessons could be learned. While the transatlantic

(English speaking) axis was important Black liberation politics in the 1960s and 1970s had a global thrust. Many of the leaders of the struggle for black liberation in America visited Britain and there were parallel forms of political action organised. (Information provided in discussion with Alrick Cambridge who was involved in this movement as a British Jamaican and one-time editor of Black Liberator.)

Chapter One
People and Race Making

Mini Contents

Introduction

Race is about *race making* just as ethnicity, too is about its own production. Everything is *made* and race and ethnicity are not exceptions. In understanding how things are made we can understand, too, their operation in the world; their grammar – the forms of social practice to which they give rise. Understanding how things are made is an important part of a materialist analysis. It is important to distinguish the understanding of *how* things are made from the understanding *that* things are made. The understanding that we have come to lean on, that race and ethnicity are socially produced, has not always offered, as it should, descriptions of the mechanisms of their production; of the ways in which they are made. Obviously race making is a complicated business and a concern that runs throughout this volume. In this chapter I make a modest start on the project of understanding race making. I refer to race making but in fact some of the best insights into these processes are worked out in relation to ethnicity, so race making in this context is shorthand for both.

Race making is about people. I don't mean that it has *something* to do with people. No one would disagree with that. I mean that it is centrally about people, enough to put people in the centre of the analytic frame so that the nature of the world and the means of its analysis are brought into alignment. My purpose in this chapter is to make the argument that race *making* is highly significant in understanding what social scientists refer to as race; and to show that race making is crucially about people. The centrality of people to understanding the operation of race and key aspects of race making are unravelled together in this chapter, which also points to some of the practical and analytical benefits of seeing things in this way.

We will begin with the argument that people are the central element in attempts at understanding race, and, in the process of developing this argument, uncover some of the social processes or mechanisms involved in race making. Let me begin by telling you how I came to this practical understanding of the centrality of people while I was 'in the field' as anthropologists refer to their research.

People and race making: some practical lessons

I was trained as a student of social categories and structures, wielding the kind of macro-analytic tool kit in which the actual *people* living in racial orders took on a hollow, puppet like quality. This was a conceptual tool bag I'd assembled in order to think about race in Britain, where I had a broad understanding of what went on under the banner of 'race'. I took this with me when I moved to Toronto, and then to Vancouver. In each place I'd open my tool kit, re-arrange things a bit and then put it all back. Defeated. Do conceptual tools work across nation state and provincial boundaries? Maybe. Certainly race in these places meant something other than it did in Britain and I was not sure what. Living long term in a particular place we develop our conceptual understanding as social researchers almost by social osmosis and don't realise the benefits of this kind of first hand practical understanding until it is gone, and, although anthropologists have ways of making themselves familiar with the unfamiliar, other kinds of social researchers do not. Anyway, no one in Canada even said 'race', they said 'ethnicity', the ethnic mosaic was the state sponsored image, an aspiration, race was too close to racism. By the time I'd decided to get back to researching race I was living in Montreal and teaching in a local university. The conceptual tool kit was looking a bit travel weary and I had even less idea what race and ethnicity meant, or how they worked, in a place where, in language terms alone, I struggled to understand everything. Being forced to start again from the beginning there was nothing lost in working from the opposite direction and seeing what I could learn from the kinds of anthropological methods, that render the unfamiliar familiar. I traded 'big picture' elements like categories and structure for lives, and tried to build a picture of the local racial order from the bottom up. I would, I decided, examine individual lives for their connections to other lives and by these means work the micro to make the macro, and back to the familiar territories of social categories and structures. At least that was the plan.

Operating on the fringes of transcultural psychiatry[1] out of interest and because of contacts I'd developed in Vancouver, I was interviewing psychiatric nurses of Caribbean origin about what it was like for them living and working in Montreal. These were highly qualified and educated professionals, and I was struck by how their lives could not be more different than those of their (black) clients whom I was also interviewing in informal community settings. Racial categories, I had started to see, obscure hugely divergent social positions, which could be unpacked and mapped onto (an interpretation of) the social fabric as something composed of *different kinds of racialised lives*. That there *are* differences within social categories is a banal and unsurprising insight; that difference can offer a starting point in a more detailed account of the operation of race and the racial texture of society is actually rather exciting. These differences between professionals and their clients were magnified when it came to strategies for dealing with racism. Psychiatric clients often developed accounts of madness structured by conspiracies generated through their interface with a range of agencies dealing with their affairs: immigration, child welfare, juvenile justice, education, the police and court system, and psychiatry (Knowles, 2000a). Psychiatric nurses dealt with a quite different range of agencies in different capacities: another highly significant difference between racialised subjects. They also dealt with employers, others in authority over them at work and a different range of neighbourhood and social networks. I talked to people who rebutted racism with expensive designer clothes, which made them feel good about themselves, and with people who went on taking courses to educate themselves well beyond the others in their workplace as a means of personal security in a hostile world. These were all ways of coping with racism in various manifestations. More mapping!

The differences between lives, which had seemed trivial when I had approached things from the opposite, macro structural direction now showed up in magnified form and demanded to be taken into account. I began to see not just that there were differences, but what they consisted of and how they might be categorised. If I wanted to understand how the things we refer to as race – primarily in this case manifestations of racism as forms of exclusion presaged on an account of differences explained by race – worked in this place then these individual differences mattered. Or, rather, if I did not take them into account then my picture of things would lack subtlety and detail because it had missed out on people as anything other than an aggregated category of puppets dancing in the formation of social structures. The details of racial orders operate in individual lives, and this was my first lesson in the importance of people. Racial orders are very uneven and racial categories like 'Caribbean Canadian' do not show up the contours of the racial landscape very well. Taking a closer look at them, conversely, exposed the racial texture of things rather starkly.

I was to learn of still more subtle distinctions from a different direction. Eager to learn about the local political, organisational dimensions of race and ethnicity in Montreal I had made contact with some of the black and community association activists funded by the provincial government as part of its ethnic pluralism[2]. It was through meeting another kind of more practical black activist who had been excluded from this professional ethnic circuit that I was told about William Kafe. William Kafe was a Ghanaian teacher who was in jail because he had threatened to shoot the Mayor of Verdun, the key municipal dignitary of a suburb of Montreal. He had made this threat out of frustration. A secondary school teacher working for the Deux Montaine School Board just outside of Montreal, he was the victim of fifteen years worth of racial taunts and harassment at the hands of his students. The students acted with the tacit collusion of his managers and the education authority, both of whom insisted that his problems arose from his inability to manage his students' behaviour and not from their racism. He fought back. He amassed documents, he took his employers to the Quebec Human Rights Commission and won, but he lost his job and his will to live in the process as his 'case' took over all other aspects of his life. People inevitably *turn* themselves into *categories* and *cases* in order to be able to fight this kind of battle, and, while these are important political campaigns, they also squeeze the life-blood out of those who fight them, and they end up feeling as hollowed out as the social categories to which they are assigned.

By the time Kafe had got out of jail and I met him he wanted to talk: he wanted to be heard, and saw me as a sympathetic female scribe. His 'case' was extensively documented: his house full of papers and tapes detailing his dealings with the school, the school board, his union, the medical insurance agencies managing the teachers' employment insurance scheme, the psychiatric agencies to whom he had been referred as part of his employment/unemployment insurance, and the psychiatrist he consulted for himself as a way of managing the stress all of this caused him. It was a researcher's dream. If I wanted to understand in detail the micro *processes* composing race through forms of racial exclusion and harassment – race making, making race matter – then here was my chance.

I learned two important lessons through William Kafe and his documents. The first built on the lessons about differentiation within racial categories I had learned from the psychiatric nurses and their clients. It was this. I learned late in our interview sessions that there was another black teacher teaching at the same school as Kafe. Did *he* have the same problems with the students? No. He didn't! Why was that? I had many theories about the differences between the two men who operated in the very same racial landscape and, on the face of it, as identical members of the same racial category *almost* down to the last detail. Was the other man a more commanding teacher the students would not dare annoy? Did he just duck the issues raised by his students' behaviour whereas Kafe challenged them? In the end I decided that the crucial difference had to be this: Kafe, but not his colleague, fought back against what he rightly perceived as injustice. His model – he had earlier trained as a Catholic priest – was David and Goliath. The crucial differences between them had to be matters of bearing, command, character and personal philosophy. Biography. If I was to understand the operation of race through the details of racism then I would have to have a framework that operated at this level of detail or, again, I would be missing crucial elements of its texture.

The second lesson I learned was that racial orders are in fact composed of myriad and ordinary everyday social processes and mechanisms with which people interface in no predictable way. Racism it seemed was nothing special but the drip, drip, drip of endless banality, which accumulates to something more sinister. It was about cumulative, incremental detail of the sorts of things that could happen to anyone – mix ups over time-tabling, being forced to operate across two campuses (which annoyed Kafe's students), the failure to constitute his probationary committee at the appropriate time and so on that had suspiciously converged on one – but not another – African man living in Quebec. Here, neither of them could be other than exotic. But one – and not the other – had *publicly* unleashed local fears of the meaning of black-ness as servility and dirt; matter out of place[3]. If I was to understand how racial orders worked then I needed to grapple with these processes and the people involved in them. I had learned that race making centrally involved people and their decisions and their actions; their ways of being who they are in the world in which they live. And race making involved myriad rather ordi-nary social processes and activities. These were to be important practical lessons in race. *People are the motor of race making* and hence deserve a central place in the analytical frameworks through which the operation of race is understood.

There are other lessons to be learned from the published work of others about the centrality of people in making racial orders. It is not just school children and education bureaucrats who make distinctions between racialised subjects; entire regimes do this, even ones that ostensibly have the most uni-form and systematic approach to racialising their citizens and sub-citizens. Mark Roseman's (2000) biography of Marianne Strauss who survived as a Jew in Nazi Germany until after the war while her family were exterminated makes just this point. Strauss survives the final solution through a combina-tion of privilege, resources, suitable networks, well-placed contacts, audacity, disposition, courage, ambivalence about her Jewishness, ambivalent connec-tion with certain versions of Germanness, mobility, youth, attractiveness, femininity and sheer strength of character. In the same regime six million other Jews are systematically exterminated. Not only does she survive, she manages to make the lives of those who are about to perish more comfortable through sending letters and parcels to the ghettos and camps in the East. One of the mechanisms by which she achieves this is a German army officer who risks death to play postman. Regimes are assembled through myriad social processes, mechanisms and routine activities: there are bound to be moments of inattention, unevenness and difference that matter. People at the point of their interface with regimes hold the key to these things, and the ways in which they pan out.

This takes us to a second and still more crucial point about the relationship between people and racialised regimes underscored in the work of Primo Levi

(2000) in *The Drowned and the Saved,* and still on the issue of the holocaust, *the iconic instance of racial classification through the mechanism of death.* Levi quite rightly argues that it was *people* who staffed the genocidal regime of the holocaust. People made decisions, did their jobs, filled forms, maintained gas supplies, ran trains, enabled other people to do other jobs (social processes) all of which ended in the systematic racialised regimes of death implemented in the concentration camps. Regimes are about people as well as systems and structures, which would lie inert without their agency, their volition, their ability to make things happen. Levi's (2000: 40–2) startling honesty conveys the layers of complicity this demanded and secured, not just among Germans, like the soldier in the Strauss story who defied the regime's demanded complicity and worked against it, but even among Jews. The regime's prime victims, argues Levi, operated 'within the gray band, that zone of ambiguity which irradiates around regimes based on terror and obsequiousness ... nobody can know for how long and under what trials his soul can resist before yielding or breaking'. Levi's point about regimes of death and terror is no less true of any other regime that '... degrades its victims and makes them similar to itself, because it needs both great and small complicities' (2000: 49).

Levi identifies a raw but insightful moment in the operation of human agency, the subjectivities[4] of which it is capable and the operation and articulation of regimes over people's lives. The unpalatable truth is that we are all complicit in our own (literal and metaphoric) annihilation and in that of others. The regime is both *of us* and *wields power over us*[5]. People (and their actions) compose (racialised) regimes. How we compose them is not a straightforward matter to understand, for we are both, as Levi contends, complicit in our own and others' annihilation and, sometimes, work against the regime like the German soldier who smuggled parcels into the camp.

A second less dramatic and systematically violent example of the complicity between people and regimes is offered in Braman's (1999) account of the mechanisms sustaining the segregation laws in the United States in the 1890s. A light skinned black man, Plessy, who was counted as white in some states and black in others because they had different definitions of blackness, was prosecuted for violating the segregation laws of the State of Louisiana by riding in a whites only railway carriage (Braman, 1999: 1394). This example shows, although the author does not make a point of this, that *implementing the social boundaries of whiteness and blackness* was only possible because of the actions of Plessy's fellow passengers, the guard who reported it, and those staffing the legal apparatus that were prepared to pursue segregation by juridical means. The point here is that racial segregation was as much the achievement of human agency as the structural imperatives of the regime's arbitrary and iniquitous forms of racial classification. This goes beyond complicity. There is reflexivity and conviction here. Volition. It is the people who compose regimes that make them work. People are a part of the operation of the apparatus of racial classification, exclusion and death. The detailed manner of this interface between regimes and people is something we need to understand. We will return to this later.

So far I have been trying to convince you that race is about race making and centrally concerned with people. By looking at people we can begin to understand the complicated and uneven nature of racial orders and their regimes. I have suggested that human action – how people operate – in racial orders is vitally important in understanding how race works. That people are the key to understanding race making. And race making is a series of small processes and mechanisms that overall add up to the making of people and the regimes administering them, in certain terms. People are the motor of race making; they take up causes, or not. They act in compliance with regimes; or undermine them. The puzzle of the person and what lies beyond is at the heart of this chapter's deliberations on race making.

Understanding race through structure

I make these points about the centrality of people in race making because I believe that people, and their connection with the social processes composing race making, have been overlooked in conceptual accounts of race. The contributions of people in the making, organisation and routine maintenance of racialised regimes is systematically occluded by the conceptualisation of race as primarily a big picture problem, and by the difficulties of moving between differences of scale and magnification. The social and political character of race is widely, and correctly, acknowledged[6]. Perhaps because race is manifest in social inequalities – there is no race but there is racism (Mason, 1994) – what are conceived as the bearers of these distinctions have been eclipsed by the bigger systems and forces orchestrating lives. Although the social and political character of race is evident in both micro and macro contexts, race analysis has been dominated by big picture dynamics which have been useful in showing up the structural and systematic organisation of race in forms of inequality and exclusion as racism. Rex and Moore's (1967) early study on housing markets and race in Britain is an example of this kind of work, but there are many others, the sociology of race is dominated by macro analysis (Anthias and Yuval-Davis, 1992; Wieviorka, 1995; Solomos and Back, 1996; Banton, 2000; Miles, 2000; Rex, 2000; the PSI reports and the numerous publications of the Institute of Race Relations). Without this kind of analysis there would be no accounts of the systematic nature of racism and no strategies for opposing it.

But the down side of this approach is that we lack understanding of the operation of human agency in the making of race, and our versions of race making are empty and mechanistic assertions about the social and the political underpinning of race, which are not substantiated with *flesh*. In the face of broader structural priorities, the operation of the individual human subject became a second order problem in the scheme of things. As I suggested earlier these are problems of focus and priority, and the difficulty of zooming in and out on race as a simultaneously big/small picture problem. This is understandable in its historical context in the genealogy of race. Structuralist and other forms of macro explanation, such as Miles' (1989) racialisation thesis for example, were hard won from the territory of racial prejudice, which claimed the person and her psychic terrain alone, as the problem to be dealt with. That we learned to think systematically about race was a good thing; but that we lost the link between structures and big pictures on the one hand, and people on the other has been to the detriment of our understanding of race. I am not for one moment suggesting a return to 60s individualism in racial explanation, but I am suggesting a drawing of connections between people and the big and small social processes with which their lives connect.

Understanding race through the cultural turn

The omission of people from structuralism and other big picture accounts of race is conceptually understandable – the focus is on the system as a whole – but the omission of people from the other, parallel, track along which the analysis of race later travelled is perhaps rather more surprising. I refer to the 'cultural turn' in the social sciences which brought 'new ethnicities' (Hall, 1991a; Modood, 1994) and individually customised versions of ethnicity-as-fragmented-identity, intended to break up the monoliths built around race and present a more finely detailed picture of things, and yet did so *without foregrounding people in its analytic schemes.* How did this happen? How did these claims upon shades of experience so squarely miss the bearers of those experiences? This happened because of the relationship between people and culture that dominates the frameworks of the turn towards consideration of black and Asian expressive cultures in film, art, music and so on. In these frameworks the individual is the vehicle of cultural expression; not in an active sense of *making* the world, but in a *representative* sense in which people are the units, but not the animators, of cultures. Rather than being the makers of their own lives or the cultural landscapes of their daily operation; people are merely puppets acting out the scripts of the bigger plot in which their lives are set? Alexander's (1996) *The Art of Being Black* and *The Asian Gang* (2000) are exceptional in taking an ethnographical approach to race in which the operation of human agency is clearly visible.

In the cultural turn then it is always *culture* as a collective capacity, and not *people* or their ways of being in the world, which needs to be understood. People operate as the units of cultural inscription. Their lives and forms of being (subjectivity) are written by the bigger text in which their lives are arranged and from which their lives can be interpreted. These theories of how people operate – and which are about versions of subjectivity and human agency as we shall see later – explain why the turn to *identity* did not bring the bearers of identity centre stage as objects of serious intellectual engagement. Instead the cultural turn secured the separation of social and cultural analysis. Alluring images of hybridity and mixity, and their self-assembly kits of ethnic identity manifest in cultural production, *worked* particularly well in exploring visual and literary (cultural) formats. But they offered nothing for the task of understanding the social mechanisms through which race and ethnicity work, and the forms of social practice – as grammar – to which they give rise, or the political forms of which they are capable. Consequently, as objects of intellectual engagement, race and ethnicity have travelled along the two parallel tracks outlined above: one concerned with the (macro and the) structural, the other with the (macro dimensions of the) cultural. The first was politically engaged: the second, more fragmented and finely detailed, had powers of description only. The leakage between these two tracks took a particular form: identity and subjectivity were given a priority while the social mechanisms of their operation remained obscured. Although *announced* as significant, people remained in a marginal position in the analytic frame. Greater progress in understanding individual lives is realised through anthropological enterprises excavating ethnicity, as we shall see later on in this chapter.

In both of these trajectories of race the individual is only implicitly *accorded* an active role in the making of social, political and cultural landscape that is, at the last moment, overshadowed by bigger forces. Despite protestations to the contrary, the individual in the last instance occupies a back seat as the *processor, not maker,* of social, political and cultural forces in both analytical trajectories. Hence my earlier comments about race making. Race making and the activities of people are all part of the same social processes. This chapter is an attempt to excavate the individual from this predicament of marginality-billed-as-centrality, and to suggest some more active ways of conceptualising the individual in the analytic schemes through which race and ethnicity are understood.

People and social categories

Race and ethnicity *are* social and political distinctions. But they are *made and sustained by individual agency,* and, what is more, there is no contradiction between these two claims. Bonnett's (1996: 151) critique of Frankenberg's (1993) study of whiteness strikes at just this point. Racial categories cannot, Bonnett claims, be at once unstable political categories, always at the point of unravelling, *and* a community of human subjects with the power of volition. If race is a social myth sustained in political landscape, claims Bonnett, it cannot also be a *real* set of social distinctions animated by the lives and people to whom it refers. This is a fundamental misconception. The ways in which *people operate in relation to the social categories and political landscapes by which they and others are identified* is one of the most intriguing problems of our time. Racial categories characterising political landscapes could not be developed and sustained unless they were meaningful for, and acted on, by human agents in the conduct of their everyday lives. Although racial categories are social and political constructs, they are also effective in the making of who we are in the world and what we do in it. They operate in the manufacture of identities and in activities composing human agency. Race is certainly not just a social myth: it is acted on and has meaning in peoples' lives. Social and political categories are never mythical, they are just that, social and political categories: ways of distinguishing people and thinking about how the world works. They don't have a force in human biology, but that is a different point. They have a *meaning in social and political organisation and human action.*

This chapter sets this point at the centre of the analysis of race and ethnicity. The category 'black'[7] so roundly unseated by the unravelling of racial categories in the new ethnicities project which asserted, undoubtedly correctly, that identities were far more delicate matters than the blunt application of blackness in opposition to whiteness, offers an example. While squarely missing the delicate texture of identity as versions of the self, 'black' was a tactical posture developed in the US and Britain in the 1960s and 1970s, which both characterised and contested the social inequalities of racial landscape. But in order to do these two things effectively the category 'black' had to make a meaningful connection with the daily experience of social exclusion and the personal feelings that came with it. In other words black *was* a category of political analysis drawn from a macro-social analysis of the racial landscape. But it also had a *deep personal resonance* in the lives of those for whom it had a meaning and who successfully waged political struggles by means of it. If it hadn't no one could have connected with it or found it an effective entry point into political strategy. That there were people for whom it was neither a useful nor effective designation is undoubtedly true, but does not rebut the point, indeed, on the contrary, it speaks volumes about differences between (black) lives and experiences. Black in America, in Britain and elsewhere, evidently evoked multiple and varied profound senses of whom one was in the world of the local (and global in the case of Pan Africanists) racial order. Of course black was also a tactical posture for combating racism: a political bargain struck over the character of the political landscape and the possibility of its transformation, which grated against existential and experiential versions of the self and individual lives. My argument is that there were forms of *personal investment and meaning* attached to political distinctions without which no political campaign could have been conceived, much less successfully waged. Those who claim that race and ethnicity is a tactical posture are right, but only in a limited sense. They have not accounted for the human emotions mobilised in tactical postures, or the ways in which people connect their personal experiences with the experiences of others[8].

So far I have been writing about *people* occupying a central place in race making as though this was an entirely unproblematic concept. In fact the term people is open to varied interpretation. What might it mean? And what does it mean in the conceptual apparatus in which I am using it as a pivotal point in my analysis? There are many aspects to these questions, but here I want to focus on two aspects that have, I consider, significance in establishing the meaning of this term. The first are theories of subjectivity, for these cut to the heart of what it means to be a person. The second are theories of human agency, which foreground important distinctions about the relationship between people and social, political and cultural forces.

Subjectivities

What follows reviews key contributions to understanding subjectivity and points to their potential in understanding race making as being about the making of subjectivity. Of course there is more to race making than people and subjectivity, but I have argued already that people are a central consideration in this. The terms in which people are made, or make themselves, are a highly significant part of race making, although, as we shall see, these things always involve more than the individual person. Race making is thus always a complicated and inter-related set of processes, which go beyond the person. First though, what do I mean by subjectivities? Or, rather, as establishing the meaning of subjectivities is the object of this entire section, what is my starting point in understanding subjectivities?

Wander (1994: xiii–xiv), Lefebvre's translator in *Everyday Life in the Modern World*, for me captures the *spirit* of what I mean by subjectivities.

> Clerks, salespersons, business executives, doctors, lawyers, assembly-line workers – must all cultivate 'winning' personalities. In a lifelong sequence of encounters with anonymous others, each of us must be able to 'put ourselves across,' to 'sell ourselves' to the other. In this kind of relationship, our worth depends on conditions beyond our control, thus any setback in the drive for success may cause a severe threat to self-esteem. Helplessness, insecurity, and inferiority threaten when the other does not respond in the appropriate manner. This undermines a sense of autonomy and independence. The feeling that 'I am whatever you want me to be'. ... Since it is not production skills that are valued in the marketplace ... but instead our attractiveness, we are led to see ourselves and others as commodities. The other becomes a button to be pushed, a link to be forged, a 'contact'. We rank the other according to officially sanctioned values, according to his or her intelligence, attractiveness, influence, or success. ... The other is someone who is better or worse, is superior to or insubordinate to me. Relationships become superficial ... The modern world fosters a childlike personality, a person who constantly seeks and needs approval, who is not hung up on the past and is not committed to a future apart from becoming a success. It fosters a person who enters into the here and now of adjustment demanded by bosses and customers, who has no principles to speak of, who remains ever alert for opportunities ... the marketing persona is of a piece with the modern world ... way of being-in-the-world.

A biting indictment of the world in which we live, inspired by Lefebvre's assessment that our world consists of forms of *commercial terrorism* and its internalised forms as personhood, for me conveys a (bleak) contemporary sense of subjectivity. In fact it displays all of subjectivities' key elements. Subjectivity is about modes of being-in-the-world; it is about the forms of personhood available to us; and it is about the ways in which the outside becomes part of our inside – although I reject its economic determinism and its passivity – and becomes part of who we are and the kinds of relationships we might form. Subjectivity is about the underlying principles of what it means to be a person in the world. Subjectivity, as Wander so lucidly shows, is always social and the subject is created and recreated through forms of praxis (Crossley, 1994: 46) composed of routine activities. It is in this way, encapsulated by Wander, that I use subjectivity in this volume, as a way of examining some of the central features of personhood which is, in turn, a basis for understanding people, and race making as a people-centred activity.

Understanding subjectivities

Wander effectively invokes the *sense or spirit of subjectivity and its social dynamics,* but we need a more systematic approach to understand subjectivity enough to see some of its race making mechanisms. Three sets of contributions are particularly useful to the project in hand. First are those that take the view that subjectivity is composed of the *packages of capacities* identified and developed by the philosopher Charles Taylor, whose work is often used in developing theories of identity. This connects with some strong sociological traditions in the insights G.H. Mead. Second are the contributions of those – like Pile and Thrift – who are concerned with examining *subject positions* instead of capacities, and mapping their relationship to the social landscapes in which they appear. Third are the contributions of Constructionist Psychologists like John Shotter who draw on the insights of Wittgenstein, Volosinov, Berger and Luckman and Harré and foreground certain *relational* aspects of subjectivity. Although these approaches operate quite different models, there is also considerable overlap between them, and it is this which melds them into a cluster of concepts from which we can grasp what it means to be a person in contemporary society as a starting point in understanding the person in race making. The social and the dialogical processes of human interaction feature prominently in these versions of personhood, and it is this which makes them particularly suited to the analysis of race and ethnicity.

Subjectivities as capacities

Taylor (1989: 35–6) concurs with Mead that the self can only exist among the other selves, which operate as its 'conversation partners', its 'webs of interlocation'. To be a person is to interact with the community and moral universe – in conversation with its thinkers, its prophets and the dead – through which one is defined (Taylor, 1989: 38). If the self is inevitably social then it is also dialogical. These conversations and the networks of which they are a part need not necessarily take place through narrative: Mead's (1952: 144) 'conversations of gestures' hints at the habitual and non-verbal conversations we have with those with whom we live in some form of community/proximity. To be a person is to interface with the networks of social relationships, which confer content and meaning: the self is always socially inscribed. Hence to be a person invokes the capacity for reflexivity and community (Mead, 1952: 136–7) – the mechanisms by which an individual *becomes an object to itself* – and not just social connection. Reflexivity is manifest in individual stories in which people speak about who they are, and give a sense of their place in the social arrangement of things.

Embedded in these are conceptions of the 'proper person'. Taylor (1989: 40) gives the example of the 'proper' modern self, framing itself in terms of leaving home and making its way in the world. It is through these and other stories that the self is understood and told as narrative. They are personal/social stories of the evolution and deployment of personhood and the living of a 'good life'. To be a person is to subscribe to certain versions of how a life should be lived: something involving a moral universe. 'To know who you are is to be oriented in moral space' (Taylor, 1989: 28). Taylor's package of human capacities composing the modern person includes a sense of inwardness, involving an interior life of emotional and moral reflection, which dates to Plato, St Augustine and so on (Taylor, 1989: 112–7). The social charting of the self does not remove the existential as a domain of individual reasoning and structured decision making in the sense in which Camus used it to indicate the path chosen among other paths. The existential belongs both to the individual and the social fabric – moral universe, shared meaning and conversation of gestures – of which s/he is a part. Even Mead's (1952: 221) charting of the self in purely social terms does not deny 'the expression of the individual himself (sic)'. Indeed the idea of an internal domain of reflexiveness would seem to underscore it. Otherwise the emotional interior of the person is the (social) outside written *inside*, and even theories of 'socialisation' do not require these levels of unprocessed social ingestion. The general point is this. A space is left in these philosophical schemes for the existential which is not fully developed, but which has analytic potential in developing accounts of raced/ethnicised subjectivities. We may be written by the societies in which we live (to paraphrase Freeman, 1993: 80) but not without remainder. The remainder is what we uniquely add, the existential, which belongs only to us as individuals in our interface with the world in which we live.

The insights of Taylor and Mead highlight the many connections between the personal and the social and the need to think these connections through in relationship to race and ethnicity. The personal/social interface is at the heart of race making. People make themselves in dialogues with the social mechanisms with which their lives intersect. There is never *just* the person. And, as my earlier examples drawn from my own research hinted, forms of social inscription are clearly calibrated by race. Neeman (1994: 136) stresses the need to understand the interrelationship between personal biographies and the invented collective text of ethnicity. And, although I think that ethnicity is more than text – it has a practical force in individual lives – this goes further in confronting social mechanisms than other accounts of race that do little more than admit that the construction of collective identities has implications for the self. Identities are always both socially and individually customised and we need to better understand the interplay between these two aspects of identity as ways of thinking about the self. The 'proper person' and the 'good life' are clearly open to infinite variation and the extent to which these might reveal moments of racial and ethnic grammar in their moral universes are important issues demanding investigation. Bhabha (1994, cited in Pile and Thrift, 1995) hints at this kind of process when he argues that the person – the cultural framework of the self – is so invested in the Western colonial project as to be irreversibly tainted (Pile and Thrift, 1995: 9). If the analysis of race and ethnicity demands other versions of subjectivity then might we not know what they are, or might be? The capacity for reflexivity, inwardness and community are likewise areas where differences in the content and meaning of these things might prove instructive in understanding the working of race and ethnicity. In Taylor's scheme of things the key features of being a person are pinned down in very general terms that we might search for difference and variation, and which might connect with race and ethnicity and then, consequently, shade into things we didn't know about race making through subjectivity.

But there is a problem with this kind of *capacities* approach, which has to do with race history. There is a vast history of conceptualising race in terms of *racial* differences in human capacities, which provided the substance of racism. This is especially evident in narratives concerned with the management of empire and the politics of decolonisation, in which racially/ethnically construed capacities for democratic participation in self-government were major considerations in granting independence (Knowles, 1992). The coupling of race/ethnicity with capacity is likely entrenched in operational conceptions of *self and others* in racially hierarchical terms, and uncoupling them would be a difficult and intricate operation. Is the capacities approach of Taylor useful in conceptualising subjectivity as raced/ethnicised despite these difficult historical associations? The answer is a qualified yes, if, as I have just argued, we can distance ourselves from racial classifications that lean on capacities calibrated around democracy and civilisation, which featured so prominently in debates concerned with decolonisation. There is unfinished historical business concerning the inherently raced nature of conceptions of what it means to be human. These need to be reworked so as to challenge some of this history of racial classification in which people and their degrees of civilisation were judged in terms of human capacities, which belonged to some and against which others were judged as inadequate. Yes, Taylor's capacities approach is useful because it opens up the existential, and with it individual difference, as an incompletely considered aspect of raced and ethnicised dimensions of subjectivity. And yes, because it offers the prospect of a more thorough examination of the dialogues between human subjects over the spoken and unspoken assumptions on which forms of human community are premised. Elements of the capacities approach – if not the approach in total – hold the individual and the social in a finely balanced tension, and allow us to examine the social processes operating at their interface. This, as we will later see, is useful.

Subjectivities as positions

Other models of subjectivity offer different tools for understanding race making as a people-centred enterprise. What happens if we shift the frame in which the person is apprehended? In place of the modern person as a bundle of capacities in Taylor's analysis imagine the person as 'subject position' mapped onto the social landscape (Pile and Thrift, 1995: 3). In this schema selves are constituted in certain terms through the social categories – like race and ethnicity and much more besides – applied to them, and through which they are socially understood. To this we can add, they understand themselves in ways that take account of the relevant forms of social recognition applied. Although we should anticipate an imperfect fit between person and category, position is useful because it foregrounds social categories and their spatial arrangement, although the lives composing them remain implied rather than analytically developed. To be a person in this frame is to occupy, simultaneously, even divergent positions on the social landscapes to which we are all connected in the webs of social consequences and practical political outcomes – which are a part of our very existence. Position resonates with Mauss' (1986: 12) 'civil persona' as the artificial character(s) of the mask distinguished, in the second century by the Greeks, from the innermost self. The mapping exercises of Pile and Thrift (1995: 4–7) underscore the significance of *space* and the *quotidian* aspects of the self in the making of personhood. Lefebvre (1994) develops this idea of the significance of the everyday. He uses it to mean: 'the dull routine, the ongoing, go-to-work, pay the bills, homeward trudge of daily existence', which is beyond philosophy and language, or, embedded in practical action (Wander, Lefebvre's translator, 1994: vii).

To be a contemporary person is to be engaged in the (specific material) details of everyday life as de Certeau (1989) and Lefebvre contend. The contemporary person is made in the rituals of daily existence. The ways in which daily life is shaped by race and ethnicity – or what these things consist of at this level of the everyday – is clearly something for further consideration. In doing what we habitually do, we make ourselves, and the fine social distinctions composing our lives. This is all part of race making as the making of raced and ethnicised subjectivities. Similarly, in producing the spaces through which lives are lived we produce ourselves in certain terms. Space[9] – its everyday use and social relationships – is an important component in the production of the person. The racialisation and ethnicisation of space have been examined in various ways, and this is the subject of Chapter 4. Social position, in this formulation, substitutes for social identities but the problem of the social/personal relationship remains in a different form. Instead of having to understand the relationship between collective and personal versions of the self we need to understand the relationship between social position and personal biography. This is, in fact, a reformulation of the same problem, which is not solved in either framework.

In addition to space and the significance of everyday life in the making of subjectivity, positional versions of personhood offer social location and the related concept of categories of public recognition in race, gender and so on, to our conceptual tool kit. This latter point helps develop Taylor's idea concerning the dialogues between people and their social/historical/moral universes. Subjectivities are also made in the interface between people and the social categories by which they are recognised and positioned in the world. In being who we are in the world we have to take into account the forms of public recognition through which we are known and placed in the social landscape. This is particularly potent in relation to race/ethnicity. I indicated earlier in this chapter that mapping the relationship between people and the social interfaces composing their routine lives was a useful way of developing more finely tuned accounts of the racial texture of the social fabric. Positional accounts of subjectivity, therefore, have a use in developing an understanding of race making, despite the fact that generally they are insensitive to individual lives: a dimension we need to add to them, but to which they are amenable.

Compositional and relational aspects of subjectivities

Shotter's (1997: 9) version of Social Constructionist Psychology foregrounds relational, as opposed to representational, understanding of the narratives in which the self is configured. While this shares the premises of both Mead's and Taylor's versions of personhood – as made in the dialogues of social interaction – the narratives through which selves are *told* are ongoing acts of *invention* and not acts or *re-presentation*. This is particularly useful in focusing us on the central issue of the *making* of raced/ethnicised subjectivities as part of a materialist analysis. Consequently, in this framework selves are *made* in interpersonal, intersubjective contexts shaped in dialogues with social circumstances and stories of personal past and present: a configuration of personal events (Yi and Shorter-Gooden, 1999: 18–19). Selves are produced in practical action and embodied forms of knowing in daily contexts of human interaction, which need not be spoken. In this, constructionist psychologists agree with Mead's conversations of gestures. Here, again, is the prospect of developing dialogues without word-narrative as one of the places where race and ethnicity is made. The self is made 'in the momentary relational spaces occurring between ourselves and another or otherness in our surroundings' (Shotter, 1997: 12). The selves made by these means have no permanent essence, they are always in the process of becoming. It is important here to stress that this is not an attempt to produce essentialist versions of race and ethnicity, but to see their production as an open set of ongoing processes. Inner lives in this formulation are neither inner nor private: thoughts are not organised in the inner centre of our being and then represented in words but organised in the 'moment-by-moment, back-and-forth' processes 'at the boundary of our being' in our daily interaction with others (Shotter, 1997: 13). The emotional interior, or inner life, is created at the point at which the individual deals with the social. It is hence integral to the person in a different way from its formulation as a 'trait' by Mead and Taylor.

Herein lies the possibility of further elaborating our understanding of the existential: it is what is uniquely taken into the interior from the social interface and processed in a life. The existential is impossible without the social: it is the social writ in *alternate form* processed in the inner thoughts and actions of the individual positioned at the confluence of the individual with the social world – the place where personhood is created as public/private activity.

'It is in the responsive speaking of our words we can begin to create with others, in joint action, a sense of the unique nature of our own inner lives' (Shotter, 1997: 17). Embodiment here has two meanings of relevance to our purpose in this chapter. It means to be both *positioned within historical processes* and it refers to the place of *corporeality – of body – in generating the person* in the practical dialogues composing the social landscapes on which we operate. Evidently both forms of embodiment – as well as the elaborated notion of the existential – have a bearing on our understanding of race and ethnicity as being *made*. To be raced is to be positioned within (racialised) historical processes and their (racialised) political landscapes; and within discourses and practices concerning (raced) corporeality. We return to issues of corporeality (and comportment) later in this chapter.

This review of subjectivity was intended to pull out some of the concepts that have a utility in developing our understanding of race and ethnicity making as people-centred enterprises. The three models I emphasise are incompatible with each other, in that they offer competing versions of this important aspect of what it means to be a person. I have pillaged them for things that help us understand race making because I am less interested in the integrity of models, than their use in developing conceptual tools for social analysis. Between them these accounts of subjectivity offer a version of personhood as socially inscribed in dialogues with others as part of a network of social relationships; as cast in the relational spaces between the self and others. The person is composed in the capacity for reflexivity and through moral frameworks; through position on the social landscape in which space and everyday practical action compose what we are, and what we can be. The person is not finished but constantly made in an ongoing set of social and spatial relationships and dialogues of practical action. And these versions of subjectivity offer an elaborated account of the existential, as what is uniquely part of an individual interior, drawn from, and impossible to conceptualise without the social, but uniquely part of each inner life. These aspects of personhood are very useful in conceptualising the things I refer to as race making; in understanding people as raced and active in making race. Race making centres on the making of selves in dialogical relationships with the things composing the social interface: relationships with others – social networks – and, through others to agencies, community and regime, the things which lie beyond the individual, and yet are intimately bound up with it and its making. Race making is centrally about people, but it is never *just* about people, for the category of the person as subjectivity – not its only but key ingredient – is always part of a bigger social dialogue. To be human is to be actively engaged with others, and more besides, as we will see as this volume unfolds.

Agency

One of the key axes of difference in these accounts of subjectivity as well as a key aspect of personhood I flagged earlier, is *agency*. We have already noted that in all theories of subjectivity the person is socially inscribed, but there is enormous variation in forms and degrees of inscription that have a bearing on our understanding of race as race making. Agency is about the balance of forces between people and those things that are more than people and have to do with the organisation of the social fabric. It is about the balance of forces between will and effort on the one hand and social forces on the other. Agency is about the scope of human action to influence the way things are. We might usefully think of human agency as comprised of a spectrum of possibilities. At the Baudrillard (see *Simulations* and other work) end of the spectrum the human subject is duped, seduced by consumption; an empty husk, the vessel of social and cultural processes in which she is participant, but not producer. People are social puppets in this formulation, doing what is required of them, doing the bidding of the bigger forces shaping what we refer to as 'the social' or 'society'. At the opposite end of this spectrum lies the domain of free choice and individual existence and its crises, in which social processes are relegated to a backdrop for individual dramas: forms of auto/biography. The position of the subject in relation to forms of social inscription is always a part of accounts of subjectivity. Judith Butler's (1997: 2–3) *Psychic Life of Power*, for example, argues (from a recognisably Foucauldian perspective) that subjection, being subordinated by power, lies at the heart of subjectivity. 'Subjection consists precisely in this fundamental dependency on a discourse we never choose but that, paradoxically, initiates and sustains our agency'. It then remains to ask 'What is the psychic form that power takes?' (Butler, 1997: 2). In this type of formulation of subjectivity, human agency is formulated within the operation of the matrices of power, which *make* the psychic life of the subject in certain terms. The scope of human agency in this formulation of things is severely curtailed.

As part of a social analysis centred on people and their contribution to race making I, of course, favour a more balanced version of human agency as a halfway point between unfettered individualism and equally unfettered social determination. This analysis *works* the dialogues between people and the social interfaces composing their lives: the relational spaces between the self and others, which admit the prospect of active human agency and the existential as a domain of unpredictability and possibility. For me to suggest that this is a *halfway point* is a bit misleading, because the pivotal point is a fluctuating point of individual/social interface which has to be worked out situation by situation. Hints of these relational spaces between the self and others surfaced in the Kafe case and in my other examples of how race making was a people centred enterprise, where human agency made a substantial difference to the ways things worked out. My account of human agency wants to admit differences and inequalities in the operation of human agency as part of what needs investigating. But it also wants to suggest that outcomes are not known in advance, that people make themselves and the social fabric of which their lives are a part in mutually constitutive ways.

This chapter is not just about the inscription of race/ethnicity in lives and subjectivities, it is about *the nature of contemporary personhood and its fabrication in the processes and relationships composing the social world in racial and ethnic terms.* Understanding race is fundamental in understanding the person and an enterprise which should be, as I have suggested, at the very centre of social analysis, just as the converse is also true. Understanding race requires an understanding of people. As Goldberg (1993) points out, as long as we have conceptualised – and we might add acted on – the modern concept of the person we have done so in racial terms: race and rights as a capacity of subjectivity belong together and have developed in tandem[10].

Making ethnicity

If social analysts have been inattentive to the social mechanisms of race making and the significance of people in race making, the same cannot be said of theories of ethnicity. Developing theories of ethnicity has largely been the domain of social anthropologists and examining what they have to say about how ethnicity is *made* is also useful for developing our understanding of race. When sociologists, on the other hand, have been involved in understanding ethnicity their efforts have been rather rudimentary. Glazer and Moynihan's (1963) *Beyond the Melting Pot* and Novak's (1972) *The Rise of Unmeltable Ethnics* (cited Patterson, 1991) are examples. Both of these authors are concerned with the extent to which ethnicity survives as a relevant variable in people's lives (Patterson, 1991: 49–50) and imply both ethnicity's optionality and its operation at the margins of existence. The equation being worked here is – person with underlying subjectivity plus ethnicity – not, as I have been suggesting, that being a person is calibrated in ethnic terms. Of course this is a matter of political context. Glazer and Moynihan and Novak are sociologists concerned with immigration as a tool of nation building: with the casting of new Americans out of old Europeans. It is anthropologists who have taken ethnicity (but not race) seriously as a detailed set of social and political processes, which have a bearing in the lives of people and their forms of consciousness. In this way some anthropologists come close to conceptualising ethnicity as part of human subjectivity, as opposed to the optional add-on of the Glazer and Moynihan and Novak approaches.

Ethnicity is manufactured through social processes underscoring both the personal and the political landscapes on which lives are set: and it is this combination of things that makes their insights particularly pertinent to our project. Interestingly, as I mentioned earlier, there are no parallel accounts of race as manufactured, apart from those concerned with its generation as a discourse and as a political category, all of which deny its veracity, while simultaneously acknowledging that it is a force in making people's lives. The conceptualisation of ethnicity as something *produced,* as the result of human effort, and not as something *primordial* emerges from Fredrik Barthes' (1969) *Ethnic Groups and Boundaries* and in the anthropological writing Barthes subsequently inspired. Here ethnicity operates as a feature of social organisation. Barthes' (1994: 18) dramatalurgical, Goffmanesque, version of ethnicity conceptualises it as being about the production of versions of selfhood, fabricated and maintained at the boundaries where the self encountered that which it was not: the other. It was on this boundary with the other – in Barthes' version of things – that the self *became itself in ethnic terms* in taking in its differences with the other. The self in this formulation is *made as ethnicity*; unlike the Novak approach to ethnicity as an add-on.

Barthes (1994: 21) divides the social processes through which ethnic boundaries are maintained into micro, median and macro processes: different levels of social landscape all intersecting with the self. At each of these levels, he says, there is silencing and erasure of the experiences constituting ethnicity, so that ethnicity is always being selectively manufactured out of the myriad of available human experiences. In this process – and contrary to our models of subjectivity outlined above – the outside political and social landscape is taken inside so that subjectivity is the *internalisation of the social in the face of what it is not*. While Barthes' model ultimately proffers only a hollow account of the subject as the processor, and not the maker, of social knowledge, he does see ethnicity as embedded in the territories of the self, and manufactured through definite social processes in some kind of dialogue between the individual and the social/political context in which the individual is composed. His model is dialogical, processual, about the constitution of social categories as experiences and lives, centered on ethnicity and provides an understanding of ethnicity as embedded in the self *and* the social processes composing the self. So it is useful, despite its rudimentary version of subjectivity and the ultimate occlusion of the individual by the social.

Hall's situational model of ethnicity as 'new ethnicity' neither goes as far as Barthes, nor acknowledges its intellectual debt to Barthes. Hall, too, stresses boundary and not content as the nexus of ethnic identity formation in insisting upon the 'other' – a psychoanalytic concept developed by Winnicott and applied to good effect by Fanon – in the fabrication of the self as not-the-other. The identity of the self in this formulation is 'composed always across the silence of the other'. The black British identities of which Hall writes are composed from what is frozen out of Englishness – driven by racism – and the political reaction of counter identities (Hall, 1991b: 52). The ethnic/racial self in this formula 'only achieves its positive through the narrow eye of the negative' (Hall, 1991a: 21). While the status of the other is problematic in this formulation – as Anthony Cohen's discussion of self consciousness will later reveal – Hall's post-Barthian, cultural studies argument concerning the significance of *political* contexts and the dialogues of the self which they unleash is a very useful one, because it underscores the significance of political struggles in ethnicity making, and goes some way towards bridging the intellectual gulf between ethnicity and race.

Roosens (1989: 13), an anthropologist in the Barthes tradition, develops this political point further, arguing that ethnicities are animated around the political landscapes of social disadvantage and this is usefully seen as one of the mechanisms producing ethnicity. In the dialogues between ethnic selves and the political landscapes animating them we derive important clues about *whose* experience counts and *how*. Verdery (1994: 37) poses ethnic identity as bound up with historic process in the formation of nation states as part of state-makers' management of populations: 'tags by which state-makers keep track of their political subjects'. They are more than tags. People have investments in these tags – indeed they have been prepared to die for them in the former Yugoslavia and elsewhere – which operate, somehow, also as forms of personal identities formed and guarded by conviction. Ethnicities are also identities[11] that work across state boundaries. Bell (cited in Roosens, 1989: 17) suggests they offer one of the few macro-level organisational forms left to belong to in the context of the erosion of nation states as meaningful forms of belonging. This would seem to be a reasonable interpretation of the forms of human community which have formed in the breakdown of nation states in the Balkans and elsewhere. Hall (1991a: 26–36) sees ethnicity as a reach for local grounding and as the place or space from which people speak (positional versions of subjectivity). These are useful insights in developing a more personal account of ethnicity as being closer to subjectivity in the context of broader social, political and administrative forces operating around the self. What seems to be significant here are the processes through which the making of selves – in racial and ethnic terms – occur at the interface with broader social, political and administrative actions and landscapes. This is an entirely productive path to follow and one we will return to in subsequent chapters.

As well as highlighting political processes, situational models of ethnicity have been concerned with another key dimension of subjectivity raised earlier: the existential. Attempts to think about ethnicity in more individual (existential) terms are evident in the (anthropological) work of Anthony Cohen and Nigel Rapport. Cohen (1994a: 61–2) says of Barthes that he treats ethnicity as a tactical posture and so ignores self-consciousness: an aspect of the existential dimension of subjectivity Cohen – but not anthropology generally – deals with rather effectively. In establishing a more complete account of the subject, Cohen (1994b), in his book *Self Consciousness* contests the significance of boundary/otherness in the constitution of the self: 'When I consult myself about who I am, this entails something more than the rather negative reflection on 'who I am not ...'. Cohen (1994a)[12] is saying that we cannot read the individual self from either the collective self or the other. This is a wholly more individual kind of research programme than most anthropologists are prepared to engage with as, in general terms in anthropological investigation even though individual selves are the object of investigation, they are taken to stand in for other selves too. And it operates a more textured version of subjectivity in which the subject is not just positioned at the boundary with the other, but in a more considered engagement with the positive content of identity. Cohen (1994: 62) takes on the (absent) self as a complex and private as well as a public, plastic and variable entity, and pinpoints the contingency of ethnicity as something with a definite appearance, but indefinite substance. The indefinite substance of ethnicity (and race) is important in establishing an account of ethnicity (and race) making in non-essential terms.

For other commentators on ethnicity the 'ethnic self' is crafted in ethnic self-stories and ethnic narratives as well as at the interface with racism (Yi and Shorter-Gooden, 1999: 19). These ethnic narratives and self-stories are dia-logically formed in the 'countless exchanges one has with one's family, friends, institutions and the broader culture' (Yi and Shorter-Gooden, 1999: 24). These insights are presented as part of a practical enterprise: the re-writing/ re-invention of the self through therapeutic contexts. Yi and Shorter-Gooden present a case of a Korean who is confronted with a version of himself as a Korean forged in the local race politics – note the extension of this argument to deal with race – of his relationships with African American neighbours in which he is forced to deal with their versions of who he is. This hits at both the individual/existential dimensions of ethnic subject formation and the categories of social recognition with which they inevitably intersect. Yi and Shorter-Gooden (1999: 25) rightly claim that ethnic identities are multi-sourced and about other (social) categories of public recognition such as masculinity. Applying similar insights on consciousness to race, Norberto and Janice Valdez (1998: 379) show how individual families negotiated aspects of racial identity through intermarriage, migration, legal processes and revised genealogies. Ethnicised *subjectivities* wear different *identities* as badges or public announcements. In fact, this works for raced subjectivities too: the political context, the negotiation with others/public versions of what the raced self means.

Ethnicity then – like race – should be seen as a part of the constitution of modern subjectivity: it is central to the concept of the person. Verdery (1994: 44) says Barthes emphasised ethnicity as a fundamental means of ordering social life: and a seminal form of political calculation of difference. Verdery asks about the political context in which ethnic difference is made significant. Politics provides the frame in which ethnicity (and race) matters (Verdery 1994: 44–7). Patterson (1991: 55) says we can conceptualise ethnicity as 'a form of subjectivity with multiple centers …'. Immigrants relearn who they are in the social contexts to which they have migrated (Patterson 1991: 14). In line with Smith's (1988) views, Patterson advances the idea that subjects are caught up in a dialectical process of both being subjected to social formations, language, political apparatuses and so on and yet at the same time never are completely determined by them. This is a useful way to con-ceptualise the general relationship between raced and ethnicised subjec-tivities and social/political landscape. Ethnicity is construed not in place, but in a moving sense of place and social landscape. We will return to these things later in this chapter. Before we consider further the interface between people and social landscape as aspects of race (and ethnicity) making, we need to consider other aspects of race making as a people-centred activity. There is more to people than subjectivity and agency. There is corporeality and comportment: things that have a strong existential dimension to them and hence form a good bridge in our discussion between people and social landscapes.

Corporeality and comportment

Bodies and their movements are important in making people in racial and ethnic terms. Corporeality refers to the physicality of bodies, to the embodiment of personhood and so it is both a material and experiential aspect of personhood. It is also the visible announcement of versions of ethnicity, race, gender, age and much more besides. Comportment refers to the ways in which bodies move or otherwise conduct themselves. The two things operate together and provide important social clues about identity and mark the character of social space as we will see in later chapters. They provide the primary surfaces on which people interface with social contexts and are hence an integral part of subjectivity, which, as we have seen, is always socially animated and inscribed.

The body is instrumental in the grounding of the self. Goldberg (1993: 60), who is concerned with race, contends that the social subject; 'Consists in the intersection of social discourses in the body'. Although he is right, discourses on race and ethnicity do alight on the body, more than discourses are implicated here, for the raced and gendered body is essentially a *practical accomplishment*; it is worked on by human agency. Following Harré, Pile and Thrift (1995: 7) contend that the body also *grounds* the self as identity. We can add that it is the notice board on which the insignia of the self may be hung. Thus, to extend Goldberg's (1993: 1) argument about race and rights, that we conceive of subjects foremost in racial terms, brings together race, identity, subjectivity and the body as a cluster of things we need to take account of in conceptualising race making. It is on the body that the narratives of genealogy display themselves in skin pigmentation and bodily characteristics. These things compose the social messages announcing local and common understanding, mapping who people are in racial and ethnic (and other) terms. The body *announces* and *makes public* these things as part of a network of shared meanings and assumptions about who we are in the world: identity. This plays a significant part in the dialogues between the self and the categories of social recognition through which one is socially placed and dealt with. The body is raced and ethnicised in the articulation and announcement of skin pigments, hair, bodily comportment and the things pinned upon it or worn around it. In this the body is more than a significant site of cultural consumption through adornment. The body *plays* as part of identity – the *self* of the neatly packaged announcement – that works to signal the self and its place in the collectivity of selves (mapping) in which meaning is always negotiated. This is, perhaps, what Goffman and Shilling (Pile and Thrift, 1995: 7) refer to as the *shared vocabularies* of the body. This kind of formulation, I think, avoids the kind of racial essentialism that often alights on the body.

In race terms we need to think about the body through its insignia, adornment (including clothes), grooming and the accomplishment of appearance through the tweaking and massaging into place of the skin, hair and other attributes composing it. Following Shotter we might think of this, not primarily as symbolic and representational – though it is also undoubtedly that – but as a part of the *making* of selves in the living of lives in the webs of raced social relationships. These things are practical accomplishments, achieved in the deliberate actions of human agency and intended as part of the presentation of the self that gives off social messages through styles incorporating race and ethnicity. We can see this as part of the *filling* or *texture* of what Goldberg (1993: 79) identifies as the empty receptacles of race and ethnicity and as a part of their manufacture.

As important as the physicality of bodies and their insignia is something not often considered but closely connected: bodily comportment. The body is also about its movements, its form of animation. The ways in which people move through and occupy space are significant aspects of race making considered in later chapters. These movements provide another account of people and their lives. The lives people *walk* but do not necessarily *talk* (Knowles, 2000: 84–6) are, I think, appropriately considered *silent narratives* which, like clothes and other insignia, announce a kind of presence as well as an archive of activity and movement. Pile and Thrift (1995: 27–8) come close to this idea in their use of Bourdieu's idea of *ceaseless flow of conduct as absorbed coping*: and we should think of this as habitual activity of the sort which is not readily reflected on, but practised instead. This practical action of absorbed coping resonates with Goffman's dramatalurgical conception of the self as (dialogically) constituted in the acts of performance: although performance implies deliberation and crafting not implied by Bourdieu's idea.

Comportment and performance highlight the significance of *movement* as a small-scale, local activity. Meanwhile movement as *travel* has become centrally important in understanding the human dynamics of global society and most significantly for our purposes here, in the framing of ethnicities and diaspora. Movement as travel also has a place in the making of the self in ethnic and racial terms. Pile and Thrift (1995: 21) contend that Hall and Gilroy are arguing for what Said called a 'politics of transfiguration' founded on difference and the freedom to move across border and boundary in pursuit of self and other. There are important gains in political and biographical terms in transcending one racial order by replacing it with another: also a theme returned to later in this book. Space is heavily implicated in the comments above concerning comportment and travel. Space is the practical accomplishment of human action (Lefebvre, 1996), and action involves the deployment of bodies. Corporeality occupies a strategic place in the making of racial and ethnic (and gendered) selves and in the making of the social landscapes and their social relationships in which those selves operate. All of these themes raised in the corporeal making of subjectivities are taken up further in later chapters. *Where* people walk, and *how* they comport their bodies in their neighbourhoods and beyond are all part of race making.

People and regimes

Now we move on to some of the social interfaces composing subjectivity. Regime covers a multitude of situations of different magnitude and scale. It refers to particular kinds of social relationships that are more than personal, although they inevitably involve personal relationships too. Regime can refer to small scale local situations organised through contact with specific kinds of agencies: those who run local and national taxation, those who dispense various kinds of aid and resources such as housing, social services, who run libraries and parks, schools and leisure facilities. It can refer to forms of municipal or national governance. Regimes can be about forms of employment that are bigger than family businesses. They are the bureaucratic networks within which our lives are enmeshed. They are more systematic and bigger in their scope than personal relationships, although they have many similarities with personal relationships and overlap with them, especially in the ways in which people comport themselves. Models of private conduct in personal relationships seep into public interactions with bureaucracies, and ways of public conduct are tried out in more personal contexts, so these things are not entirely separate. They are about relationships with *others* which extend beyond family and friendship and which, in the current climate of performance management and measurement of effectiveness and efficiency from school league tables to hospital waiting lists in Britain, extend into the minutiae of our being, our subjectivity. In the spirit of Foucault we can think of these things as parts of the matrices forming our lives as systems of public interactions: but within which there is room for certain kinds of decision-making over directions to take, how to comport ourselves and so on. Regimes and their components are a large part of the social interface against which we develop our human subjectivity, the things that make us people.

I raised the social interface at the beginning of this chapter in the context of the differences between William Kafe and his colleague, and in the context of Levi's and Roseman's work on the holocaust, which noted important differences in the manner in which regimes deal with their racialised subjects. This was a part of my general argument, which was that people make regimes, are part of the race making that makes regimes as well as people in racial (and ethnic) terms. We also saw earlier in the case of Roseman's soldier playing postman in the Jewish ghetto, that people can operate various levels of compliance and non-compliance with regimes. Herzfeld (1992: 33) sees the complicity between regimes and its subjects as part of a broader problem. In charting the 'social production of indifference', the 'destructive, routinised inaction', which becomes an 'inevitable dimension of everyday social experience' and takes many forms from the benign to summary execution; Herzfeld (1992: 56) suggests that: 'All bureaucrats and their clients alike are potential bricoleurs, working both within and upon "the system" ...'. What they produce becomes a part of the fabric of everyday life:

> Once in being, a nation state has to establish a pervasive reinforcement of its culturally constructed logic in every aspect of daily life. The main framework consists of a set of national categories: those that define who belongs and who does not. These categories are relatively simple, few in number and rigid. They suppress the relativity of all social categories in daily use, so that one may no longer claim different identities in different situations. (Herzfeld, 1992: 65)

In relation to the operation of nationalism, Herzfeld (1992: 49) recognises the role of ordinary people in working on the grand images of their political leadership and recasting them in more familiar terms. In uncovering the symbolic roots of indifference he reveals 'an intimate, two-way relationship between manifestations of state power and the numerous levels at which a sense of local community is realised'. Hence, he concludes 'The roots of official intolerance and indifference lie in the popular attitudes upon which official discourse builds to make its own case'. It is this that makes genocide possible. The conceptual models are already in place 'perhaps less violent, but certainly no more tolerant of social or cultural differences' (Herzfeld, 1992: 49).

> The real danger of indifference is not that it grows out of the barrel of a gun, but that it too easily becomes habitual. It is the opium of the state drudge. ... Hierarchy and egalitarianism, tolerance and genocide, kindly hospitality and brutal indifference: these are not mutually exclusive opposites, but the dialectics of differentiation in what we are pleased to call the modern world. (Herzfeld, 1992: 184)

While the search for a general connection between people and regimes is not where my own argument is going, preferring instead to search for specific mechanisms and processes, Herzfeld's general point, that the lives and thinking of ordinary people are significant in the production of regimes, is very relevant. As Levi points out, there are great and small complicities and they are all important: they collectively compose the racial fabric of regimes.

The fabric and fabrication of subjectivity and the regimes in which subjectivity is made are, then, but two aspects of the same set of processes. People make the racialised social orders through which their own lives are cast at the same time as they make themselves as the subjects of their own biographies with their own crises of existence, at the same time as they deal with the imperatives of the regimes in which they operate. As I suggested earlier, it is *people* who operate racialised regimes. It is people who give substance and meaning to racial categories in their daily lives. They are able to do this, according to Herzfeld, because the symbolic roots of their own lives and the assumptions and structures of popular thought on which their lives are based are the same as those which operate, at another level, in the calibration of the regime. Race and ethnicity are not just aspects of political structure or the categories by which people are dealt with. At the core of race and ethnicity is the interface between subjectivity, the underlying basis of what it means to be a person in the world, the operation of human agency and the political landscapes on which it is all set. Individuals live with, and give meaning to, political landscapes and social categories with which they have deep connections.

It is in the interface between people and the regimes managing their lives that private and public notions of racial and ethnic identity are staked out and negotiated. It is here that we confront, contest and collude in, publicly calibrated notions of who we are in racial or ethnic terms. It is here that what it means to be us is struggled over. In racialised societies what it means to be white Irish, to be Indian, to be a Jamaican or Korean is transacted at this boundary between the self and the collective other at which subjectivities are manufactured. Not because we need the other to be ourselves, but because public, social conceptions of race and ethnicity always negotiate private, lived, interior, existential versions. Both are part of race making and lives are about living around and accommodating the gaps between, these two things. Who you think you are in racial or ethnic terms is very important. It shapes the decisions you make and the manner in which you conduct yourself in the world in which you live. But this always takes into account public and social perceptions of who you are and your life will be about the forms of accommodation and complicity this entails. I am not suggesting that there are agreed versions of these. They are always interpreted. In societies configured by forms of racism, in which forms of racial exclusion and social injustice operate as part of the regime, then racism too is a significant part of the making of race: a very important part. It sets the character of the political landscape and the ways in which racialised subjectivities operate within it. As we make ourselves and the world in which we live, so we make race.

Looking forward

I have argued in this chapter that it is *race making* that we need to understand. In arguing that race is *produced* I have tried to identify some of the *mechanisms* active in composing it. I have argued that people are central in race making, making themselves and their social environments and regimes in racial terms. The mechanisms composing race are minute social processes bound up with the ordinary activities of living and being who we are in the world. I have argued that race is made in the deep texture of subjectivity. We know, from the templates of personhood we reviewed, that subjectivity is always socially engaged, that it acts dialogically with the fabric of the social, making it and the self in social terms. Of particular significance at this person/social interface are the dialogues with administrative action, the ways in which we are dealt with as people and as constituents of social categories made in racial, ethnic and other terms. It is here, at this interface, that categories of public recognition negotiate the internal, existential and unique aspects of personhood. It is also in mapping the character of these types and numbers of interfaces that we can map race and ethnicity in more detailed terms, terms that take account of other aspects of social position and biography. At this interface with the social we see the significance of social relationships and, later, we will see the importance of the social organisation of space. It is at the social interface that we see the operation of racism in the interface with social agencies and with others in social relationships. It is *political contexts* that make race matter: contexts where race is a force in generating social distinctions of a particular character, forms of racism play a crucial part in the making of race. They too are the products of human agency. It is here at the social interface that we see the importance of body and movement, as the self projects itself, asserts itself, in the networks of social relationships of its own composition. The body with its insignia, grooming and comportment grounds the self and launches it at the other, social, parts which are effective in the making of the self. Subjectivity is integrally raced and always in the process of becoming, always incomplete, at the point of unravelling and becoming something else. Subjectivity is a part of composing the raced social fabric and at the same time made by it in the dialogues of mutual composition. It follows that attempts to excavate race or ethnicity from either its human agents, or from the texture of the social fabric in which it is embedded, are futile. Consequently race and ethnicity are best left 'in place' and reviewed in the political and social (situational) contexts in which they occur (Knowles, 2000: 152–7).

Maintaining the unique, the existential, at the interface with the social and the systematic means that race making is both systematic and biographical, with a wild card that can show up and move things in unpredictable ways. Race making is hence always something that needs to be unpacked as, and when, and where, it operates. There are no templates from which to predict what may happen. It is always situational, simultaneously personal and social.

There are many advantages of seeing things in these terms. The person-centred forms of analysis I suggest in this chapter provide a far more detailed and highly textured account of race than many others. It allows far finer social differences and distinctions to become apparent. We get a detailed, up-close, look at how race operates by untangling the ways in which it is made. In exposing the detailed operation of race through looking at how it is produced we can begin to piece together the racial grammar of our societies and our time. Exposing the mechanisms by which race is made we gain a picture of the forms of social practice to which it gives rise, but in a way that exposes race as an actionable target. Something we can do something about. If we make the world in which we live in racial terms then we can unmake or remake it too. And this approach places the political impetus with people and forms of human agency. If it is *we* who make the world in racial terms, then *we* can remake it in terms that are less racially offensive and objectionably divisive and unfair. Volition raises questions of culpability. And culpability is an invitation to political action and change. We can ask – what is involved in being who we are in the world in racial terms? How does this impact on other people? And on the making of the social fabric in racial terms? Are there ways of changing who we are and what we do? What leeway is there in the existential to effect significant social change? Those – kinds of (white) people – who are the beneficiaries of racial orders need to ask themselves, ourselves, critical questions about the forms of our collusion with the regimes in which our lives are set and think about ways in which we can disrupt the complicities on which racialised regimes depend. But those who are on the other end of things, whose forms of social disadvantage are structured by race, need to ask similar questions establishing collusion and culpability, uncomfortable questions too, which have implications for our forms of being in the world. There are fundamental personal and political issues, which come from placing people at the centre of the analysis of race.

Summary

- Race making is about the many things that go into producing race *in people* and *in social and political systems*. People are the motor of race (and ethnicity) making and contribute significantly to the fabric of racialised regimes.
- Subjectivities are significant in making people in their interface with the social world. Three models of subjectivity provide important information for formulating what it means to be a person in the contemporary world: explanations of subjectivities as bundlers of capacities, explanations that think about subjectivities in terms of social positions and those fore-grounding relational and compositional aspects of subjectivities.
- Ethnicity and race and bound up with subjectivities, versions of person-hood as socially inscribed in dialogues with others as part of a network of social relationships, as cast in the relational spaces between the self and others. The raced and ethnicised person is composed through reflexivity and moral frameworks; through positions on the social landscape in which space and everyday practical action make us.

Race making: This forms a part of a materialist analysis, the idea that race, and ethnicity too, are 'made' or produced and that people are central in making race. Race is made in the ways in which people conduct themselves in every-day life, in moving about the world, in how they look and what they wear and in their interactions with each other and the social and political regimes in which their lives are set.

Notes

1. The Jewish General Hospital and the McGill University form an established centre for the study and practice of transcultural psychiatry and produce a journal of the same name. This was a good place from which to study the production of race in psychiatric regimes.

2. See Vered Amit-Talai (1996) for a discussion of ethnic activists in Montreal.

3. See Knowles (1996a)

4. Subjectivity refers to the underlying principles of what it means to be a person in the world, the cornerstone of modern philosophy in which the individual is the centre of politi-cal, social and theoretical thought (Dallmayr, 1981: ix). The version of subjectivity advanced in this volume is based on Merleau Ponty's concept of situated subjectivity which has the advantage of a social and embodied sense of human agency that stresses habitat as the con-text for thought and action and through which we take on a habitual relationship to the world we do not necessarily reflect on (Crossley, 1994: 8–14). Patterson (1991: 15) argues that human subjects are caught in a dialectical process of being both subjected to social for-mations but never completely determined by them.

5. This is sustained in Foucault's account of power as disciplinary networks. See *Discipline and Punish* (1977) for a fuller description of this; and Knowles (1996a) for a simpler discus-sion of power as discipline.

6. Race and ethnicity are conceptualised as social and political distinctions in most cur-rent accounts of race and many accounts of ethnicity. See for example Goldberg (1993), Patterson (1991), Barthes (1994), Roosens (1989), Hall (1991a), Cohen (1997), Miles (1989), Winant (1994a) and Cambridge and Feuchtwang (1992).

7. *Black* in Britain and the US at this time was a reference to an expression of a common experience of exclusion and a common political identity, forged through resistance to exclusion and as the assertion of new and positive meaning (Miles, 1994: 195).

8. See Portelli's (1991: 1–29) discussion on the relationship between individual memories and public events.

9. Conceptions of space draw on the work of Lefebvre (1996). Lefebvre's concept of space is etched by human agency; the product of the uses to which it is put; the purposes for which it was made; the interests it serves; and the social relationships which take place within and through it. In this formulation space both etches and is etched by human agency.

10. Goldberg's (1993) race and rights thesis is eloquently set out in *Racist Culture*. He claims that in modern/postmodern culture we conceive of social subjects first and foremost in racial terms. He suggests that modernity's subject is 'abstract and atomistic, general and universal' and that race furnishes the subject with a specific identity. This is partly the result of liberalism, which deals with race through tolerance and denial, insisting on sameness. As we began to conceptualise the individual we did so as the bearer of rights (developed in political philosophy) and as the bearer of race (Goldberg, 1993: 1–42).

11. Identities are an aspect of subjectivity, but subjectivity is the more fundamental category, the models of personhood on which we build embellishments and insignia composing identities. Subjectivities are the templates of personhood, identities are about detail.

12. This reference refers to Anthony Cohen's lecture in Amsterdam of the same year, 1994, as his book *Self Consciousness,* published in Vermeulen & Govers (eds). Both are useful sources of reference in thinking through ethnicity in more individual terms.

Chapter Two
Lives and Auto/Biography

Mini contents

Introduction

People's lives and deaths are the central object of auto/biography[1]. In auto/biographical writing we see the texture of individual lives; the connections between lives in the form of social relationships; the interface between people and broader social and political landscapes and processes; the everyday and the extraordinary; and personal and social transformation. Auto/biographies produce the existential elements of lives in their broader social context. They contain these elements, noted in the last chapter, as essential in producing an understanding of race making and consequently, the racial grammar of societies; grainy, detailed, pictures of the social fabric. In the last chapter I signalled some of the analytic advantages of focusing on people, and showed the lessons of my own biographical approach to understanding the operation of race in Montreal through the life of William Kafe, some psychiatric nurses and their clients. In this chapter I want to examine what can be learned about race and ethnicity by examining published auto/biographical work. This chapter then, concerns the deep texture of lives, subjectivities and the social and political interfaces in which people are made in racial and ethnic terms. This chapter explores what race and ethnicity might mean in the contexts of people's lives.

What does auto/biography do?

It would be a mistake to think that auto/biography is the life of a person rendered in textual form. Auto/biography neither *captures* subjectivity nor the lives it calibrates, but it does reveal aspects of the substance of lives and hints at forms of subjectivity. Auto/biography reveals something of the texture and mode of operation of a life and the social world of which it is a part. Subjectivity, as we saw in the last chapter, is the bigger project, it concerns the templates of personhood from which specific modes of being in the world and actual lives are hewn. The person is drawn from the *category* of the person and auto/biography is able to deliver moments, insights, vistas onto the life of a person and the principles through which it is calibrated. Auto/biography is not the *living* of a life but its *telling,* in partial form. Lives are made and activated in their living, not in their telling, but, in so far as telling is part of living, it is also part of the fabrication of a life. Telling as auto/biography then, is indirectly, a part of the constitution of a life. It is primarily a narrative stringing together of fragments and moments made in memory, which mesh with plausible versions of the self. Auto/biographies narrate what it is possible to tell about a life. Much is left unsaid; un-narrated and un-narratable. The un-narrated and un-narratable parts of lives are unconscious. They are either part of the 'unconscious' in the psychoanalytic sense and/or they are embedded in the habitual repetition of practical action, in its spatiality, or in the taken for granted assumptions which move bodies in and through space and habitus. Auto/biography cannot capture all of this. It is inevitably a partial story, offered by its subject or another claiming detailed knowledge of its subject, concerning the strategies deployed in their being and operation in the social world. Auto/biography is inevitably flawed by its limitations.

It also has numerous advantages and enough of them to make it a viable methodology for understanding key aspects of racial grammar. Auto/biography is uniquely positioned to allow the investigative gaze to wander simultaneously in two directions. Individual lives – and their partially captured forms of subjectivity – and their social context are brought together in the same frame. Auto/biography looks inwards and outwards at the same time. It displays the existential as some of the unique features of lives, at its interface with the social landscape. The story of the self inevitably involves others and hence also inevitably opens onto the social landscape. Auto/biography's capacities particularly suit it to the task in hand which is to provide a way of conceptualising race and ethnicity that places the individual subject at the centre of the analytic frame. Subjectivity, as I suggested in the last chapter, stands astride the existential and the social. So too does auto/biography and this makes it a most suitable approach for some of the things we want to know. I suggested in the last chapter that race and ethnicity are deeply buried in the texture of subjectivity and that bits of subjectivity as an existential/ social enterprise are revealed in auto/biography. Because of their ability to direct the analytical gaze in two directions at once auto/biographies contain accounts of individual lives as textured by race/ethnicity, in the political contexts in which these things are animated and given meaning. *In the contexts in which they exist and matter.*

Auto/biographies open a window on individual lives and their crises of existence, at the same time as they open onto the political landscapes in which those lives are made. Although the views from this window are restricted, as I suggest above, auto/biography is a useful conceptual and methodological tool for capturing (raced) subjectivity and the political/social context of its making. Auto/biography simultaneously reveals the subject, the social categories through which forms of public recognition are transacted, and the political landscape on which all of this takes place. Auto/biography then is capable of capturing big and small pictures, micro and macro focuses, in the same frame. The micro-framing of the social through biographical work has a long tradition in sociology. C Wright Mills in the 1950s saw the sociological imagination as generated in the interaction between life experience and history (Erben, 1993: 15) as we saw in the Introduction. Modern hermeneutical biography was founded by Wilhelm Dilthey, in the nineteenth century, for whom history was the composite study of individuals (Erben, 1993: 15–16). Robert Merton (1988), Norman Denzin (1989) and Daniel Bertaux (1981) provide more recent examples of its effective deployment in social understanding and analysis. Forms of biographical method are most effectively used in social policy (Chamberlayne and King, 2000), in expositions of methodology (Wengraf, 2000) and much more besides.

Auto/biography reveals the nature of human volition and the systems in which it is operative. It reveals some of the consequences of this interface between volition and systems. Above all it reveals some of the dynamics of lives and the activities of living. Because of this it reveals racial categories as more than a tactical posture, in exposing the substance of the lives in which ethnicity and race operate tactically because it takes in the dialogues between lives and political landscapes.

I argued in the last chapter that British analytical engagement with race and ethnicity had neglected individual lives – the project of auto/biography – as a site of social knowing. The exceptions to this are one or two anthropologists interested in auto/biographical methods (Nigel Rapport) or self-consciousness (Anthony Cohen). A growing band of social analysts who are prepared to work auto/biographically have been interested in gender but not in race. Interest in auto/biographical approaches to race and ethnicity has, however, surfaced in the reclamation projects[2] of British oral histories detailing the individual/collective stories of diasporas. These provide accounts of race as Jewishness and as blackness and while these often draw some of the links between people within communities, their focus has remained squarely local and they have generally not been interested in connecting lives with the bigger picture of the racial order of things in which racialised and ethnicised lives are arranged and have meaning. Because of this they are of limited use in the analysis of race and ethnicity. An exception is the autobiography of Yasmin Alibhai-Brown (1997), which details her move from Uganda to Britain. As I suggested in the last chapter, this gap shows a lack of preparedness to move between different magnitudes of scope and scale. There are problems with detail too. It is also rare that the texture of race and ethnicity in lives rendered in auto/biography are fully enough described to make them analytically useful. In generating my own biographical account of the making of race in William Kafe's life, I was fortunate enough to have available his own detailed records. Auto/biographies are not generally written in this kind of detail, as they are not usually intended to contribute to the analysis of race, but to offer a description of a particular tranche of raced or ethnicised lives.

While British analyses of race have neglected auto/biographical accounts, American analyses have not, and so my examination of the analytic value of auto/biographical enterprise in this chapter focuses on American race writing that takes this form. American auto/biography lies much closer to the *analysis of race* because of the intellectual/political context in which it operates and which sustains the generation of 'ethnic studies' as African American, Hispanic studies and so on in American universities[3]. This, in itself, is the product of a political culture of race consciousness; a sense that race matters, albeit in a restricted way, which operates in popular as well as in intellectual culture. America has produced an ethnicised/raced auto/biographical genre which *operates in close proximity* to the *analysis* of race in the universities and which also stresses its importance in popular mythology and culture. This is a genre that suits the purposes of this chapter, which is to put some lived auto/biographical flesh on the skeletons of people and their subjectivity and so provide examples of the ways in which race making is about people and the lives they live. This is the product of a political context in which race and ethnicity are acknowledged as being close to the surface of political and individual life. The US, of course, provides this context.

This chapter then, explores auto/biographies' contribution to the analysis of race and the connections between lives positioned by race and ethnicity and the broader social and political contexts in which they operate in the United States. It chews on the interface between agency and structure, which, as I suggested in the last chapter, are not distinct but related domains of analysis and the practical arrangement of race and ethnicity in the lives they organise. In particular, it reviews the intersections between lives and the operation of racism, and here captures some critical aspects of race making, showing how people make a difference in regimes.

Auto/biographical narrative

This is a useful point at which to review our operational understanding of the self, the object of auto/biographical narrative and to say something about the character of auto/biographical narrative. In the theories concerning the formulation of the self as subjectivity in the last chapter, I stressed Shotter's approach in which the self becomes an ongoing project of constant composition. The self is continually composed in many places through many processes and highly significantly, in other, less reflected-upon, forms of (spatial/habitual) composition-in-action which will be discussed more thoroughly in Chapter 3. One of these places in the composition of the self is auto/biography. It is important to understand that it is the compositional, not representational, aspects of the self in auto/biography that mark it as part of a material, not discursive, analysis. Auto/biography is a narrative activity involving reflection, theorisation and the translation of living, rendered as stories, into text. I have already noted that while life and narrative, living and telling, are not the same thing, they *are* intricately connected in that *telling* becomes part of living and *living* becomes part of telling. Auto/biographies are hence compositional narratives, which form an integral part of continuous processes of self generation. They are also a *particular* way of accounting for the self, a particular *kind of narrative*, a particular *mode of self understanding* (Freeman, 1993: 28). They consist in acts of writing and sense-making 'by which individuals are responsible for seeing present moments of being in the context of past and future ones...a creative act by which an individual gives meaning to his or her own individual life...' (Rapport, 1999: 3). In the interpretative acts entailed in auto/biography – with their in-built theorising and distanciation – the self is constantly written and rewritten, constituted and reconstituted. New relationships between past and present, collection and re-collection are constantly established (Freeman, 1993: 30–3, 45–9) in auto/biography. The selective and socially configured operation of memory creates new bargains struck between personal past and personal present. The self is always an interpretation based on the selective garnering of experience rendered in narrative, but not in narrative alone, as we shall see later in the book.

The simultaneity and interconnection of living and telling, past and present, is replicated in the operation of what is referred to as the 'existential' in Chapter 1 and also in the social (and administrative) aspects revealed in auto/biographical work. At one level the articulation and configuration of the self is personal and existential: '...a means by which individuals existentially apprehend their own lives' (Rapport, 1999: 3). And yet at another level, and simultaneously, the self is intricately *socially* etched as the last chapter showed in reviewing different theoretical formulations of the self *all* of which concurred on the point of the self's social character. The self, manifested in the narrative genre of auto/biography, is inherently social: produced and communicated through social conventions and revealed in particular ways in auto/biographical convention. Existential paths are inevitably cut *through* social landscape and by the *means* of social landscape, which provides the material manipulated in rendering the self as an existential/social being. Multiple dimensions of social landscape come into play in this connection.

Erben's (1999: 18) discussion of Walter Benjamin and Franz Kafka – relevant for our purposes here as an exposition of ethnicity-at-its-intersection-with-race as Jewishness – settles on two key components of social landscape in the etching of the existential (Jewish) self: myth and the quotidian. The two men, Erben tells us, shared '...an ability and desire to explore the tension between the experience of the mythico-traditional and the endlessly negotiated activities of modern metropolitan life'. The two men would have grazed on mid-European stories that captured some of what it meant to be *them* as a category socially positioned at this point, and in this place, in the twentieth century. The more prosaic (non-mythical, quotidian) part of their social landscape concerned the daily activities of what it meant to be Jewish in the context of German city life. Hence, and significantly for the discussion which follows, the vicissitudes of social landscape operate between the imaginativeness of myth and the banality of everyday existence. Rapport (1999: 5), drawing on the work of anthropologists such as Lévi Strauss and Edmund Leach, points to the significance in myth, music and ritual as the means by which individuals transmit collective messages to themselves about themselves, concerning the eternal structural verities of their societies and world views: verities which not only claim an unchanging world but whose telling and retelling effects a stasis or lack of change.

Myths, music and ritual operate as cultural forms synthesising and disguising acts of individual communication and truth making (Rapport, 1999: 5). Whether the existential is occluded by, or leans directly and visibly upon, these highly significant aspects of social landscape does not matter: it is their interconnectedness that is significant and worthy of note. Myth, music and ritual are, in this formulation adopted by Rapport, seminal aspects of social landscape and constitutive (not representative) of both lives *and* the scenes on which they are lived. Worthy of note is their relationship to narrative: they both transcend narrative *and* they operate through it. Again this points to the significance of non-narrative forms of communication, through action, gesture and emotion, in the processes of collective being which draw the individual into the collectivity of souls. But being habitual and embedded does not preclude these non-narrative forms of communication becoming articulated in narrative. They may or may not be expressed in this form and where exceptional reflexivity allows them to be converted into narrative, it should be noted that *substantial work of translation* has already been performed on them.

Race, ethnicity and auto/biographical narrative

Philosophers and sociologists of race and ethnicity have claimed that race and ethnicity play a fundamental part in the cauldrons of human existence. Race and ethnicity are evidently seminal in who we are existentially and socially, and in formulating the positions we might occupy on any social landscape. It was argued in the last chapter that race and ethnicity were indissoluble elements of the self: and it follows in this chapter that as selves are composed in auto/biographical narrative so too are race and ethnicity. The generation (and excavation) of racially and ethnically positioned selves in auto/biographical narrative is, of course, the subject of this chapter. Some introductory remarks on some of the contours of race and ethnicity and the relationship of these concepts (and their contours) to the means by which lives are lived and told, are thus appropriate.

Indissoluble elements in the composition of life, race and ethnicity share elements of their constitution with life itself: their circumscription by the prospect of death. Race and ethnicity are as much a part of death as they are of life: they exist at the centre of the crises of existence and its extinction. Life and death and the race and ethnicity embedded in life and its forms of extinction as death, are part of existential trajectories and the social and political landscapes upon which they are etched. Erben's (1999) biographical essay on Kafka and Benjamin touches on this theme in revealing what is fundamental about both men's ethnicity as Jewishness. Proposing Kafka as the 'formally creative version of his [Benjamin's] philosophy' (Erben, 1999: 14), the 'Jewishness' of novelist and philosopher is played-out in the proximity of their lives to the regimes managing Jewish death. Jewish life, at this point in the twentieth century, was organised around a reckoning with the political organisation of death: genocide. Kafka's lover was shot by the Stalinist regime in Russia. 'Had he lived (he died young) and been unable to flee the territory of the Third Reich he would have joined his three sisters in Auschwitz' (Erben, 1999: 14). The impact of the political organisation of death on Jewish existence at this time and in this place is impossible to overestimate. The prospect of life itself – quite apart from its peculiar arrangement in quotidian detail – is suffused with the political strategies managing race and ethnicity, as this example of the lives of Kafka and Benjamin, explored by Erben, so poignantly shows. Reared in a lethal form of anti-semitism, it is not surprising that Kafka's work should display the precariousness of life itself and the certainty of death in its untimely conclusion. 'All Kafka's greatest work…is the history of a central protagonist's regression from the confident certainties of normal life to a state of overwhelming psychic bewilderment, and, eventually, death' (Erben, 1999: 14). Uncertainty, born of the prospect of systematic and untimely death, connects with other, less lethal, aspects of the marginality of Jewish life.

> If Kafka's sense of failure and the fact of his Jewishness set a theme for Benjamin's connection to him, this theme is played out, in oblique and unstraightforward ways, through an appreciation of the vicissitudes of modernity, and a recognition of the universal in the prosaic. (Erben, 1999: 13)

Here Erben (1999: 18) points to the substance of the ethnically/racially organised existential in what Benjamin and Kafka shared through their Jewishness, and the social landscapes in which it was articulated. This is played out in the dialogue between the myths of the cultures in which selves are moulded and the quotidian aspects of everyday life: and the ultimate conclusion of life (but not myth) in death. Erben also rightly points to the obliqueness with which ethnicity and race are manifest in lives. It is this very obliqueness which makes the analysis of race through the window of auto/biography a challenging approach.

What follows is an exploration of the popular and intellectual manifestations of the (American) genre of raced biography. This exploration is concerned with how the fabric of (raced) subjectivity and the fabric of (raced) versions of everyday life are revealed in this material.

Popular versions of African American lives

The development of cyberspace technologies serves well the project of valorising individual lives and struggles edited out of the nation's compositional record of heroes and circumstances. The Internet has not only widened access to the means of dissemination of hitherto little known information. It also facilitates the transgression of previous boundaries between public and private in that private struggles and experiences can readily be rendered public in this form. The Texas and Ohio Historical Society web site collections, for example, showcase the biographies and activities of prominent local African Americans, especially those who engaged in local struggles, which extended the civil rights of all. This selection of those who made a difference in race making of course suits our purposes in this chapter and this volume overall. Ohio's digital collection, 'illuminates specific moments in the history of Ohio's African-Americans and provides an overview of their experiences during the time period 1850–1920 in the words of the people that lived them.' These are offered as a part of the account of the 'American Memory' – an online resource of the Library of Congress (http.//ohiohistory.org. africanam) – from which they were previously excluded by the (racial) power geometries structuring historiographies[4]. Similarly, the Ohio Historical Society National Afro-American Museum and Cultural Center aims to provide a public education service on African American history and culture 'from the African origins to the present by collecting, preserving and interpreting material evidence of the Black experience' (www.ohiohistory.org/places/afroam). The museum's permanent exhibit animates what are described as 'typical' fifties black lives as well as detailing social changes and developments in black rights throughout that period.

The reinsertion of these lost heroes, heroines and experiences into accounts of American history is evidently the project here. At the same time this material underscores the *recent* nature of black civil rights and the political contexts in which they were demanded. Race and rights, struggle and experience, are all part of this enterprise which serves to tweak the national conscience in replaying the recent history of the relationship between the nation state and its black citizens. Lest we forget! And we should not forget because this is still very much a live issue. This catalogue of suffering and struggle against injustices inflicted by white Americans of European descent resonates with a present of continued and renewed forms of racial injustice. It also highlights the dynamics in which the racing of blacks is guided by, and rebounds as, the racing of whites[5]. Those whose lives were more than ordinary[6] in their contribution to the struggle for civil rights; Christia Adair, for example, an otherwise unknown heroine from Texas was active in the NAACP[7] in the 1940s and through whose efforts black Texans were able to serve on juries or be hired for government jobs. One of Adair's smaller, but significant, achievements was the desegregation of the changing rooms in the local department store: an assault on the feasibility of segregation in mass consumption urban America.

These stories are also testimonies. Individual lives are shown to be 'making a difference'. Agency triumphs over the injustices embedded in structure: and the fault lines of the structure shift and realign themselves slowly but surely. Structure unravels in the face of determined human agency. And we see racial orders being made and remade by individual and collective action. An account of social change, Adair's story is more than a political statement about social justice. It is also an invitation to ongoing political action to further refashion the racial order. Web sites serving the projects of local oral histories are a good place to publicise these otherwise little known struggles, placing them in the national tapestry from which they were consigned to obscurity by more prominent struggles organised by the NAACP leadership. To 'tell' lives is to rescue them from the obscurity to which they are consigned by *the racial order and its dominant modes of opposition*, both of which have the effect of rendering them insignificant. To 'tell' lives is to imbue them with meaning and dignity: to reposition them in the racial order and the regimes of its opposition. Web sites and the collections they popularise are monuments to America's racial past and the continuing struggles of a racialised present in which they are given new meaning and poignancy.

Academic accounts of racialised and ethnicised auto/biography

Academic and popular accounts share the project of social critique as a prelude to social reform and the work of historical reconstruction on which it is based. What differentiates the popular and the academic is the extent of their elaboration, the level of their theorisation and the extent to which they are prepared to engage in social analysis. For these reasons rather than any intrinsic worth, academic accounts form a basis for the kind of discussion this chapter demands. Academic accounts are more likely to be mobilised in the service of detailed and abstract social analysis and are hence often more explicit in articulating and defending their political project. Otherwise there are no substantial differences in content and orientation although popular accounts have the benefit of broader appeal. This – academic – writing is marked as a genre by its attempts to understand the mechanisms of individual lives and the collectivities of which they are a part *organised through the modality of race*. Race, as the means by which the (American) nation state has collectivised subjectivities and dealt with its citizens from slavery onward, lies at the centre of this genre as its central principle of social organisation and individual identity. Social and emotional landscapes are intricately connected and the excavation of lives and the social structures in which they are embedded usually proceeds in tandem. The contestation and reconstruction of the existing racial order occupies a central place in this genre. Auto/biography, with its access to the social and political order as well as individual lives, is a prelude to a politics addressing racial inequities. This particular combination is examined more closely in reviewing selected themes found in recent African American auto/biographical writing.

Slavery and sameness

On the surface, African American auto/biographical writing is a vehicle for the exploration of *individual lives*. Closer examination quickly reveals the social templates from which these lives were cut. Slavery occupies a pivotal position in the production of African American lives, identities and activities and many auto/biographies make reference to the particularities of a slave heritage in collectivising and articulating this set of lives. Davis' (1999: 151–5) account of black female slave narratives argues that they were a vehicle for shaping black women's identity: this in itself is a political act. In their less-than-human-status slaves were denied common humanity and identity, and their narratives are presented as a part of their relentless search for self-definition (Davis, 1999: 151). In speaking their lives – slave narratives were part of an oral tradition pre-dating written auto/biography – slaves confirm their existence and articulate a 'voice' asserting and validating a version of life and identity – 'being' itself – a set of activities that inevitably included the demand for freedom.

> ...the female slave narrative was written to define and create black identi-ties...female slaves examined, interpreted and created the importance of their lives [in the face of a system of erasure which insisted upon their insignifi-cance]...make statements about the system as well as relate events that occurred in their lives...Understand herself as a product of the forces against her...alter and later abolish the institution of slavery....(Davis, 1999: 156)

Slave narratives, in common with later versions of black lives and their sub-jectivities, articulated through segregation and later still the acquisition of formal equality, are a rhetoric of the self which is *capable of imagining and asserting new versions of the self that transcend its social context*. The black slave self is simultaneously *in place* and *transcendent* in the journey beyond its place to other places where it can be what it is capable of being. The seminal impor-tance placed on slavery in accounts of African American lives rests on their paradigmatic reconstitution of the self from its sub-human to its human form, able to take its place alongside other forms of human life.

This claiming of humanity forms the very bedrock of the self. Thus slavery acts as a reminder of what can be accomplished and as a tribute to those who endured it, challenged it and imagined a life beyond it. Interestingly slave narratives occupy a quite different place in the narratives of African Canadians. Possibly because of its position in the British Empire and because of the anti-slavery movement developing in Britain, the slave origins of Canadians who arrived from America with the United Empire Loyalists and others who worked in domestic slavery in Montreal were obscured, and have only recently been excavated. The acknowledgement of Canadian slavery contradicts the liberal version of Canada as a place of slave emancipation and escape through the underground railway. Thomson (1979) details this history in *Blacks in Deep Snow*. There has, in fact, been a settled African Canadian population in Nova Scotia for three hundred years (Williams, 1989) and yet narratives of racial exclusion and protest have not developed as they have on the American side of the border where slavery has an iconic status in the calibration of black disadvantage and oppression. This shows that similar historical forms generate quite different political reactions and narratives.

It is evident from these few examples and the commentary they sustain, that the concept of a (black American) life – and the ability to reflect upon and narrate it – is composed of three elements arranged in a dialogue with each other. There is the self and its identities and potential identities – the things of which the self is capable. Second there is the daily unremarkable (quotidian) life. Third there are the (more remarkable) moments of social transformation. The individual self and its circumstances – a life – inevitably invokes the collectivity of lives of which it is a part. One is a slave demanding freedom along with other slaves forced into opposition with those (whites) who compose the texture of slave society. In these dialogues of slavery between the individual and the social context in which that individual operates, the 'social' and the 'structural' are dominant and the myth of sameness is ascendant. Accounts of the individual hence sometimes work against the individual. Distinctiveness cashes-out as common experience and the basis of political claims; and the existential is eclipsed by the social. Slavery played a significant part in establishing and sustaining the unity of African Americans as a *social category*. Hence the project of exploring lives through biographies was always conceived as an exploration of the basis of collective life, although it looked like auto/biography and had auto/biography's potential to reveal the racial texture of lives in acts of social transformation.

Diversity

Once dominated by the myth of sameness, a sameness originating in slavery and which underwrote the politics of counter assertion as a protest against the social locations African Americans occupied, African American auto/ biography now displays all the vicissitudes of diversity. This is a recent and important theoretical shift in it as a genre. It is not a shift *from* the social templates of slavery but takes these as given and proceeds with the task of diversification through biographical complication. In this shift individual lives gain a new importance, not as units of structure, but as its active constituents. Conyers (1999b) *Black Lives: Essays in African American Biography*, for example, assembles a cast of characters that chronicle the diversity of lives and complex identities *written beyond the templates of slavery*. Conyers' volume – a good example of contemporary writing – includes McClinton's biographical essay on Vinnette Carrol. Carrol was a director of musicals and playwright operating from the 1940s to the 1960s, whose work combined a version of Brecht, and the German theatre traditions in which his work was set, with her own roots in African American musical performance. McClinton's biographical essay stresses Carrol's relationship to the broader African American community that she drew upon as a source of inspiration in carving out her craft and repaid with the provision of opportunity and role models for young actors, producers and so on. Carrol's biographer describes her art as:

> ...both specific and universal in addressing the human condition and the spirit of human kind through a multi-cultural theatrical expression...Carrol believed that in order for African American theater to be totally complete, it must first be rooted in its communities, it must take pride in its unique history, it must remember and embrace its past, and it must use its own talents. (McClinton, 1999: 23–24)

Carrol's work (as her biographer describes it) was open to other traditions and to entering the mainstream. This was no ghetto theatre. Neither was her's a ghetto life. Her biographer contends that her work moved from what it meant to be black to what it meant to be 'alive' (McClinton, 1999: 28). Addressing the human condition and asserting the African American condition into *the* human condition, Carrol's life and work (and identity) is firmly placed within a matrix of traditions that have no single source in slavery but which complete the political work of the anti-slavery movement in claiming a common humanity with others.

Other essays in Conyers' collection chronicle the lives of Richard Allen who shaped the African Methodist Episcopal Church and General Daniel James a 'warrior who hated war' and who was in active service in Vietnam (Bracey, 1999: 37). This is a very contemporary collection showing how far African American biographical traditions have opened out beyond the icons of sport, music and religion. This, too, shows auto/biography is a vehicle for social reconstruction: in this case a bid to leave the 'ethnic fringe' and enter the mainstream. Inevitably this is a project with individual lives at its centre. The existential, by implication, takes priority over the collectivising of experience and its source in the oppressive regimes of slavery. But it is only able to do this because its form of conceptual and political organisation have shifted to more fragmented forms.

The shift from slavery as a form of (sub)human 'being' to be transcended and the more recent diversification of African Americanness are all a part of the broader issue of racial and ethnic identities and the lives and narratives in which they surface. Questions of identity span and connect individual lives with the networks of social categories to which they can have connections. Identity lies at the confluence of the social and the individual/existential. It is simultaneously personal and social although the mechanisms composing this are rarely specified.

> The Afro-American biography generally has racial and social meaning larger than the particular life portrayed; the life comes to exemplify the need for reform...Identity, of course, is the core ingredient in any biography. (Conyers, 1999a: 3)

Individual lives stand for the collectivity of lives: a connection that takes a particular turn in relation to African Americans. This is the point at which individual biography opens onto the social landscape and its racialised social categories. While this foregrounds individual people, it backs away from the uniqueness of lives by aggregating them in this way in order to support claims about social categories. The anthropology of ethnicity, examined in the last chapter, takes a similar stance and aggregates lives drawing on the examples furnished by *some* lives. This is inevitable. The question is – which lives are chosen?

Race and nation

Collective identity issues raised in African American auto/biographical narratives operate on at least two connected levels. Authentic versions of African American identity are occluded by slavery: '…"Who am I really?" persists as the essential question to be asked and answered, as with all blacks who were born in slavery…' (Huggins, cited Conyers, 1999a: 3). We will return, later in this chapter, to this dimension of racialised identity as it is linked to comments above concerning diversity. Being African American is framed by their status as Americans; as citizens of the nation state and the history of that relationship in slavery and segregation. Authentic versions of *personal identity* are closer to the existential and less mediated by social structures. Authentic versions of *social identities* have the opposite characteristics. And so we see that personal and social identities undermine as well as reinforce each other and give each other political substance. All are selections and involve forms of silence and erasure. There is no authenticity: all involve forms of aggregation and editing. This is so in the formation of even personal experiences, which are inevitably highly selective. These questions of citizenship and diversity – of different ways of being American – run through the auto/ biographical genre. Being American is inseparable from race: it is race that structures the relationship between the individual and the collectivity of nation. Race has profound currency. '…to be American is to be shaped by the "device" of "race"…' (Kenan, 1999: 6). Our first set of social identity questions then concern the level of nation: what it meant (and means) to be American. This is about the national landscape itself on which all citizens are positioned and repositioned and which in turn mediates more closely existential versions of the self.

In settler societies ethnicised immigrant experiences articulate the defining moments in the building of nations. In North America the founding myths of struggle against hostile environments and aboriginal peoples are told as the story of white Northern Europeans (Dyer, 1997). In America (and in Canada) agricultural activity and settlement in the great trudge westward proffered the people-fabric, as well as the defining moments in the building of nation through the conquest and control of land and the forms of identity valorised by it. The farm – for example – was the moral centre of settler life symbolising the fruits of human effort (Knowles, 1999): the tenacity and struggle required to shape a landscape wrested from (unrecognised) forms of aboriginal land tenure and use. Agricultural settlement also settled its heritage on those of European descent. Their suitability for this form of enterprise targeted them as nation-builders and differentiated them from both aboriginals and other would-be settlers from Asia (aliens) and the Caribbean. American and Canadian immigration throughout the twentieth century upheld this version of nation and the distinction between 'settlers' and 'aliens' who were imported as cheap labour to be returned. In Canada it was this version of nation-building in which agriculture became a right of passage to becoming a (British) Canadian citizen that structured migration around the British empire. The conquest and tilling of soil invoked the selective validation of ethnic experience in much the same way as the US and upheld the 'white Canada' policy, which only finally collapsed in the mid nineteen sixties. As in the United States, immigrant experiences were about ploughing, planting and quilting. 'Canadian nation-building was predicated on the view that certain races were better suited for citizenship' (Iacovetta, 1998). America's version of this settler scenario was one in which the lives and exertions of some, rather than others, were valorised: slaves and other versions of settler 'ethnic experiences' went uncelebrated and unacknowledged in the texture of nation. Hence the significance of slave narratives and the other ethnicised memories silenced and edited out the nation's myths of origin. Rice (1996: 158, citing Boelhauer) says that beneath the political map of the United States there is an ethnic memory theatre that reads a countervailing reality 'below the cartographic surface of political representation'. Nation is the selective weaving of individual and collective ethnic and racial experiences and efforts. This describes some of the conduits connecting people and their lives with the bigger political units of nation: a connection made, and later maintained, in racial and ethnic terms. Part of race making.

Speaking in the silence

In this context African American auto/biography is understandably dedicated to recovering the memories of these unwritten and unsung histories: the silenced memories of the alternate cartographic surface. Conyer's biography of Karenga – chair of Black Studies at California State University and author of many significant works – charts Karenga's contribution to developing an alternate version of (black) nationalism. Edited out of the national fabric, this remembered and celebrated its own (silenced) forms of building 'struggle' and 'community' (Conyers, 1999: 9). 'For the disinherited African American, power comes through a knowledge of origin, of at-homeness, which works against a racial oppression which marginalises'. This brings its own Afrocentric perspectives and cosmology (Conyers, 1999a: 4: 16–17); its own social landscape, its own heroes, rituals and celebrations: the construction of a tradition of freedom, uplift, self respect and belonging (Kachun, 1999: 47). African American auto/biography is about asserting an alternate collectivity of individual lives with its own means of belonging. Identity is one of the mechanisms through which this is achieved. Auto/biography is not just about great lives but the context, mechanisms, networks and purposes served in commemoration (Kachun, 1999: 45–7). The collectivising of identities for these purposes acts as a centrifugal force in African American auto/biography. This in turn produces other silences around alternate versions of African American lives and experiences.

Individuals and social processes

In this collectivising of social identities the individual reappears as the model for fragmentation and complexity and as conduit and conductor of social processes. Auto/biography is the ideal medium for expressing this complexity. Fragmentation pulls in the opposite direction to the centrifugal force of collectivising, which produces African Americans as a collective identity. It is a feature of this genre that it supports both of these opposing tendencies, and that it has been slow to examine in any detail the social processes implicated in individual lives in a way which goes beyond the ethnic composition of the fabric of the nation. The diversity embedded in social identities breaks open around individual lives allowing confession of the complexity of social identities. This has led to modification concerning the all-encompassing nature of race. Having acknowledged that race is deeply ingrained in the American imagination Kenan (1999: 6–7) goes on to say 'Yet race is only one element of being black, only one side of the multi-sided rubric of understanding of who "we" are'. He goes on to describe the landscape of North Carolina, the site of his own becoming black:

> Here I inherited a vision of being black embedded in the trappings of daily life: These signs and symbols were the air I breathed in the rituals, cuisine, fashion, music, language...culture...wound around and worn daily...and later New York. The real estate of my mind. (Kenan, 1999: 8)

The fragmentation of identity here takes place around two axes: the axis of daily life and the axis of place, a step beyond the customary generalisations concerning the ethnic and racial fabric of nation. In both axes – the everyday and place – the unexamined, the taken for granted, becomes significant. The quotidian nature of this 'being black' life, he says was taken for granted. By definition it was the unexamined:

> We were never given to define or dissect our blackness...[it was taken for granted] that this tapestry, this ever-reaching back fabric was what being black was all about...(Kenan, 1999: 7)

Consequently Kenan (1999: 8) says he grew up believing 'the lie' – should we call it a tactical position which served an earlier political agenda? – of the sameness of being black all over America. Kenan's book is an attempt at unpacking the lie. His journey around America includes biographical interviews with people in different locales in which he sets out to discover how 'black folk' live and think about themselves. The collectivising pull of locale and the quotidian underwrite his project, in place of the collectivising pull of history. A more textured account of the racial fabric of American society emerges.

These smaller (than slavery and subsequent forms of exclusion) collectivities imposed by place and the quotidian details of daily life collapse together when confronted with *individual* experience. Kenan confronts them with his own experience: something that is as well served by the genre of auto/biography as the project of describing individual relationships to forms of collectivity. Auto/biography, it seems, simultaneously sustains and undermines the concept of collectivity. It is able to do so because of the sliding place occupied by the individual. The individual can serve as exemplar of community or its living sovereign constituent. These are matters of emphasis and the power accorded to human agency, which was raised in the last chapter. In these matters Kenan walks over the line drawn by earlier uses of African American auto/biography outlined above. In order to sustain the collective identities of African Americans, Kenan goes beyond the fragmentation of place and daily life. In future if there are to be collective identities they must be capable of containing and expressing individual experience. They must be capable of expressing Kenan's *own* experience as an African American. This, he admits, is socially etched by the shifting social landscapes of our time. It is not that social processes are neglected in Kenan's analysis: but the individual life takes centre stage as the means by which these new social processes are expressed. Kenan points to two sets of processes which, it seems, fundamentally undermine previous versions of the meaning and significance of African American identities: they are high levels of geographical mobility and the disembodiment which accompanies contemporary modes of human communication and interaction, on the telephone and the Internet, in which visual manifestations of race as skin play no part.

Kenan is concerned about black and collective selves in the cyberspace re-shaping of what it means to be American and what it means to be human, and hence, what it means to be black – 'Terminal blackness' (Kenan, 1999: 619). Does this mode of cyber human interaction (he asks) erase race? 'This thing we call being black, does it exist outside of our bodies? Where, indeed, am I black? On my skin? In my mind?' (Kenan, 1999: 621). Online we are all, he says, 'netizens' (Kenan, 1999: 621–3) '...how could you be black on a computer screen?' (Kenan, 1999: 623). Of what does African Americanness consist in these disembodied forms of human communication? And in the new contexts of geographical mobility?

> I am as itinerant as the fabled wandering Jew. I have changed my address more in one year than my grandfather has in his entire life. I could easily live in California or Brazil or Japan or Ireland or South Africa. My friends come from all over the world...I am emblematic of my generation. Despite my rural background I am now a netizen, a paradoxically rootless American whose home is reluctantly the world...the concept of being black or Negro or African American (has) changed indelibly...But what is black any more? Who is authentically black in a country, within a culture, where one's very existence has always been the shifting identity of survival...who can be authentically black when every black person holds the codes and the blueprints of that blackness. (Kenan, 1999: 625)

Kenan worries about how to fit the black self into the collectivity of selves in the face of these new social processes (Kenan, 1999: 16). In doing so he exposes the nerve of African American identity as reliant on skin and recognizes the meaning of skin as pigmentation and the continued significance of traditional notions of community as the geographical units on which daily life is presaged. Movement takes priority over stasis and what it means to be black must be rethought in the light of these circumstances. Geographical notions of stasis as community and skin as pigmentation are central planks in African American identity in the genre of auto/biography and beyond it. What has shifted is the relationship between individual and collective identities and the political contexts in which identities – individual and social – operate. These delicate questions of balance and the matrix connecting individual lives and the broader social landscape on which it is set are excavated a little further in the two auto/biographical examples which follow.

Case study 1: The auto/biography of James McBride

McBride's (1996) *The Colour of Water: A Black Man's Tribute to His White Mother* is literally auto/biography, in that it contains his account of his own life, as well as a biographical portrait of his mother and the many threads connecting the two life stories. It lies in between the distinction made earlier between academic and popular accounts. Herein lies it strength. It provides extensive detail of the relationship between people and political contexts but has no conceptual axe to grind on the relationship between human agency and its social templates as academic accounts tend to. The narrative switches between McBride's story of the family in which he grew up in New York in the 1950s and 1960s, shaped by the twin forces of his Jewish mother and the politics of civil rights, and his mother's story of her early life as a Polish Jewish immigrant to America. Very much a 90s piece, this is a self-confident account of blackness in which the dignity conferred by the oppression of slavery and the missing black voices in the making of national culture is both already won and an ongoing battle. It is the product of a political context in which the complexity of blackness can be admitted and in which blackness does not need to be defended in the same way as earlier valorisations of blackness were defended through roots. What makes this a noteworthy piece of writing, from the point of view of the project on which this book is embarked, is its awareness of race in the texture of personal lives *and* in political and social landscape. Consequently race operates as a series of practical accomplishments embedded in the details of everyday life, just as it operates in the broader social and political circumstances in which those lives are conducted. The individual/ socio-political relationships of this auto/biography are finely tuned. Individual lives and the forms of social agency they exert, though highly significant, are in constant struggle with the circumstances in which they are cast and in which the outcomes are unpredictable. This is a socially positioned form of fragmentation in which the mechanisms connecting the individual with the social are clearly displayed – hence its usefulness.

McBride's parent's relationship straddles the racial distinctions of segregation which rendered it illicit, rendered it a relationship which could not take place, a relationship, like others, consigned to the interstices of the racial order. The racial landscape on which it is set is not just etched by difference and inequality but by persecution and death. His mother, Rachel, born in 1921, leaves Poland as a child in an orthodox Jewish family in 1923. The context in which she and her family depart for America is particular. Russian soldiers regularly arrive in the community where her family live, line up Jews and shoot them. Despite the gravity of these circumstances immigration was no simple matter: 'You just can't walk into America' (McBride, 1996: 12). Networks of Polish Jews facilitate migration to the New World and this plays a significant part in the negotiation of immigration regulation. Rachel's father's work as an itinerant Rabbi takes them to the South, the heartland of Jim Crow, segregation, the Klu Klux Klan and the undercurrents of popular support and individual agency that produced and sustained it. In this particular cauldron of race and ethnicity Jews are neither black nor white, but surrounded by the forms of summary judgement and death attendant upon local black/white relations. Rachel tells us that:

> ...death was always around Suffolk...it was like a bomb waiting to go off. I always felt that way about the South, that beneath the smiles and Southern hospitality and politeness were a lot of guns and liquor and secrets. And a lot of those secrets ended up floating down the Nansemand River... (McBride, 1996: 84)

The death-dealing activities of the Klan were underscored by the racial hostility of the poor white communities where the Shilsky family lived: '...the white kids hated Jews in my school...its that feeling that nobody likes you; that's how I felt, living in the South'. (McBride, 1996: 64). This aspect of Rachel's political/emotional landscape coincided with a set of family circumstances in which she was sexually abused by her father and consequently felt worthless as well as homeless.

Across the divide of death and local racial segregation Rachel fell in love with a 'nigger'. This caused race problems in two directions. 'If there was one thing Tateh (father) didn't like more than gentiles, it was black folks...' (McBride, 1996: 81). Her family 'sat shiva' at her symbolic death as a Jew when she finally married a (different) black man in 1942. Second, '...the regular white folks in the town would've killed him...half of them were probably the Klan anyway, so it was all the same' (McBride, 1996: 84). Here we see some of the least attractive forms of local white volition and social agency. Being a Southern Jewish woman descended from Polish refugees who had fallen in love with a black man unleashed multiple racial tensions with potentially lethal consequences. Rachel repositions herself in the North[8], in New York City, living in Harlem with another black refugee from the South, Dennis McBride's father. New York, in the 50s and 60s offered another (differently) racially charged landscape, but one in which it was at least possible for Dennis and Rachel to live unmolested by the Klan, and raise their black children. Dennis had a ready-made social context in Harlem, which Rachel entered with difficulty. Being a white woman and the mother of black children in the groundswell of Black Nationalism and Civil Rights in which whites were *de facto* the enemy, was another difficult social position on the racial landscape to negotiate. The young McBride with his growing political awareness admits 'I thought Black Power would be the end of my mother' (McBride, 1996: 19).

On this most difficult and dangerous of political and social landscapes, Rachel construes her own, practical, lived, version of family life in which she resourcefully draws upon the best that local African American and Jewish networks have to offer. Refusing to openly confront issues of race and identity, indeed refusing to explain to her black children why her skin was a different colour from theirs and that of their neighbours, Rachel's origins and early life become a no-go area for family discussion. McBride details her attitude to racial identity:

> ...she had little time for games, and even less time for identity crises. She and my father brought a curious blend of Jewish-European and African American distrust and paranoia into our house...the best and worst of the immigrant mentality; hard work, no nonsense, quest for excellence, distrust of authority figures, and a deep belief in God and education. (McBride, 1996: 21)

Families speak silence more than any other language. Rachel 'worked' Jewish philanthropic contributions for her children's school scholarships, haggling for clothes (from Jewish traders) and education (from Jewish benefactors) and places in sought-after schools.

> It was in her sense of education, more than any other, that mommy conveyed her Jewishness to us. She admired the way Jewish parents raised their children to be scholastic standouts... (McBride, 1996: 67)

The determinedly unnarrated, practical accomplishment of living was the mechanism of her Jewishness and one of the sources of the family's ambiguous racial location.

> The question of race was like the power of the moon in my house. It was what made the river flow, the ocean swell, and the tide rise, but it was a silent power, intractable, indomitable, indisputable and completely ignored. (McBride, 1996: 72)

Working the local Jewish networks to secure educational and musical opportunities for her children, Rachel cast her life in the black community of Harlem, where she did more than survive its heady politics of black self assertion and the implications this had for whites. She contributed substantially to that community. She worked with her husband in establishing the New Brown

Memorial Baptist Church, and she worked with 'one of the most dangerous and neglected housing projects in New York City...the only white person in sight...' (McBride, 1996: 23). She made friends and played a part in the building of the 'spirit' of the local black community. This life of community contribution is starkly counterpoised to the McBride's staunchly defended private family life in which the children were encouraged to reveal nothing about their lives to outsiders. The personal and the collective were kept strictly separate. Constructive community participation is balanced by the siege mentality that pervaded family life. In crafting this story McBride conveys a sense of his mother building and sustaining, through enormous effort, a mother-dominated family system that launched a number of its children on successful career paths as surely as it fell apart as the children grew up and became influenced by other versions of blackness forged in the spirit of 60s revolution. The young McBride's 60s version of blackness contrasted sharply with the more old fashioned Black Southern church-going education-based existence that Rachel and Dennis (and later when Dennis died, Rachel's second husband) offered as the philosophy of family life.

In this story we see the tensions between lives and their racialised political context. Emotional connection across racial divides worked against the odds. These were not cultural templates repeated at the level of individual lives. They were alliances forged against the grain of the racial order: transcendent and multi-layered versions of blackness forged in the practical living arrangements provided by the racial landscape in which they were set. These are forms of race making through the practical accomplishment of living. McBride exposes the existential in his text and shows how it encounters and negotiates political culture. In his own adolescence and his descent into a life of drugs on the street from which he eventually removed himself he quotes his elder sister on this very matter. 'You have to choose between what the world expects of you and what you want for yourself' (McBride, 1996: 125). Similarly an elderly Jew from his mother's community said of Rachel towards the end of her life when McBride was researching his book: 'She picked that life for herself and she lived it, that's all' (McBride, 1996: 177). To this his mother adds by way of explanation: 'I stayed on the black side because that was the only place I could stay' (McBride, 1996: 182). Agency negotiates structure, because it is part of structure, imbued with structure and yet capable of transcending structure. Lives are lived in the conditions in which they are formed and in which they can make a difference.

Case study 2: Oprah Winfrey: a different kind of black life (story)

Published auto/biographies of course are shaped by their authors' narratives wielded by, or on behalf of, their subjects. They are as varied as the race-awareness and theories of their composers. While McBride's story details the racial *self* generated in a dialogue with the racial politics through which it is forged, in Oprah Winfrey's biography the self transcends racial politics in a different way. Winfrey's biography displays the subtle shift in balance in which the self occupies centre stage and political landscape retreats to become yet another obstacle overcome in the progress of a life. Winfrey's biography illustrates some of the pitfalls evident in the retreat *to the self* as the centre of a politics supporting differentiation to the point of complete fragmentation. This is in part a matter of narrative genre as well as the configuration of individual agency and politics. Winfrey's life is massaged into a popular Cinderella cartoon in which the beautiful, and hence deserving, self is engaged in a struggle against the odds – in which race is just one of many other obstacles – for success. The 'celebrity genre', of course, demands this kind of narrative of an American TV chat show host and mega star. This is inevitably a story of progress from rags to riches, obscurity to fame, detailing obstacles overcome en route. Inside this well-worked parable of success lies another more political narrative in which some of the contours of the political landscape are drawn, but only as background. Winfrey is the product of some of the same elements of the (racial) political landscape as McBride. Her family, too, leave the South in the 50s migrations of blacks northward. But apart from this, and a passing reference to her slave and Baptist heritage, there is little intimation that Winfrey's flight northwards is contextualised by anything more than a flight from the grinding poverty of Southern life. Winfrey's biographer, Nellie Bly, like McBride, spends a good deal of time exploring the emotional dynamics of her family and her place in *its* (abusive) emotional economy. But her story is told as a one-dimensional way in which her inner turmoil, pain and other experiences are shaped by the evil intentions of other *individuals* whose actions are not placed on the broader social landscape of which they form a part. It is in this respect that the Winfrey story most resembles the Cinderella story: Winfrey struggles against the cruelty of her family and their refusal to recognise her talent and beauty. Episodes in this saga punctuate the biography and this is clearly a narrative template that precludes a more textured version of the emotional economy of the Winfrey family, its circumstances and the fabrication of both of these things by the politics of race.

The central project in this story is a contemporary version of the (American) self. The central struggle is about control over the life being narrated: control that is wrested from other characters with more suspect motives and less beauty or talent. It is a story in which the self struggles for *career success* measured in ratings, in the number of TV stations controlled, jockeying for pre-eminence over other famous chat show hosts. It is a story in which Winfrey's physical features are manipulated around current versions of (American) beauty, and a constant struggle over weight, itself an important marker of self-control and self-directedness, as well as a particular version of beauty. These struggles against others and her own body – as well as her struggle against her family and their cruelty – mark Winfrey's story. This is a story about the struggle for ratings, fame and money, rather than *rights and community improvement*. And this is a squarely individual rather than a collective project. In this quest the reader is also assured that Winfrey has become an important black icon for African Americans. We are told that she has been honoured by NAACP and the National Council of Negro Women, and that her financial contributions (evidence of her kindness to the less fortunate) send black kids to college on scholarships providing opportunities they would not otherwise have had. We are asked to believe that her confessional style of TV show is 'good for people' and that she helps people with their lives through her shows. In this trajectory the self is 'good' as well as successful, beautiful, rich, famous and deserving on account of early poverty and enduring struggles against her mean family and her exploding body. That this self is also black is not central to the plot: it is an adjunct of early poverty and later largesse. Race has only a walk-on part in this story in which the self is de-raced. The problem with this account – at least for our purposes in this volume – is the status of race as incidental as well as the narrative position of the self.

Concluding comments

Winfrey's and McBride's auto/biographical efforts point to the fine line between the project of the (raced) self as motivated by the mythology of individualism in which advancement is about competition, and the collaborative project of the raced self operating as part of a collectivity of selves in the service of social transformation. In the Winfrey story the social bonds are incidental obstacles to be overcome. In the McBride story social bonds are integral to the articulation of selves in concerted forms of political action. In the former the self is abstracted from social and political contexts. In the latter the self operates in a tension with social and political contexts. In the former the story is about the self overcoming its social landscape so that the existential transcends the social context constraining it. In the latter the self is product and producer of social landscape: an existential/social project articulated in a set of political circumstances. In the Winfrey scheme of things the project of the self is articulated by the search for fame, money and stereotypical notions of beauty. In the McBride scheme of things individual success is linked with the success, survival and betterment of others similarly positioned in the racial order. It shows the personal struggles of a single family but in concert with others. The McBride story interfaces with social categories and the political strategies through which these categories can be redesigned. Whereas in the Winfrey story the self only has to overcome these categories and its social order: it takes no hostages and needs no allies. It only has to change one life, not many lives. But for some of the details of the forms of social disadvantage the heroine of the Winfrey story could be white and poor. She needs no politics, only the motivation of self-interest in pursuit of wealth and fame. Although both stories involve *transcendence,* one is inevitably individual, and the other a more collective enterprise. Despite the movement of black biography towards the fragmentation of experience (a project echoed by Hall), of place and the details of everyday life shown in Conyers, Kenan and McBride, the self is always already a political project cast in a relationship to others similarly positioned on the racial landscape. This is the key difference between *these* versions of raced lives and Winfrey's. For auto/biography to operate as a tool of social analysis the subject must be captured in relationship to the social categories through which it is positioned and in relationship to the political landscape or regimes on which its meaning is configured. For it is only in these social locations and relationships that race and ethnicity – whether as forms of blackness or as forms of whiteness – acquire meaning. The social landscape, its forms of politics and its categories of social recognition can only be *read* in auto/biography because they are already known by other means. Otherwise we would have difficulty in recognising them in the biographical material we examine.

What have we learned about race and ethnicity in examining the interface between agency and structure, between people and political landscape, revealed in auto/biography and its social framing? We see some of the ways in which race/ethnicity *work* as forms of volition, in that we see who decides to do what in what circumstances. Possible paths and outcomes are exposed in auto/biographical work. Athletes, soldiers, theatre directors and political activists all make their lives, in different ways. They do so against the grain of the racial order, and yet it is *possible* for them to do this; and the conditions of possibility and impossibility are significant. Volition is not just the property of extraordinary lives, but ordinary lives too. We see race and ethnicity in operation in the details composing lives. Who lives where? Goes to school here or there? Lives in a certain way in a large or a small family? How is time spent in this way rather than that: as it was used in the McBride house to study or learn music rather than deal drugs or run rackets? Who is exposed to which set of political circumstances and reacts to them in any particular way? We see these things in the *flesh*, in their particularity, in auto/biographical work. In this chapter we have seen race and ethnicity in operation as a means of life, as various versions of possible life-styles and as versions of death. We have seen race and ethnicity in myths of founding nations and in the quotidian details of everyday life: in the cauldrons of human existence and in its forms of extinction. Race and ethnicity are ways of life and death and involve different forms of politics from Black Nationalism, to the desegregation of changing rooms to the lethal activities of the Klu Klux Klan. All of these circumstances involve seeing the individual as standing for the collective in a way that does not happen in white auto/biographical enterprises which are much more inflected with the individual as unique and facing existential choices.

White, as well as black, subjectivities, lives and auto/biographies are made by the processes indicated above. So why do I focus on blackness, on African America lives? White lives are also raced and ethnicised by different but related means. Race is less transparent in white auto/biographies for a number of reasons. Stories of racial privilege are less dramatic than stories of disadvantage. Privilege imposes less upon its subjects and their consciousness. Privilege is, in the main, taken for granted: it is disadvantage that makes itself *felt*, and in being felt irrupt into narrative and politics.

Particular versions of experience, struggle and rights cohere around blackness. Whiteness at this time and in the places covered by this chapter was deeply buried in the fabric of nation and its founding settler myths. Whiteness brought choices about forms of association with blackness. It brought other avenues of employment than those available to African Americans and it occupied a quite different relationship to slavery and segregation: systems in which whites were beneficiaries although not in any straightforward way. Whiteness as Americanness issued and continues to issue its own web of invitations to political action: from liberal support for civil rights to the more violent activities of the Klan. This chapter could equally have discussed whiteness (a later chapter does). White American volition is the other side of this story. In this chapter we see whites as Klan members, as beneficiaries of slavery and in other positions beneficiaries of the racial order in which they live. And, we can see them as its dissidents. There are choices of allegiance to be made.

Auto/biographical rendering of lives, as I suggested in the last chapter and I hope, have demonstrated throughout this one, provides a closer picture of the racial and ethnic social fabric: so exposing elements of its racial grammar. It exposes detail and it does so from a people-centred frame, foregrounding the actions and agency of people in their interactions with others who occupy the same racial categories and circumstances, regimes and political landscape. These are all part of race making. In particular, this chapter stressed the balancing of individual and collective action; of individual lives and the collectivities of lives from which they are drawn and which they exemplify in an edited sort of way. McBride and Winfrey provide opposite examples of this balance and its social mechanisms. They show different positions in the sliding place of the individual in political regimes, although we have to look through the manner of their narration by putting together divergent descriptions of the same thing. We learned that auto/biographical telling itself is a political act and part of race making: compositional narratives in which the self and its political landscapes are generated. Auto/biographical telling composes political landscapes just as it recomposes them. Telling transcends and transforms, just as it also confirms and reaffirms. And auto/biographical telling reveals the dynamics between people and systems in which transformation and affirmation are accomplished. It tells us how people put together everyday lives and the ways in which race and ethnicity make those lives. We saw how Rachel lived her life as a practical accomplishment in the interstices of the racial order. How she made sense of what she was and organised the lives of her children in certain terms, positioning them to transcend the social place that had been marked out for them as African Americans. These are some of the advantages – the analytic value – of approaching race through the medium of auto/biography. Of course auto/biographies written by others are limited by their conceptions of the self and its place on the social landscape. But when the researcher generates her own auto/biographical accounts many of these limitations are overcome.

Summary

- Auto/biography tells us about people's lives, the social categories through which forms of public recognition, like race and ethnicity, are transacted and the political landscape on which this all takes place. Auto/biography is very good at revealing the social texture – the details – of lives and social systems.
- Whether the researcher generates her own auto/biographical accounts through interviewing as a way of studying race, or uses the published auto/biographical writing of others, we can learn a lot about race in a macro as well as a micro sense through auto/biographical writing.

Racial order: This term appears in this and the last two chapters. It is used by Winant (1994a: 267) to refer to the structuring of societies by race. Examples of racial orders persist in most societies, and the places Winant writes of – Brazil and the Unites States – have quite particular forms of racial structuring, racial orders. Racial orders are made in the operation of race in shaping the contours of societies, in organising the relationships between societies through globalisation and they work on personal identities and sub-jectivities of people living in those arrangements. As racial subjects we shape and are in turn shaped by the racial orders in which we live and operate.

Auto/biography: This is a formulation used in the British Sociological Association calling itself 'Auto/biography' and that runs a journal with the same name. It develops sociological analyses through auto/biographical means, examining individual lives for their broader social significance. Autobiography is where the subject is also the author, and biography is where the subject and the author are different. But biographical writing often has autobiographical connections, as biographers approach their subjects through the prism of their own life.

Notes

1. Auto/biography is a formulation used by a British Journal and British Sociology Association Study Group of that name and refers to the collection of a broad range of biographical and autobiographical life story material. This term also suggests that biographical material is strongly autobiographical: that these are not two sharply distinguished genres (Editorial Introduction to the Special Issue on Auto/Biography in Sociology, 1993, *Sociology*, Vol. 27, No.1. The two genres are used together in this chapter in both of the senses indicated here, and is distinguished from more thorough and philosophical studies of black phenomenology developed by A.X. Cambridge (1996).

2. There are active racial/ethnic reclamation projects in British Oral History as the journal of that name demonstrates. See for example Darshan Singh Tatla (1993) 'This is our Home Now: Reminiscences of a Punjabi Migrant in Coventry' *Oral History* Vol. 21, No. 1. This volume in particular contains similar material concerning Palestinians and Ukranians. But the paper by Darsham Singh Tatla also contains an insider history of the (British) Indian Workers Association as well as an account of what it was like to arrive in Britain and make settlement decisions as a worker from the subcontinent in the 1950s and 1960s.

3. The ethnic studies genre in American universities is important in developing these categories for critical analysis. They are also responsible for foregrounding whiteness as a defensive position and showing that these categories involve dialogues of oppression/privilege.

4. 'Power geometries' is a term used by Massey (1991) in relation to globalisation in order to discuss the ways in which individuals and social groups are placed in relation to social processes. Historiographies have their own power geometry in conferring status and validity on the experiences of some rather than others.

5. The racing of blackness rebounds in the racing of whiteness in the dialogues of race politics. The naming, content and implications of blackness made white folks white: as the dichotomies of oppressor/oppressed massaged skin tones into political categories. Gallagher (1995) discusses the backlash (or white feelings of racial antipathy and disadvantage) among American college students as affirmative action began to unravel. This shows the difficulties involved in white culpability.

6. More than ordinary in the sense of challenging and transcending the racial order, although ordinary lives are valorised too because possibly just living against the grain – the homeward trudge of daily existence – involves its own forms of transcendence. In this all lives are more than ordinary and deserving of attention and note. The alternative is the great people theory of historical accounts.

7. National Association for the Advancement of Colored Peoples.

8. One of the Southern Oral History and folklore projects in a local museum in Durham North Carolina makes a claim now widely made that Northern blacks were really no better off, that the South was no more lethally racist than the North. This results from a more detailed examination of the racial texture of both societies the South traditionally damned for its closeness to slavery.

Chapter Three
The Place of Space

Mini Contents

Vignette 1: Ghetto or car park?

In 1987 a utilities company digging in Frankfurt unearth a thirteenth century Jewish ghetto. A dispute ensues about whether it should be preserved, and if so, in what form. The Jewish population of Frankfurt – many of them migrants from Eastern Europe – become the keepers of other, German, Jewish memories; and local Germans confront the difficulty of remembering and dealing with their past of anti-semitism and genocide. Should the ghetto be left where it lies beneath the spot where the municipality plans to build a car park, or dug up and restored to commemorate the victims of the holocaust? [Example taken from Henri Lustiger-Thaler's, 1996, *'Remembering Forgetfully'*].

Vignette 2: Shrine or disco?

In the early 1990s a group of African American pilgrim/tourists protest at the way in which Ghana has treated its former slave castles, once used as holding tanks for slaves awaiting transportation from Africa to the New World. To the local Ghanian population, not resettled by slave traders, the castles hold no special significance. Once serving as post offices, some were converted into night-clubs and discos, given a fresh coat of paint and bright lights. Are these castles shrines to slave-memories or nightclubs?

Vignette 3: Farmland or slave cemetery?

In what are known as the 'townships' to the East of Montreal in Quebec in the mid 1990s, a farmer unearths a collection of bones while ploughing. Closer inspection reveals that the bones that have surfaced are human remains. An African American historian from the other side of the world's longest undefended border points out that the farmer's field was once a slave graveyard used to inter those who worked as slaves in wealthy Montreal households. This unmarked graveyard contradicts the 'official' story of liberal Canadian multi-culturalism, which holds that the Canadian soil at the end of the underground railway – used by slaves to escape American slavery – was a place of emancipation, and not another place of enslavement. The French Canadian cornfield is also an African Canadian burial ground containing what remains of the bodies erased from official histories of the nation. What some need to remember, others need to forget. Or, to lean on another racialised conflict in recent Canadian history, and a conflict that blocked the Chatugay Bridge in Quebec for weeks in the summer of 1990 in a stand off between natives and the military: some people's golf courses are other people's sacred burial grounds.

Introductory comments on space

These three vignettes contain some important lessons about the relationship between race (and ethnicity) and space, and so form a useful starting point for our *exploration of the spatial dimensions of race making,* which is the purpose of this chapter. I hope in this chapter to convince you of the analytical advantages of grasping the spatial character of race. I hope to show you that understanding the spatiality of race teaches us things about race we cannot know by other means. Once we understand how race making takes place through space we have more important detail about the racial texture of the social fabric, and a better grasp of racial grammar as the forms of social practice to which race gives rise. Space is both part of these processes and it defines their jurisdiction. Which society? What parts of the social fabric? These are all matters of space and place.

Some lessons from the vignettes above serve as an entry point to this chapter. There are many, but let me identify three simple lessons, which sketch in something of the general character of race making through space. First, it would appear that race and ethnicity become attached by a number of social mechanisms, including stories, to physical space or territory. This chapter will examine these mechanisms and the ways in which they operate, for although space has become something of a focus in contemporary social analysis, the rigour of its theoretical development as a concept is not always matched by a detailed understanding of its social and political means of operation. This chapter aims to unpack some of the mechanisms through which race and space connect. The (Quebec) cornfield and the golf course are unlikely sites of racial memory. What makes sites of memory is that they contain the ghosts of untold stories, which have a resonance with the racial politics of the present. Race and the cornfield and race and the golf course, are connected by a series of filaments – mechanisms – that can be identified, and which create the racial substance of space.

Space – and this is the second lesson of these vignettes – is evidently etched by time, so that (selected elements of) a racialised past and a racialised present confront each other. Canadian multiculturalism confronts its history of slavery, just as the modern liberal democratic German state confronts the racial politics of the Third Reich. This agitates its un-mastered relationship with anti-semitism. The spatiality of race is highly political and easily invokes the past as a way of settling the present.

Third, the relationship between race and space is not just about difference. Differences compete with each other spatially and hence demand to be resolved. The racing of space inevitably involves forms of contestation. The same slave castle cannot be *both* a sacred shrine *and* a disco because these sustain incompatible practices – dancing and the reverent contemplation of origins – which compete for the same space. In this the castles are unlike the Sea of Galilee in Israel, which sustains tourist disco boats *and* the image of Christ walking on water in the same place. This is possible because one of these things is a set of practices and the other an image and, although one disrupts the other, it does not make it impossible! This example shows that the same space can serve multiple interpretations, uses and valorised lives; but these differences are also often brought into conflict with each other. This image of conflict between competing versions of place unsettles, as is intended, the comforting mythology of multiculturalism's have-it-all-ways model of ethnic mosaics, in which differences coexist in a pretty pattern. Struggles over space frequently demand the casting of personal and political allegiances in one direction or another when settling the uses of space from among its contending possibilities.

This chapter is about the ways in which race and ethnicity are a part of the texture of space. It points out that space is in fact a composite, active, archive of politics and individual agency, and is, in this capacity, part of race making. This chapter marks a shift in our analytic focus from people, to the *relationship between people and places*. I argued in the last two chapters that people are central in race making. Race making also occurs, as I hope to show you, through place and space, but it does this through the agency of people. It is the lives, activities and social relationships of people that establish the social character of space. I want you to think about space as produced by who people are, by what they do, and by the ways in which they connect with other people. Space is an active archive of the social processes and social relationships composing racial orders. Active because it is not just a monument, accumulated through a racial past and present – although it is also that – it is active in the sense that it *interacts with people and their activities* as an ongoing set of possibilities in which race is fabricated. Space itself *potentially* has social agency in the same way in which *things* potentially have social agency. But space's agency – its meaning, effectiveness and potential uses – is released by the activities of people. Alone it is inert. It is activated, given meaning, texture and substance, by human agency. Through this chapter and the two chapters following I want you to think of space in this way: as the practical accomplishment of human activity. I hope to persuade you that space exposes further contours of human agency *not* exposed in more purely narrative forms such as auto/biography. It exposes what is not accessible by other analytic means.

People remain at the centre of our analytical framework but now they do so in their dialogues with space and place. Place and space are not the same. I don't want to say too much about either of them at this stage as the character and meaning of both unfolds in this and the following chapters in their relationship with race, which is how we need to think about them. At this point it is enough to say that space is the general category from which places are made in more specific terms. In this respect place is like identity, indeed places have identities. Space on the other hand is a more general category, like personhood, which supplies the basic material from which identity is made. (See discussion in Chapter 1.) In specifying a *particular space* we get place, as a building, a neighbourhood or region. For a better discussion of the distinction between places and spaces see Massey (1994).

In establishing the relationship between race and space this chapter reviews the work of others and summarises what we have learned about race by paying attention to space. It then unpacks the racial texture of space still further, suggesting other avenues of understanding and investigation. Race making is a spatial practice, and space contains important information about racial grammar as forms of social practice to which race gives rise. Space, then, is one more point of entry into the complicated puzzle of understanding the meaning and operation of race and ethnicity today.

Sociology's implicit spatiality

Space is, of course, part of the domain of geography, but has recently become a significant focus for contemporary social analysis across a range of disciplines and notably in sociology, which is a discipline centrally concerned with the business of social analysis. There is a certain amount of debate concerning sociology's spatial credentials, which need not detain us here too long except in so far as it relates to race. Lechner's (1991: 195) claim that space was always peripheral to sociology's analytic concerns is not, I think, entirely true. Space is *latent* in classical – late nineteenth and early twentieth centuries – sociological (grand) narratives, rather than an explicit category in the analysis, which instead focused on things like the relationship between the individual and society, or elements of social structure.

In the work of the sociologist Simmel, for example, who was lecturing in Berlin between 1903 and 1910, space is both socially framed and a context for human action. Social interaction and social relationships, in Simmel's work, assume a spatial form: providing a means of thinking about the 'geometry of society' (Lechner, 1991: 196). Simmel's work contains the early echoes of current concern with spatiality both in social geography and in sociology. It was concerned with the social organisation of space; its occupation by certain groups rather than others; and the exercise of authority and forms of domination by spatial means. Simmel's concerns spanned both personal and city/state space and Lechner (1991: 196–99) describes them as hovering between spatial determinism and social constructionism. Earlier still, in Marx's major work, the spatiality of the social organisation of capital is implied rather than explicit as it is with Simmel, but it is certainly there. The factory-model on which Marx's analysis of the operation of capital rests, is above all else a particular kind of space, servicing the social relationships of production. Lefebvre in *The Production of Space* (1974/1996) elaborated a Marxist interpretation of space in which he asks crucial questions about the social relationships and uses of space. John Berger, also writing in the 1970s discusses the intersections between time and space in his work on the French peasantry, which is concerned with the intricate intertwining of lineage and landscape. Foucault sees the spatiality of the operation of power in Bentham's panopticon (Soja, 1989: 17), the model for disciplinary society, in which power is exercised through architecturally organised surveillance. The panopticon is the archetypal architecture of power, its spatial form, replicated in the school, the hospital, and the army barracks: models for disciplinary society. Goffman's (1986) *Asylums* is a brilliant and detailed account of the social relationships of a particular (enclosed) space, etched by the architecture of containment, but refashioned in its use by the social agency of its inmates. Goffman shows the interface between human agency and space in asserting the territories of the self over the architecture of their containment.

It is not that sociology in particular or social analysis more generally has ignored or overlooked the spatial: it simply has not *prioritised* it as an explicit dimension of analysis. In its (indirect) attention to the spatial, sociology has contributed to the apprehension of space in social terms, significantly, for our purposes in this chapter, recognising it as an *affective* context for both micro and macro social relationships and contexts. Sociology has also recognised the connection between power and territory in the ways in which groups take hold of territory and exclude others. These are important lessons in drawing some of the social contours of space in the *workings* of race and ethnicity.

Space and the Chicago School

Space was not implicit but a central analytic concern, in the early (and later) sociology of the Chicago School. Moreover Chicago accounts of space were developed explicitly in relation to race and ethnicity. The spatiality of race and ethnicity developed conceptually in a *particular relationship with space as urban environment*: an association maintained in *contemporary* social analysis and which has marked the development of race as a concept over the last 40 years. It is through this route that urban landscape became *the* place of race, both in America and in Britain[1]. In this context race and ethnicity is narrowly interpreted as blackness and as various ethnicised forms of otherness, but *not* as whiteness. In Britain the countryside became – first by default and, later, more explicitly (Urry, 1995) – a domain of whiteness as Englishness. It was by these routes that the binary categories of (British) race sociology (as blackness and whiteness) became established in spatial terms. These racial/spatial binaries are equally true of Canada and the United States, as we will see later.

Seminal versions of urban sociology, represented in the research and writing of the Chicago School with its clearly spatially arranged concentric circles as zones of occupation, produced the dynamics of (urban) modernity in racial terms. Burgess, Park, Janowitz and their collaborators were fascinated by the combination of movement and stasis responsible for generating *urban* forms of human community and modern subjectivities. A certain level of human mobility fostered the dynamic of modernity itself:

> ...it is in the process of locomotion – involving as they do, change of scene and change of location – that mankind is enabled to develop just those mental aptitudes most characteristic of man, namely, the aptitude and habit of abstract thought. (Park, 1967: 157–159[1925])

Too little movement produced pre-modern forms associated with the entrenched mentality (and subjectivities) of the peasantry. The non-urban resident in these schemes of thought was literally *planted* in the countryside[2]. Too much mobility on the other hand, produced its own forms of urban social pathology in crime, delinquency, murder and homelessness. These pathologies were seen as signs of social disintegration: the hobo is mobile but lacks direction (Park, 1967: 158[1925]). Continuing this line of thought Faris and Dunham (1965) in the 1930s, mapped mental disorders onto the city map of Chicago and produced a (racial) typology of mental breakdown sustained by overactive patterns of urban mobility. Modern society – of which the urban environment was the archetypal form – was a 'moving equilibrium'. The 'fact of locomotion' 'defines the very nature of society' and its forms of location and local association: an ideal balance sustained human community without disintegration or disorientation. These, of course, were major concerns of the nineteenth century French sociologist, Durkheim. The urban environment in these schemes was both product and producer of modern (urban) subjectivities.

Modern subjectivities and patterns of mobility, the human material of which the urban environment was composed, were always seen in racialised and ethnicised terms by the Chicago sociologists. Park (1967: 18[1925]), quoting W.I Thomas' *Source Book of Social Origins*, claims that Jews are the archetypal modern (urban) subject. The 'wandering Jew' acquired through mobility the 'abstract terms with which to describe the various scenes which he visits. His knowledge of the world is based upon identities and differences, that is to say, on analysis and classification. ...'. The modern city subject acquired the capacity for abstract thought and the apprehension and analysis of difference *through mobility* – by moving through a succession of scenes on which life could be lived. This critical social exposure was the product of the *right* amount of mobility. Modern city life and the market system, on which it was based, also required the capacity for constant adjustment. The human capital of the American market system and the lives composing the fabric of the city-in-constant-flux was provided by waves of European migration. These waves had their own forms of movement and inevitable orientation towards urban magnets. Burgess' (1967: 58[1925]) famous concentric rings detailing zones of immigrant settlement in Chicago, were the product of large-scale human dis-location and 'routine movement' around the city. The 'pulse of the commu-nity' and the fabric of city life itself were all conceptualised in terms of race and ethnicity (and class).

Between the inner city loop, the zone of transition and the zone of work-ingmen's homes, Burgess maps out the 'ethnic ghettos' comprising the city of Chicago and the onward trajectories of its more settled populations, who cede their space to newly-arrived migrants. The spaces of ethnic occupation, Park's (1967: 27[1925]) 'immigrant colonies', are informal territories or 'neighbour-hoods' manufactured through distinctive forms of local (ethnic) political and social organisation and sustained by newspapers and other ethnic media. In this particular formulation these are voluntary arrangements sustaining the distinctiveness of the communities they serve. But they are also the product of other (racialised) social processes and social relationships. Park (1967: 10[1925]) also writes of the 'isolation of the immigrant and racial colonies of the so-called ghettos and areas of population segregation' in which 'physical and sentimental' – prejudice is seen as an aspect of sentiment – 'distances reinforce each other ...' in creating racial segregation. Immigrant ghettos were *simultaneously* the product of immigrant self-placement and networks *and* the reception immigrants received from those who were longer settled and among whom particular versions of whiteness, entitlement and capacity pre-vailed and formed an association with place. As Burgess (1967: 146[1925] insightfully observed of another city, 'Kansas is not a geographical location so much as a state of mind.' Place is associated with types of lives and ways of being in the world.

The dynamically spatial concerns of the Chicago School tied the urban landscape to the problematic of race and ethnicity in ways that revealed the forces of individual agency, and which became central to the ways social analysts think about urban populations, their movements, social relationships, subjectivities and patterns of settlement. These formulations set a template for later investigation and theorisation of race, which remained attached to *urban landscapes associated with immigrant settlement*. The spatiality of race *works* a particular version of urban space shared by racially and ethnically diverse populations. What follows is an examination of the relationship between race and space in post-Chicago School sociology in Britain and, sometimes, the United States.

Race and space

The (urban) spatiality of race has four, interconnected strands which will be (unevenly) reviewed in this chapter. The first, and most closely connected with the Chicago School, concerns racialised patterns of urban segregation. The second arises from the first and concerns the consolidation of an ethnic neighbourhood as territory under 'foreign' occupation and a hardening of social relationships into various forms of (racial) conflict. Policing lies at the hub of this version of racialised space. In these versions of territory police failure to protect neighbourhoods from racist attacks combines with aggressive policing. These two aspects of policing had far-reaching consequences in the British urban disturbances of the 1970s and 1980s. They have cropped up again more recently in the northern cities of Bradford, Burnley and Oldham. Third, the spatiality of race replays these local conflicts over turf – which themselves mimic nationally conceived conflicts – as battles over forms of *national belonging and entitlement* and are preoccupied with immigration and asylum as forms of access to the territories composing the nation. This, of course, takes us back to the situation in Southampton outlined in the opening of this volume. Fourth, the spatiality of race consists in the replaying of the preceding three dimensions through the prism of history as a disguised set of current concerns. Commemoration and memory – referred to in the vignettes that opened this chapter and revealing some of the significant characteristics of space – focus on place and different versions of the significance and meaning of place and the lives it valorised. Because this aspect of the spatiality of race rehearses the characteristics of the other three, and because it featured in the introduction, these concerns, though highly significant, will not be further explored in this chapter. The other three surfaces of race and space are each considered in turn through some of the literature concerned with the analysis of race from the late 1960s onwards.

Urban residential segregation

Conceptions of the racial dynamics of city space developed by the Chicago School provided the intellectual context for later studies of patterns of residential segregation in the United States in the 1950s and 1960s, and in Britain in the 1960s and 1970s. In the United States, in the context of desegregation of schools and other public facilities, residential segregation was measured, with some anxiety, using an index of dissimilarity. Using this empirical measure, Jackson (1981: 117), for example, plots the highly segregated residence patterns of blacks and Puerto Ricans in New York City to discover that Puerto Ricans are less segregated than native US blacks despite their status as recent immigrants. In the case of professional African Americans, Rose (1981: 127) found racialised housing sub-markets with black people occupying distinctive areas even where they had moved into white suburbs. *White flight and black 'preference'* form the two sides of these patterns of segregation, which admit the significance of human agency and decision-making. America's barometer of the success of desegregation – the loosening of racial patterns of urban residence – operate as visible markers of more general patterns of social distribution and entitlement. The racialisation of residence carries an edifice of meaning, which extends beyond where people live. British (political and intellectual) interest in racialised patterns of urban residential segregation carries a similar burden to its United States counterpart, despite the absence of a history of formal segregation in Britain. In the British context residential segregation was seen as the visible reminder and consequence of other forms of racial discrimination in jobs, income and social opportunities. In this way it also served as a marker of other things.

Racialised patterns of urban residential segregation became an object of serious sociological consideration following the first waves of mass New Commonwealth (black) immigration to Britain in the post-war period. This was, of course, a quite different, and newer, migration context from that operating in America and which prompted the interest of the Chicago School. The situation in US cities, with their racialised urban underclass noted by William Julius Wilson (1999), is taken as a warning in Britain of the can of worms that can be opened by immigration-without-dispersal-policies. Post-war immigration, of course, did not bring the first waves of black settlers to Britain. Hesse (1997: 94) drawing on Little's (1948) research argues that there was a proliferation of 'pre-war coloured quarters' in British cities and ports that worked as conduits serving post-war immigration and its patterns of residence. The British experience with racialised patterns of residential segregation, as we know because it is now well documented, is much older than this. Indeed residential segregation was a familiar template operating in the organisation of British colonial occupation in which European quarters were usually separate. The programs in Eastern Europe had produced a steady flow of Jews into particular sections of British cities from the 1870s onwards, attracting racist agitation in various parts of Britain in the 1920s and 1930s (New Statesman and Nation, 3 November, 1934: 615, 16 June 1934: 904–5; Benewick, 1972; Fishman, 1975; Knowles, 1992) so residential racial segregation was far from new. As Farrar says of the Chapeltown area of Leeds:

> Anti-semitism found its spatially defined targets in which gangs objected to what was seen as alien culture through their attacks on Jewish homes and people in the period after the end of the first world war, prior to the area being 'seen as black'... (Farrar, 1997: 113)

John Rex and Robert Moore's (1967) classic 1963–1965 study of racialised residence patterns in the Sparkbrook area of Birmingham[3] provided significant clues to the social morphology of the urban landscape into which British New Commonwealth immigrants were received. Later, Rex (1981: 32) maps 'housing class' as types of housing and housing tenure onto a differential system of racialised access. Forced to buy by discriminatory public housing allocation policies – or so the Rex and Rex and Moore argument goes – black immigrants become concentrated in certain neighbourhoods in multi-occupation situations in which some owned dilapidated property and rented rooms to others in their (ethnicised) social network under the exclusions of racism. Urban residence, reproduced and displayed patterns of allocation and access operating elsewhere in other systems of (racialised) social distribution. This argument was challenged by Badr Dahya's (1974: 77–8) study of Pakistani settlement in Birmingham and Bradford for failing to understand the immigrant relationship to Pakistan – through remittances and myths of return – or local systems of mutual aid and letting rooms as a form of entre-preneurial activity. This kind of argument, in which residence patterns are in part the outcome of decisions and courses of action taken by immigrants themselves and who, by extension, are not the passive targets of discrimina-tory allocation systems, is repeated in more recent work on residence patterns in other places.

Smith and Torallo (1993: 63–6) show that the social networks based on family and ethnicity – mediated by the Catholic Church – account for the settlement patterns of New Mexican, Central American, South East Asian and Chinese migrants to California. Patterns of residential segregation, once deployed as part of a broader politics as a key barometer of related forms of racial exclusion or the persistence of informal segregation, are more recently seen as matters of immigrant decision and experience – spatial forms of race making through active agency – on both sides of the Atlantic. It should be noted that these are not mutually exclusive arguments. There is inevitably a dynamic between forms of exclusion and the operation of networks and other aspects of circumstantial decision or 'choice' by migrants marked by race and ethnicity. It is likely that exclusion plays a big part in decision-making 'choices'.

Residential racial segregation in recent sociological writing no longer carries the burden of 'standing in' for many other forms of racialised distribution and access. Neither does it carry the burden of statistical demonstration of spatialised difference in indices of dissimilarity. Instead it carries the weight of 'popular impression': the multiple associations formed between area and ethnicity. Cohen (1996: 170) notes, in the context of race in East London, the maxim of Wallace Stevens that 'people do not live in places but in the descrip-tion of places'. Susan Smith (1993:129) helpfully differentiates residential segregation from the 'idea' of 'racial segregation'. Popular impressions of racial segregation are matters of shared imagery and these have many sources. The race politics climate is highly significant. So is the impact on an area of the aesthetics (the look) of ethnic occupation; and the ways in which an area is used and by whom. There are clearly other factors, but these three are highly significant in understanding the (residential) spatial aspects of race (and ethnicity) making.

Place embodies conceptions of race and ethnicity *in what it is and in how it is seen* rather than in there being a relationship between two entities, one referred to as 'race' and the other as 'place'. Smith (1993: 129) discusses one aspect of this rather well. 'Racial segregation' she suggests 'is a collage of political ideas which may bear little objective resemblance to black people's urban experience'. Racial segregation, says Smith, became a justification for immigration control in the conflation of two different political issues. Racial segregation then involved the *local* adoption and working-through of political narratives *applied to the nation state as a whole*. Racial segregation, or at least the *appearance* of racial segregation, offered a warning of the potential results of unfettered immigration in the transformation of local space, and it offered a rational for policies curbing the influx. Local residential space became a way of thinking about national space and its evidently permeable boundaries. The local is evidently a locus of individual experience in a way in which the bigger-than-local is not. It was in the political narratives surrounding the racialisation of Britain facilitated by permissive immigration control that residential (spatial) segregation acquired a significance it might not otherwise have had and did not deserve. It became emblematic of broader political considerations. Smith (1993:137) refers to this as a 'racialisation of culture': the conflation of race with culture and *its* forms of categorisation and subjugation.

Racial and ethnic marking of place

There are still further aspects to race making through the *race politics of place* to consider. Often, forms of local political organisation service and pursue particular ethnic agendas. And there are political forms for responding to (and objecting to) the manner in which ethnically and racially defined populations are seen and treated: anti-racist coalitions and campaigns for example. These kinds of political campaigns often involve the kinds of elision of political units of different magnitudes of scope and scale of the sort Smith refers to. They may involve a blurring of national and local political arenas as well as national and local forms of political and social organisation. John Eade's (1997) research with Bangladeshi residents of Tower Hamlets in East London offers an effective discussion of some of these aspects of local politics. Tower Hamlets was settled by people migrating from Bangladesh in the 1960s and 1970s, so that by the time of the 1991 census they constituted a quarter of the borough's population and the biggest concentration of Bangladeshis in Britain. By virtue of their size and concentration, and the *impression* this sustained – such things are not literally imagined – they made:

> a significant impact on the local political structure, local administrative services and the education system. … The youth clubs, cultural centres, prayer halls, traditional education centres, mosques and political rallies were *visible markers* (my emphasis) of the contribution which these three generations were making to the localities within which they lived. (Eade, 1997: 138)

The second generation of Bangladesh's who made their mark on forms of local social and political organisation in the 1980s, did so against exclusionist versions of local belonging and against which they marshalled global versions of themselves through Islam (Eade, 1997: 139) as a force to be reckoned with. If these forms of urban residential segregation were the conscious creation of forms of self-assertion, belonging and self-defence, they served a different purpose for the local white population, which saw itself as 'indigenous', by adding to their sense of siege and displacement. This is demonstrated in the local electoral success of neo-fascist parties which successfully lent on a racialised version of the locale as composed of the indigenous and entitled *displaced* by foreign invaders.

In relation to quite another set of social differences – the siting of a group home in the US for those with learning disabilities – Wilton (1998: 174) suggests that spatial separation, of course, visibly facilitates the maintenance of social boundaries. Moments of proximity represent challenges to the established social order and the integrity of collective identities when something is 'out of place'. Wilton reminds us that the cartographies of racism, exclusion and intolerance, which Pred (1997) discusses in relation to the reception of refugees in Sweden, are also *internalised and produced by the individuals* actively involved in them through their daily lives. The permeable structures bounding social life and political life are not just political inventions sustained in the demarcation of national and local space, but deeply embedded in individual psyches and lives which give them a materiality; and efforts to overturn them need to take account of these personal investments. This, of course, is an argument I made in Chapter 1 in relation to race more generally. I am now applying it to space as a feature of race making. Racialised conceptions of space are malleable, permeable and highly political.

The *aesthetic markers* through which race imposes itself on place are closely connected with the forms of political and social organisation as well as individual psyches and lives just discussed. Aesthetic markers – the *look* of ethnic occupation – sustain popular images attendant upon place. Visual aspects of ethnic occupation and its successive styles are 'architecturally encoded in the territory ...' (Farrar, 1997: 113): in its shops, its houses, its restaurants, its mosques and other buildings and collections of buildings. Arrangements for worship and assembling the right kinds of food are, among other things, important in 'branding' a territory. There is more to it than this. The style and clothing of bodies, their habits and manner of occupying or moving through space are equally important aesthetic markers of ethnic occupation. Between architecture and the marking of buildings and the clothing of bodies, their habits and skin and other physical markers of racial and ethnic difference, the once unnoticed and familiar becomes 'foreign' territory for those whose lives are *not* expressed through these processes, while simultaneously offering a comfort zone to those whose are. The prospect of a locally configured belonging *is* offered to those whose lives *are* expressed through these processes and their 'beliefs in myth and magic ... (in) tales, rituals and incantations' (Sack, 1980: 144). Popular images attach to these styles of occupation. From Chinatown to Little Italy 'a spatialised, politicised aesthetic' (Soja, 1989: 22) is construed through this fabrication of space utilising the buildings, shop fronts and bodies of ethnic occupation.

Anderson's (1991: 9) study of Vancouver's China Town uses David Lai's characterisation: 'a concentration of Chinese people and economic activities in one or more city blocks which forms a unique component of the urban fabric'. The urban fabric is occidental so that its oriental parts – the argument is applied to North American cities – form an idiosyncratic enclave. The aesthetics of ethnic occupation also carry more sinister social meaning. Vancouver's Chinatown, to pursue Anderson's example, construed from the human material of *alien invasion* and not *legitimate agriculturist settlers* who were, in terms of the political debates of the 1920s and beyond, of European descent, was historically associated with unacceptable and clannish social habits and crime. Third generation and newly arrived affluent Chinese settlers were still the source of Vancouver's 'Asian gang' mythology in the 1990s[4]. This indicates an important point about ethnicised aesthetics. They convey other terrible social messages. Farrar (1997:114) says that Chapeltown in Leeds (UK) became 'black' – shedding its earlier 'Jewish image' – in the period from the 1950s onwards. Black in this case was contextualised and given meaning by the activities associated with vice and drug dealing. These associations with blackness, and this is a familiar story, attract police attention and so become *territory* in another sense discussed in the next section.

The aesthetics and reputation of an area – and the consequences of this in terms of the policing – are mutually reinforcing. Reputation, and the aesthetic markers on which it leans, are vitally important in shaping the lives that can be lived in a place. As Cohen (1996: 107) points out, the reputation of an area impacts on its inhabitants, the value of property, quality of schooling available and so on. Thus urban imagineering around race and ethnicity acquires a basis in the practical conduct of lives as people act on what they believe to be the case. Image obtains a material force in practice and consequently influences the ways in which urban space is used. Urban imagineering – as Cohen discovered in his research on the Isle of Dogs in East London – sustains notions of safety and racial danger on the urban landscape: construing a popular poetics of place (Cohen, 1996: 171). Older local whites interviewed by Cohen (1996: 190) were keenly aware of the 'creeping Asian invasion' and its displacement of 'indigenous' whites. In the 'personal maps' by which people navigate their way round the city, says Cohen (1996: 190) 'the association between space and race is very close: it is about the demarcation of territories of belonging and its forms of 'autobiographical anchorage'. Lives and conceptions of belonging also constitute race making through place.

Race making through urban space exposes aspects of social morphology and extends well beyond the urban landscapes of their immediate impact (Soja, 1989: 50). This is because what happens in the city is also about the broader political unit of national territory in which it is set. This will have its own political narratives and imaginings[5] which impact locally and which form the source of immediate experience on which people base their assessments of broader than local trends. It is people, as skilled interpreters, who make the links between small and bigger political units. The shifting emblematic status of racialised patterns of residential segregation on both sides of the

Atlantic is justified in the alliance between jobs, income, neighbourhood and the resources such as education and other life chances supported by different neighbourhoods. Patterns of racialised segregation contain, express and produce multiple aspects of the social morphology of race and ethnicity. Hence their significance. But the social processes involved in their production need to be better understood.

Battle lines and local territory

Residential segregation and neighbourhoods distinguished in terms of racial and ethnic association have sustained the battle lines drawn between police and the residents of certain areas. Previously little-publicised parts of British cities – Toxteth (Liverpool), St Paul's (Bristol), Notting Hill and Tottenham (London) – became *places* in the ethnic topography of Britain precisely *because* of these conflicts. They did so in particular circumstances. They were placed on the popular ethnic map of the nation by the urban disturbances, which erupted in these and other places, throughout the 1970s and early 1980s. These racialised urban geographies were drawn in police/community conflict that followed a common pattern and which *transformed ethnic neighbourhoods into territories*. I will say a bit more about this common pattern later. First, some comments on the transformation of *place* and *neighbourhood* into territory, as this is one of the key spatial elements of race making.

Farrar (1997:107–8), who was concerned with the shifting racial morphology and conflicts of the Chapeltown area of Leeds, utilises Sacks' (1986) conception of territoriality to underscore some of its salient features. Territoriality is 'the attempt by an individual or group to affect, influence, or control people, phenomena, and relationships, by delimiting and asserting control over a geographical area'. Territory is shaped through conflict and is about the exercise of controlling force in the task of displacing other forces. This was the starting point of this chapter and the central point of the three opening vignettes. Without short-circuiting the conceptualisation of space, the unravelling of which (in relation to race) is the object of this chapter overall, it is possible to draw some of the contours of territory from a series of examples. The conversion of (racialised) neighbourhood *place* into territory draws on some of the following processes.

Legal processes are highly significant. The Special Areas Act in South Africa (1950) offers an extreme case of the demarcation of place as racial territories in defining black and white access to land and is often used as an example. Naturally these legal arrangements required precise definitions of who counted as white and who counted as black. This particular set of race calculations used biological notions of race as blood-line, or lineage, to underpin and determine the ambiguities of skin. These biological distinctions running beneath the surface of the skin, displaced historical association between people and territories and *its* versions of belonging and entitlement. They were replaced with biologically worked conceptions of 'right' guided by the new (colonial) maps of racial capacities that marked and rewarded those deserving of resources and opportunities through (white) blood and lineage.

On quite a different political landscape, equally biological notions of race in the calculation of blood and lineage underpin the establishment of Canadian native status and the reserves of territory set aside for native use. These are arbitrary allocations and territory is as central in their calculation as blood-lines. Natives are routinely moved in the siting of hydroelectric dams and their traditional land, established through centuries of use, is unrecognised in the calculation of relocation. Native reserves function both as monuments to Canadian ethnic cartography and as compensation for displacement and the absence of a more broadly-based set of rights and entitlement. They are monuments to the fact that natives have lost the political argument concerning the rights attendant upon aboriginal occupancy to (white) settlers. Reserve natives have a distinctive relationship to taxation laws, law enforcement, education facilities and the Canadian state: forms of tutelage instead of citizenship (Dyck, 1991). In this particular case a constellation of social and political circumstances mark native land as territory. These circumstances include special status (but not citizenship) entitlements for those who fall within the stipulated (biological) determinations of race. They include (arbitrary) allocations of land by the Federal State in regions remote from metropolitan Canada and for which there are few other uses outside of mining and flooding to generate electricity for metropolitan centres. They include legal contests over the ownership of what was traditionally native land, referred to as 'land claims'. And they include the legal and administrative powers of the Federal Government over native affairs through a special ministry. It is these processes that mark native land as *territory* and, Dyck (1991) argues, make natives wards of state instead of citizens. Territories are scenes of dispute between (in this case racially defined) populations with unequal relationships to political power and the means of legal enforcement through police and military patrol in cases of insurrection. These circumstances hold for both of the extreme cases of territorialisation – South Africa and Canada – just described. They also describe territory under colonial occupation: all spatial forms of race making.

A version of some of these processes just described was in play in British inner city areas of marked ethnic occupation in the 70s and early 80s. Some general features of territorialisation – in the relationship to power and means of enforcement – are the same, although the mechanisms of their operation and social and political contexts are quite different. British scenes of 'urban disturbance' were marked by excessive police patrolling; and by the forms of *coercion*, harassment and disruption that came with it [6]. They were marked by resistance and self defence by the people who lived in and used these areas. And they were marked by an unequal relationship to law enforcement, to civil protection and by the granting of 'special' status in race equality legislation in lieu of full civil rights. These processes produced the racialised geographies of the 70s and 80s in Toxteth, Brixton, Tottenham and the rest. They produced the concept of the 'front line' in urban battlegrounds staked-out between the police and residents: territories in which the balance of forces had a central importance.

The pattern of events that produced territories out of Britain's inner city neighbourhoods is by now familiar. All of these areas, of course, had substantial non-white populations with immigrant backgrounds. Torquay has neither produced the same pattern of events nor attracted the attention of race researchers. These areas all had a particular relationship to police versions of territory that ignited the local alchemy of race. The meanings associated with 'blackness' in the characterisation of 'neighbourhood' are inherently unstable and shifting: but in the circumstances just described would settle briefly into a pattern. Whatever the relationship between the popular and the police 'imaginary' – which is certainly a set of processes we could better understand – it was not unusual for black areas to become associated with petty forms of legal infraction such as small time burglary, drug dealing and so on (Kettle & Hodges, 1982). By these means certain black neighbourhoods commanded excessive police attention. From the police vantage point these areas were territory to be tamed or brought back into law and order: rescued from their forms of alienation as 'no go' areas. Kettle and Hodges (1982: 26, 78–82) document the over policing of black events such as the Notting Hill Carnival throughout the 1970s; the police raids on black meeting places such as the Mangrove Restaurant in the same area of London and the Black and White Café in Bristol as inflammatory. The summary 'invasion' by the police of black homes, clubs, premises and meeting places in the exercise of law enforcement antagonised local people. Operations such as SWAMP 81, the now famous saturation policing of black areas of London in search of muggers and robbers, condemned in the Scarman Enquiry into the Brixton riots (Kettle and Hodges, 1982: 93, 105) turned neighbourhoods into territories containing different versions of place, local residents and their civil rights.

Forms of retaliation and pitched battles in which police fought local residents for 'control' of the area ensued. Feuchtwang's (1992) account of police and residents' versions of these neighbourhoods strongly support the view that they were 'territories' in both police *and* public calculation. Describing the canteen culture sustaining police racism, Feuchtwang (1992: 101–4) characterises policing in these terms:

> Police work involves tedium, watchfulness and excitement – these characteristics it shares with any state of patrolling, such as guard duty or watch over a challenged territory. ... All these boundaries [including between beat officers and superiors], starting with the police/public shield itself, have their territorial and physical surfaces.

Citing Holdaway's insider study, Feuchtwang (1992:104) correctly identifies public disorder as understood by both sides in terms of *territorial and physical surfaces*. Police jealously guard their territory: 'The area policed from [the] station, the 'ground' as they call it, belongs to the police' (Holdaway, cited in Feuchtwang, 1992: 104). No go areas have to be repossessed. 'The public/ police relation now appears as a geography of defences insecurely separating different privacies ... ' (Feuchtwang, 1992: 105–6).

Territory and empire

For the people who lived in these areas another version of territory was in operation. Areas of racial and ethnic occupation are, historically, subjected to forms of racial violence directed at residents and their property. This ranges from organised anti-immigrant agitation to the informal hostilities of gangs randomly and speculatively roaming an area. Historically, people who live in these circumstances have rightly pointed out that they live in jeopardy, improperly protected by law enforcement agencies. These kinds of spatial race making often involve the elision of different places and even eras around the recognition of a form of social relationship. Quoting a young black woman's report to a journalist in Brixton (1981) about the raid on the house where she lived, Feuchtwang (1992: 106) shows that for her 'These invasions carry traces for black people of historical colonial transgressions'. The occupation and control of their territory by administrative means and by armed force, clearly plays into the popular memories of formerly colonised peoples in ways that are not always recognised and taken into account. There are connections, encapsulated in this kind of memory, between life in inner city Britain and the experience of colonial subjectivity. Fanon powerfully describes the parallels between the territories marked out, occupied and defended by colonisers and their armies, and the colonisation of the territories of the mind and its versions of *occupied subjectivity*. This colonised imaginary isn't fantasy. It is a set of interpretations enacted in people's material lives and routine movements around the streets, a prism through which everyday life is interpreted.

Any British Asian whose ancestral memories include the pitched battles fought throughout the subcontinent between police/army units and the independence movement will inevitably have a grasp of colonial violence enacted in defence of empire. Here is a snapshot of some of this. The records of the All India Congress Committee (AICC) for the 1930s provide graphic detail of the sheer extent of military repression involved in maintaining British occupation of India at that time. Surveying its districts, the All India Congress Committee reported 54,480 arrests for March 1932 alone[7]. It details the frequent use of lathi (baton) charges by police to disperse crowds often leading to death and serious injury of protestors (Annual Report of AICC 1931–2). Nehru himself complained in 1929 in a letter to Colonel Bridgeman of the (British) League Against Imperialism[8] that the 'police have completely lost their heads such is the level of arrests, round ups and transportation out of town' [Source in AICC Annual Report]. Similar details in different formats are repeated for other colonial occupied territories.

There were, of course, other meanings of territory, than conquest and the imposition of certain versions of public order, in colonial conquest. The activities of occupation imposed still further meanings of territory in this context. Between the 'club' and the 'Government Residential Area' occupation brought its own diverse patterns of racialised and ethnicised residence and the social and political relationship attendant upon them. Colonial occupation produced these particular versions of territory. But there were others.

British occupation of India involved the detailed mapping of local land use and ownership: the 'maps of settlement', which were minutely detailed descriptions of local land use describing who used it and how. These maps were a tool of administrative action used by Settlement Officers and District Magistrates to settle disputes between the inhabitants of a district (Richardson, 2000)[9]. The maps and their manner of deployment convey particular (fixed) notions of territory (justified in use), and reveal something of the local social relations of empire. Territories were jurisdictions managed by (British) Indian Civil Servants: justly, judiciously and sometimes violently. Like Brixton, Toxteth and, more recently, Bradford, Burnley and Bolton, *these areas of colonial jurisdiction were also territories because those whose social practices, actions and daily lives constitute them behave as if they were.*

The contemporary significance of empire remains to be fully investigated. It needs to be understood precisely for the reasons I have indicated: because it still matters in so many ways. It occupies the minds and ancestral memories of empire subjects who are now British citizens and living in circumstances in British cities that re-invoke the social relations of empire on new surfaces and in new contexts. These are better placed squarely on the political agenda for discussion than left hovering beneath the surface of urban discontent and the manner in which it is dealt with. At least some of the stories of race making through space clearly indicate that white Britishness has an un-mastered relationship to empire; and in the twenty first century it is high time this was acknowledged and dealt with, not least because it hampers our efforts at multiracialism, social justice and effective policing.

Territory as nation, belonging and entitlement

Our third dimension of race making through space concerns national space. Race and ethnicity have always been highly significant in the configuration of nation-space and asserting forms of association between people and space as 'belonging': in transforming persons into a 'people' and a 'population'. Nation – as the conversion of territory into enduring political space (Williams and Smith, 1983: 503) – becomes the repository of shared collective consciousness and memory (Williams and Smith, 1983: 503) captured in the assumed durability of race and ethnicity [10]. Cohen's (1996) discussion of 'narratives of nativism' on the Isle of Dogs in differentiating 'Islanders' from outsiders, especially Bangladeshis, offers a racial mapping of the 'popular poetics of place' (Cohen, 1996: 171–2) and the 'symbolic landscapes of race, place and identity' within which the local population of that area operate. The ways in which this constellation of things operate in East London is worth understanding. The Isle of Dogs in this analysis is simultaneously a place of foreign migration and a place of little Englander nationalism: something that sustains attacks on local Bangladeshi families and support for the British National Party. Cohen shows how race and space – as locale and nation-space – are closely related. Local territories and the autobiographical grounding they produce in local whites serve as a basis for a narrative of white entitlement overwhelmed by foreign invasion *at the level of nation space*. Lineage is set in landscape as Soja (1989: 21) notes from Berger's work on the French peasantry. But Cohen shows that this nativism is *not* an impermeable category: indeed the opposite is true. The rites of sea passage transform foreign invaders into potential kith and kin (Cohen, 1998: 12) in the making of the island race: 'it is their natural islishness that gives the English a genius for ruling other races, and a superior capacity to assimilate cultures other than their own' (Cohen, 1998: 14). The instability of Englishness is exposed: it is easily unravelled by its readiness to absorb others.

This is the other side of imperial dominance. Britain is a place of arrival as well as departure: an open conduit of a Britishness that is inevitably mongrel. In this version of Englishness the sea operates as a porous boundary that is both a source of strength and grandeur (Cohen, 1998a). The (unmastered) white British relationship to empire is a source of *both exclusion and inclusion*. Here is another demonstration of the power of individual and political agency. White Englishness, and its anchorage in the nation, are *both* embedded in the landscape of the white cliffs of Dover and always at the point of unravelling. The relationship between people and nation space is a more hopeful story than at first appeared to be the case. We will return to this argument in Chapter 6 in our analysis of whiteness.

Commemoration and memory

The salient features of race making through space in acts of commemoration, replicate and consign to the past many of the issues already raised in our discussion: the relationship between race and space in nation and belonging, police patrolling of territories and neighbourhood and urban segregation. Commemoration is about who counts and who and what should be remembered (and how) and what and who should be forgotten.

Commemoration is about political landscapes and their (present) calculations. It is about conflict and difference and their temporary resolution in the ways in which we 'get on' with things. It is about the selective operation of memory and its salient political and social contexts. Place and space are etched by time. They have temporal depth. In this sense past and present live side-by-side, occluded and revealed. Cities, like all places, are evidently textured by 'accumulated times' (de Certeau, 1989: 108): by the monuments and markings of past and present activity (Lefebvre, 1996: 78–9, 84). Cross and Keith (1993: 8), concerned with the city of the popular imaginary and articulating the dimensions of race which are not missing but unspoken, maintain that 'Race is a privileged metaphor through which the confused text of the city is rendered comprehensible.' The preceding sections of this chapter sustain just this point, that race is, analytically speaking, a point of access to the city, to understanding what it is and how it is composed by thinking through the place of race within its schemes.

So far I have shown some of the ways in which race and ethnicity surface as spatial concerns in social analysis and I have suggested that we think of these things as spatial dimensions of race making. It is now time to move on and develop further our understanding of spatial dimensions of race making, by building on some of the writing we have already reviewed. What follows is intended to suggest further avenues for research and reveal something of the racial texture of society and with it the grammar of race as a form of social practice to which it gives rise.

Spatial dimensions of race making: further possibilities

Hopefully something of the character and meaning of space is by now unfolding from the preceding discussion, but this is a useful point at which to summarise its key features. Space is about the people who occupy or use it, about the activities in which they are engaged. It is about the nature of social relationships. It is about an understanding of, and response to, local and national political contexts in which lives are set. It is about the reputations and social meanings with which space is associated. It is about the aesthetic making and modification of the built environment. And space is about the calibration of forms of attachment and sense of belonging or ownership that individuals and groups exercise over the areas in which they operate or live. Space acquires social significance only in a symbiotic relationship with the people using it, and the social categories and their meaning, through which those people are understood and understand themselves. It is the meaning, use and character of space that makes place (Massey, 1994).

Four sets of processes, which make space in racial (and ethnic) terms and which develop and re-arrange the sociological insights offered in others' work, occupy what remains of this chapter. These four sets of processes are about the *composition of space* and are heavily influenced by the work of Lefebvre and its development by Doreen Massey. Both writers aptly, concretely and with political astuteness, indicate something of the nature of space and hence offer a starting point for the consideration of our four processes. I should point out that neither of these spatial theorists directly applies their analytic apparatus to race or ethnicity. Massey (1994), guided by Lefebvre, indicates the *instability* of space in its ability to pick-up new meanings, activities and people. We can think of this as place making. Space is usefully conceptualised as a *moving landscape* with *no predictable relationship to race/ethnicity*. The racing of space, or what we have been calling spatial aspects of race making, occurs through the meanings attached to its occupants and users, their activities and their lives (codified as forms of social recognition); *and* through the meaning attached to space as place. These things, of course, are established on a case-by-case basis. There is no general formula here. Lefebvre (1996) proposes a grid of questions through which the meaning of space can be understood. For whom? By whose agency? Why and how is it construed? Space, as I have already suggested, can be understood for its grammar: not the underlying principles by which it works but the *forms of social practice to which it gives rise* and which are walked and talked by human bodies operating in particular ways, spatially and temporally. Lefebvre's version of space asks about the social activities marking a space, its codes and behaviour and the arrangement of bodies within it. Our four sets of processes are also influenced by the insights of de Certeau concerning the significance of everyday practical activities and trajectories involved in daily life and its spatial arrangement.

The four processes making space, which are most amenable to the analysis of race and ethnicity, are:

1. the architectural politics of the built environment;
2. the embodied performance of lives and their social practices;
3. movement, pathways and journeys; and
4. social relationships.
    Some of these processes were raised in the last two chapters in relation to people and their race making activities, and this is a good point at which to remind you that people are engaged in dialogical relationships with the spaces in which their lives are set. People make the spaces through which their lives are made and given substance. In this they do not exercise control over space, but interact with it.

Architectural politics of the built environment

A detailed discussion of the (racial and ethnic) politics of architecture is beyond the scope of this volume and the competence of its author. What is built and where it is sited has an enormous impact on our lives, and yet these decisions, taken by architects, urban planners, and those with vested interests in the commercial possibilities of space, such as developers, are matters on which most of us are rarely consulted. The built landscapes on which we live and on which we operate are only formally and technically subjected to democratic processes through planning consultations and the like. Our previous discussion of residence and neighbourhood has already suggested some of the ways in which race and ethnicity operate through built environments. Architecture is 'the taking place of the political, the process by which public space is constituted and configured' (Caygill, 1997: 25). It is highly political and yet its forms of politics are not apparent: indeed they are obscured. Part of their obscurity is that built environments are configured by the politics of the past. We inherit and inhabit a built environment which is not of our making and which may or may not be easily adapted for our use. The built environment contains the monuments and marking of a past that celebrates some lives and, by implication, sidelines others. The imperial Victorian architecture of Calcutta captures a moment of racial (imperial) subjugation, then moves on and services other lives and other interests, being infinitely adapted by those who operate through it. Following Lefebvre – 'by whose agency and for whom was it generated?' (Lefebvre, 1996: 116) – we can think about whose interests and activities, which set of lives and their forms of public recognition, are expressed and serviced in built environments.

This line of enquiry offers forms of dissembling and critique. British cities, like others, contain the monuments and marking of other times, versions of territory which service the defence and extension of empire and factories for the extraction of the surplus value of workers. Particular versions of white Britishness, dissected by class and property, are serviced and commemorated in these landscapes. This exposes further layers of questioning. On what terms do we make the built environment – built for other purposes – our own, 'articulating those pleasures that can be accommodated and seeking ways of weaving in those pleasures for which the space was not planned?' (Roderick, 1998: 4). Mazzoleni (1993: 289) says that architecture is not an array of monuments but 'an array of continuously open processes, in which constriction is simply a phase in a complicated life which continues without limits infinitely to manipulate the habitat.' Yet architecture appropriates and favours some uses over others, some lives and activities are privileged over others.

Issues tangential to these were raised in the literature reviewed above. Those who came to Britain as immigrants in the 1960s and 1970s and perhaps later as refugees or dependants and who live in enclaves in inner cities have adapted built environments which could not – when they were built – have anticipated the array of lives which would be lived here. Cinemas are converted into mosques, supermarkets are adapted with particular iconography and products, and *of course* this is a continuous and open process that follows and expresses the ethnicised contours of city residence and the means of acquisition and use of space. These are complicated matters of *aesthetics* and *adaptation* often raising fierce political battles concerned with usurpation, belonging and entitlement. How people deal with what is imposed upon them is an important sociological question (de Certeau, 1989: 31–32). The built environment, seen through the lenses of race and ethnicity, is the product of human agency and the local political configurations in which that agency is mobilised. A proper visual ethnography attending to the aesthetics of place as environment-in-the-making and marking by ethnicity would make a valuable contribution to our understanding of the texture of ethnicity and race. So too would an analysis of the architecture and layout of built environments; noting the ways in which these are used and adapted in their use; the ways they mesh with or grate against the lives they service and produce. The making of Sikh temples out of disused cinemas is intensely political and contentious locally and raises issues that should be confronted. Built environment is, of course, only one element in a complex kaleidoscope of moving parts of the ways in which people deal with what is around them. This brings us to *embodiment and performance*, a prelude to the composition of space through *movement and the social relationships of space*.

Embodied performance

We touched on this embodied performance as a people-centred aspect of race making in Chapter 1. But I did not point out then that these are inevitably spatial practices. Analytic concern with body and space *combine* to produce the appropriate sense of the *embodied performance* of race and ethnicity. Creative and selective borrowing from the work of Lefebvre, Mauss and Foucault allows us to develop an approach that approximates this embodied performance sense of the spatial dimensions of race making. On the face of it this concerns the *occupation* of space in the sense in which it is implicated in residence patterns examined above. But it is more than this. It is about the practical and social uses to which space is put. *Who* occupies space and how do they do so? (Lefebvre, 1996: 12). *What* occupies space and how does *it* do so? This implicates bodies and actions: a version of space as textured by its deployment in human action (Lefebvre, 1996: 8–9). Raced bodies are manifest in the spaces within which they are simultaneously product and producer (Lefebvre, 1996: 170). The occupation of space is about the daily routines and actions of bodies. It is about the ways in which bodies walk and talk – the rhythms and movement of human traffic – and the many uses to which space is put. The movement involved is local and about occupation, not the passing-through which also etches space and which is considered in the next section. This local movement is about a particular range of social activities – the running of shops and restaurants and the manner of their use, attendance at the mosque, the combinations in which pubic and private space feature and the relationship between them. Local movement is about what goes on in the spaces in which a population goes about its daily activities of shopping, going to schools, visiting clinics, meeting and religious worship. These are the everyday routines and their tactics (de Certeau, 1989: 38) composing space. The extent to which these things are textured by ethnicity and race as aspects of routine and a range of activities and mode of interaction with the built environment, may be seen as contributing to the *racing* of space.

MacGaffey and Bazenguissa-Ganga (2000: 61–5) describe some of these processes in the impact of Central Africans on certain parts of Paris, particularly the market around the Chateau Rouge metro:

> ... for Congolese in Paris, eating the foods they used to eat at home is an important token of cultural and self identification. By the second half of the 1980s, African foods such as manioc, peanuts, salt and smoked fish, a variety of vegetables and mangoes were widely available ...
>
> Many African women in Paris continue to dress as they did at home. They wear *pagne*, or lengths of wax-print cloth, as a wrap-around long skirt...[and others wear versions of designer wear].
>
> Beauty products include skin lighteners, soaps and lotions, hair straighteners and wigs, and hair extensions for braiding into elaborate hairstyles ...
>
> Modern African popular music is heard at all times in shops, in African cafes and *nganda*, and in people's homes and in their cars: it is a vital component of urban immigrant culture.

The ways in which these products are provided mark the Parisian urban landscape in ways that are highly visible and audible. We could equally describe the Bengali impact on London's Brick Lane; the African-Caribbean influence on Brixton's street market; or the British impact on Hong Kong. These areas are animated by the lives and performances of which they are a part. This concept of performance suggests, and is so intended, an element of artifice, volition and public statement. Street theatre!

Within these local movements and their forms of ethnicity-in-motion-in-everyday-life are forms of movement that are still more local. The 'techniques of the body' (Roderick, 1998, using Mauss): its postures, movement, attitudes and habits, the ways in which bodies move, sleep, sit, wash, dress, groom and eat, combine the habitual and the ancient (Mauss, [1934] 1992: 475). These are the result of the 'corporeal apprenticeship' (Roderick, 1998: 1) of child-hood training and acquisition (Mauss, [1934] 1992: 457–61). In a Foucauldian sense the body is both object and target of disciplinary power. Ilcan (1998: 5) refers to these techniques of the body as 'mobile habits' and suggests, quite properly, that there is an interconnection between space and the forms of dress, gesture, speech – knowing how to act in a given situation – that it sustains. Spaces elicit certain routines and have many contesting uses (Ilcan 1998: 12) but mobile habits have no architecture to supervise them. They are none-the-less orchestrated and Mason's (1996: 302–3) notion of 'performance' as *knowing how to act* captures this. Social performance – from weddings and other formal occasions to shopping – concerns the rituals in which we participate. These are both planned and scripted and chosen from a repertoire of possible actions, *and* at the same time have a random spontaneous element. The rules and expectations through which these performances are organised remain implicit (Mason, 1996: 304). Public and private space are governed by different conventions so that the public space we share 'submits to no single individual. Public space is produced (in a given set of circumstances) by its community of users and becomes the site of constant negotiation' (Mason, 1996: 306). 'If social space itself is a field of contention, then social performance becomes a means of urging that contention, of expressing difference, asserting ownership and displaying relationship ... ' (Mason, 1996: 307).

Race and ethnicity are a part of this. The performances of others make up the crowd in the street and become the material from which the street, the neighbourhood or the section of the city is raced or ethnicised as a public display though its subliminal tropes. Performance in-fills (Stewart, 1996: 4) the street with the things that texture it – modes of walking, ways of looking and gestures – the proximity of bodies in space taking part in the carnival of local life. In this 'each participant confirms to every other, through speech, inflection, facial expression, gesture, posture and walk, the value of their mutual presence ... ' (Mason, 1996: 317). Local and particular, these social performances 'back talk' (Stewart, 1996) other versions of neighbourhood belonging to other uses, other ethnic groups, other versions of community. This is an area of ethnography that needs attention and which would take us beyond standard descriptions of food, clothes and music as elements of race and ethnicity making. As well as focusing on the making of 'ethnic neighbourhood', it is important to think about how these spatially configured performances make whiteness.

If these things seem trivial, it is important to note that their outcomes can have serious consequences. Ethnic, raced, non-white performances of lifestyle attract censure and heighten fears of invasion as transformations in which one set of (white) images and performances fear displacement by others. This is the missing racial texture in Cohen's account of white fears on invasion in London's East End. Space is always in danger of being ceded to assemblages of other bodies, other sets of performances, ways of walking, talking and being: 'we live through a space which brings with it its own structuring of use into which we might inject our own *kinaesthetic* (my emphasis) sense' (Roderick, 1998: 3 citing Davies, 1990: 59). These kinaesthetic elements of race and ethnicity are clearly important in in-filling versions of neighbourhood. They form the substance of white neurosis concerning invasion. It is in a performance/kinaesthetic sense that bodies encounter other bodies on the street, moving through doors, negotiating the pavement. It is precisely here that antagonisms and hostilities fuelled by difference in skin, body, dress, movement and activity, are produced and are negotiated. Remember the example of the Hispanic man and woman and the white woman at the LA bus stop. This is the racial *stuff* of human interaction in public space. And yet, it rarely features in analyses of race or ethnicity.

Performance has other analytic value too, as well as revealing the substance and public interaction aspects of race. The observation of performance provides narratives on race that are not rendered in words. Researching ethnicity and community mental health provision in Montreal in the 1990s I encountered performances of (versions of) African-Caribbean Canadian ethnicity using Nation of Islam slogans on T shirts and other stylistic markers, hair styling, music allegiances and specific ways of moving, speaking and spending time. Often these stylistic decisions jived with spoken narratives of ethnic identity and versions of neighbourhood. But often they had a more perplexing relationship to it. Public narratives of race and ethnicity in Canada are heavily laced with a human-unity-in-difference perspective sponsored by government multiculturalism, as I mentioned earlier. And yet I noticed that sometimes the person delivering their version of this narrative of race blindness sported dreadlocks, a Bob Marley T shirt, lived in an area heavily infiltrated by the Nation of Islam, and socialised with others with similar location and views. If race was immaterial why was it marked in this way? Was it race and ethnicity that was being marked? What did these stylistic markers mean in someone's life? While we should not make assumptions about what this means, it is certainly worth further investigation. In the same research context I also noticed the interplay between performance and skin. Where the messages of skin were ambivalent in carrying social meaning, exaggerated performance was wielded in support. Of particular note was a young man of Dutch and Haitian descent with very light skin who turned up for an interview wearing padlocks and chains and repeating a narrative of black enslavement.

Spatial dimensions of race making then, take place in the interplay between bodies and their mobile habits of gesture, dress and speech. As I suggested earlier, it is important to think of the performances composing whiteness in these terms too. The same sorts of processes make Tower Hamlets Bangladeshi, as make Budleigh Salterton in Devon white-English. Tea rooms stuffed with elderly white folk, some of whom have returned from the service of empire, make Budleigh Salterton a particular kind of place. To use an historical example that draws on these particular contours of white Britishness, no-one was more conscious of dress codes and etiquette than British colonials who, even in the most adverse circumstances, observed what they saw as 'propriety'. Mary Kingsley, a nineteenth century traveller in West Africa and political activist in the service of empire reform, was much preoccupied with the ways in which African and European bodies were clad, used and occupied space and related to each other. Even in adverse circumstances she counselled on the need for a 'good thick skirt' announcing that one has 'no right to go around Africa in things you would be ashamed to be seen in at home'. It was important, thought Kingsley, to be able to 'face Piccadilly' (Kingsley, 1982: 19). The letters of Mary Waterston, the no-nonsense nineteenth century Presbyterian missionary doctor working in South Africa, make extensive reference to her own dress in 'black silk and soft, white polonaise … dainty slippers … and beautifully fitting kid gloves … '. (Bean and Van Heyningen, 1983: 59): clearly part of the production of nineteenth century white British femininity and a way of making fine social distinctions. The present day occupants of Budleigh Salterton tea shops are no less adamant on these issues. I have listened to many elaborate descriptions of seating arrangements, dress codes and social hierarchy at colonial-styled dinners in Mombassa and other places by those more recently returned to Budleigh from Africa on the winds of independence. Social space is, as Lefebvre (1996: 73) contends 'the outcome of a sequence and set of aspirations' which are inherently bound up with who and what we are in racial and ethnic terms. Who and what we are has a vast hinterland of quotidian detail. And it is in this detail that the fabric of race and ethnicity is produced.

Pathways and movement

The small local versions of movement just discussed as the occupation and use of space, mobile habit and social performance, intersect with bigger movements composing the extra-local trajectories of lives. The threading together of place through movement composes the racial grammar of space. What appears to be *placed* or *occupied* is about the moment in time when the analytical reading is made. Lives are *not* fixed in place although they compose place, but in the process of many journeys from one place to another. Cities, towns and rural habitats are less zones of occupation – as the Chicago School conceptualised them – than intersecting matrices (Soja, 1989: 6) composed of the journeys people make around the routine (and non-routine) activities of their lives. Space is etched by the feet traversing it as pathways: and pathways are about jobs, home, shopping, use of facilities, social networks and social activities and the configurations they bring to bear upon it. Areas are occupied, passed through, used and not used: they are about accumulated knowledge and habit. Lives are not lived in place, but in the threading together of places as sequential scenes in the trajectories of lives. It is also in the activities of lives and bodies *connecting places* that the racial grammar of place is made, configured through the agency of lives. Race and ethnicity are inscribed in the nature of these journeys, the scenes in which they are set, and the nature of the activities and processes connecting them as elements of social fabric. Such movement takes place within the context of bigger movements, which are also about the manufacture of race and ethnicity, in the journeys made between towns, cities or rural habitats and, in the case of transnational migrants (the subject of a later chapter) between countries. Tracing these journeys, their purposes, their social networks and their outcomes, significantly connects lives with place and its routines of movement. Who goes where, why and how, and the connections drawn between places by lives are highly significant issues to which we will return in Chapter 5.

Social relationships and social practices

Social relationships are the fourth dimension of space to be expanded in order to elaborate our understanding of race making as a set of spatial practices. Massey (1994), using Lefebvre, establishes the social character of space by conceptualising it as composed through *networks* of social relationships. Obviously social relationships comprise great differences of scope and scale from the intimacy of personal relationships, to more formal aspects of the networks connecting people with organisations or regimes. Building on a point I made in Chapter 1, about mapping people in terms of their interconnectedness with particular kinds of agencies and regimes, the significant thing about social relationships is their nature and character. A simple mapping of types of social relationships would be useful in revealing the kinds of lives sustained by a particular place. Social relationships formed through work, forms of consumption, leisure activities and schools are quite different from those composed of the social relationships with the benefits office, social services, school, police and the local housing department. But the quality, and not just the fact of these social relationships, is also significant. British African-Caribbeans, for example, have long complained of their fraught relationship with the police as we saw in the discussion on territory. Often they, and British Asians too, live in areas sustaining a set of social community relations composed by *violence and intimidation*: attacks on their persons and property in which they are improperly protected, as well as over-policed for petty legal infractions. Whether the social relationships of a place are hostile or cordial are matters of great importance in how people comport themselves and deal with the world around them. We could learn a great deal about the details of race making as a set of spatial practices by examining the nature and character of social relationships.

The social relationships of the mobile are particularly interesting. Wong's (1998) description of China Town in the San Francisco Bay area offers a different slice of the (ethnic) relationships of space in his description of the work/family interface among Chinese immigrants to that area. He cites Mr Chan who, in response to questions about his success in America offered the following:

> Hard work and willing[ness] to put up with adversity is important. You have to understand what is needed in the economy and the opportunity available. One must have a vision. I was also fortunate to have my old friends in Chinatown who supported us. There was a saying in China that when you are at home, you depend on your family. When you are abroad, you depend on your friends. My friends got me jobs, loaned me money and gave me emotional support. My wife and my children assisted me all the way in the family business. They are the ones that you can trust. They also save me a lot of money. Trusted and inexpensive labour cost is very important to all Chinese ethnic businesses. I also came at the right time…We saw the opportunity and we seized it. (Wong, 1998: 5)

As the focus shifts from economic/work-based versions of family to the emotional side of migrant family life, so another version of this business/ family relationship becomes visible:

> The Chungs' major problem arose not from their business but from their marriage. Mrs Chung was happy to be in the United States, but her husband was not. Mr Chung was unhappy because he felt that his wife had become his boss. He often felt left out because he could not speak English. There were other personal conflicts: frequent quarrels at home and disagreements at the restaurant. Once, after such a disagreement, Mr Chung walked off his job as cook and Mrs Chung had to replace him for the day. Mr Chung became uncooperative, on occasions singing loudly in Chinese or shouting from the kitchen. [Eventually they sell the restaurant and divorce]. (Wong, 1998: 83)

What makes this story of American Chinese relationships particularly interesting are its gender dynamics and the conflation of family and work relationships, which clearly both have a strong emotional aspect. Ilcan (1998: 5) suggests that the relationship between space and cultural practice is loosely textured 'full of potential permutations and transformations'. He is right, and we should be careful not to reduce these to crude generalisations, but instead take an investigative approach, which sees race and ethnicity as an open and shifting set of spatially configured social relationships. For Lefebvre (1996: 15) it is social practices as well as social relationships of space that constitute it. These two things are inevitably connected and both offer us access to more dynamic accounts of race and ethnicity through the spatial practices in which they are constituted. I have suggested that, as Lefebvre contends, space is, in part, composed through the social relationships it sustains, and that these form part of the texture of race and ethnicity.

Concluding remarks

In this chapter I have reviewed some of the ways in which space has featured in the analysis of race and ethnicity. Developing the insights of other writers using conceptual work on space, I identified four sets of processes – social relationships and social practices, pathways and movement, embodied performance and the architectural politics of the built environment – through which race making takes place, and which consequently offer potential for more detailed analysis. Adding space to the operation of human agency, discussed in earlier chapters, allows us to discuss in detail some of the surfaces on which people engage in race making activities. People make race in space. I have identified some of the detailed mechanisms through which space absorbs and expresses race. Race is generated in the social texture of space, and so the analysis of space reveals its racial grammar as forms of social practice to which race gives rise. I have argued that we learn things about race from space that are not revealed by other means; not revealed in the stories people tell about themselves. The use people make of space tells other stories about their lives. We found a striking example of this in our research in Montreal (Knowles, 2000a). We had collected the stories of two young men living in a shelter for the homeless who identified themselves as 'Jamaican' although their relationship to Jamaica was not at all straightforward or written in skin. In discussing their relationship to the city space they used they produced a slick story of street wisdom and bravado. When we subsequently spent the day with them on the street another story of their use of city space, told by their walking but not verbalised by them, emerged. It was a story of marginality, of being unable to use spaces used by others except on highly qualified terms. It was a story of uncertainty and enforced mobility as they meandered around the city for the day able to only use the edges of public space, intended for commercial activity, for limited amounts of time. Space has its own narratives in the movement and uses of it by raced bodies in pursuit of routine activities; and these add significantly to the stories people tell about themselves. Space also reveals the social priorities composing it. Commercial space does not sustain or tolerate the socially excluded. It is itself a commodity, and we must pay to use it.

Summary

- Race making is a people-centred set of spatial practices. The racial and ethnic texture of space is made through the social activities a place sustains, the way it looks, its performances, its buildings and its social and political relationships.
- Existing analyses of space are concerned with racialised patterns of residential segregation, forms of policing that turn neighbourhood into territory and national belonging and entitlement.
- Further exploration of the racing of space leads us to consider traces of race/ethnicity in the built environment as a *concrete* form of politics, embodied performances, pathways and movement through space, social relationships and social practices.

• Traces of (minority) ethnic occupation display themselves in many areas and can be photographed and described in discussing the racial/ethnic texture of space. These may be about buildings and people and social activities. Spatial aspects of race and ethnicity are very visual and can form the basis of a sociological photo essay.

Notes

1. Race is historically seen as an urban issue from the time of the Chicago School. Cities were historically the site of migration. The race sociology of rural Britain remains an unexecuted and urgent project both as a source of versions of white Englishness and the social relationships of those with recent immigrant genealogies. How the owners of the only Asian restaurant in a Dorset town operate locally and globally, is an interesting question, especially given the connections with empire of some of the white residents of this sort of town.

2. Narratives of national belonging frequently use horticultural terminology. Political debates in Britain surrounding Indian independence in the 1920s and 1930s used horticultural images to discuss citizenship potential. The Indian peasantry, for example, were so rooted in a rural landscape as to be unable to overcome this and participate in decision-making processes. Even in Labour Party calculations the Indian peasantry 'with an outlook confined by tradition and environment' was incapable of participating in anything bigger than local, village political processes (Labour Party Home Affairs Department, 1930: cited Knowles, 1992). Horticultural images were also used in the same period to discuss and control immigration to Canada from India. Fending off potential Indian agriculturalist immigrants, the Canadian Federal Parliament recorded a number of speeches about the superior suitability of Northern European agriculturalists for 'rooting' in the Canadian soil. The problem with 'aliens' as opposed to immigrants of nation building stock, was that they had to be 'transplanted' to but did not 'grow' naturally in 'the country of which they were ignorant' (Neill, 1923: 4645) whereas others took more naturally to 'Canadian soil'. Climate as an adjunct of agriculture was also significant in moderating who could belong: who could become Canadian (Knowles 1996: 906).

3. There was a large literature on race and residential patterns of segregation in Britain in the 1970s, including Peach (1975), Peach, Robinson & Smith (1981) and Rex and Moore (1967).

4. Local student mythology had Simon Fraser University library staked-out by rival Asian gangs which occupied specific floors which put them out of bounds to others. Locally there were also stories of Chinese Triads operating in Vancouver.

5. Whether the city is, as Soja (1989) claims, a 'summative metaphor for the spatialisation of modernity' is another matter with which we are not here particularly concerned.

6. There were a number of sources on police harassment of black British populations in the 1970s and 1980s: Kettle and Hodges (1980), Gordon (1986), Holdaway (1996) and Daniel James (1979).

7. The oral history archive of the Nehru Memorial Library in Delhi contains numerous sources, recorded interviews and letters which detail the political agitation surrounding the Indian demand for independence from Britain. Specifically the records of the All India Congress Committee, which oversaw the different regions' Congress Committees had extensive records of civil disobedience activities. But there were many other groups also involved in boycotts and civil disobedience including a highly splintered Trade Union Movement.

8. The Nehru Memorial Library in Delhi has a collection of Nehru's correspondence to various people. The 1929 letters between him and the British-based League Against Imperialism and its leader Colonel Bridgeman are a source of information on this point.

9. Richardson's (2000: 94) memoir set in India in the aftermath of the First World War talks of being appointed Assistant Settlement Officer in the Settlement Operations in the Districts

of Patna and Bogra. 'I had to spend some twenty days in the month riding across fields to inspect the accuracy of field plans which were being plotted for the Food Settlement Maps. Later in the season I also had to ascertain that the names of everyone who had an Interest in the land and the amount of rent or remuneration they were under obligation to pay, were correctly recorded'. Settlement maps made, by law, a true representation of all the interests in the land in an area. MacPherson (Richardson, 2000: 117) used these in 1935 to settle a Moslem/Hindu dispute over the demolition of a local mosque.

10. Williams and Smith (1983: 504–12) note the characteristics of national territory in habitat, folk culture, scale, location, boundary, autarchy (the idea that a territory might contain a resource deposit), homeland and nation building upon a given landscape.

Chapter Four
Globalisation

'In bringing down the twin towers of the World Trade Center and destroying a section of the Pentagon with diabolically contrived human bombs, Jihadic warriors reverse the momentum in the struggle between Jihad and McWorld, writing a new page in an ongoing story. Until that day, history's seemingly ineluctable march into a complacent post-modernity had appeared to favour McWorld's ultimate triumph – a historical victory for free market institutions and McWorld's assiduously commercialised and ambitiously secularist materialism. Today, the outcome of the confrontation between the future and the radical reaction to it seem far less certain'.
Benjamin Barber 2001: xi

Mini contents

Introduction

Globalisation[1] is about time/space distanciation[2], and the realignment of distant and local social forms, so that connections between social contexts are networked across the earth's surface (Giddens, 1990: 64). Globalisation is the story of multiple forms of interconnection; of networks of social, political, economic, technological and scientific activity spanning the globe. Its intensity and velocity are made possible by developments in the technologies of transportation and communication. Its popular rhetoric captures the zeitgeist of our time (Held, McGrew, Goldblatt and Perraton, 1999: 1). It is a concept that has slipped easily into popular currency, while simultaneously occupying a paradigmatic status in the social sciences (Robertson, 1995: 1). It is at the centre of academic debate about whether 'as an analytic construct [it] delivers any added value in the search for a coherent understanding of the historical forces...shaping the sociopolitical realities of everyday life' (Held, McGrew, Goldblatt and Perraton, 1999: 1)[3], or whether it effectively delivers no new insights into the operation of grand scale social configurations. Social scientists and chattering classes alike are much occupied by these forms of connection, and their impact on the models we use to think about the social world. The circulation of commodities, money, people and images are some of the key connectors on which interest in global networks settle. I refer to these things collectively as 'globalisation theory'[4].

Globalisation theory brings significant insights to our understanding of contemporary social organisation, and has, as yet, unrealised potential in helping us to understand the operation of race and ethnicity. This was suggested earlier in highlighting the plight of the refugees who have arrived in Southampton. Race is not just composed in place, but, as I suggested in the last chapter, in the connections between places. Race making takes place on a global as well as local scale, in the networks connecting places. This chapter is about the global character of race and ethnicity. But globalisation theory has a difficult relationship with race, so we begin our exploration by thinking about this difficulty and the balance sheet of advantages and drawbacks on which it stands.

Problems with globalisation theory

There are a number of problems with globalisation theory that need to be reformulated if it is to deliver an effective analysis of race. Although it offers a framework that foregrounds space and movement, globalisation theory operates in a way that obscures the social organisation of the trans-societal flows it is trying to explain. Social aspects of globalisation, as I shall demonstrate later, are occluded as its economic and technical forms take priority, and globalisation is seen as a series of *economic and technical changes that carry social implications*. Globalisation theory, as I shall argue, is not *social theory*, but *economic theory with social consequences*. This needs rethinking if we want to pursue an analysis of global social forms involved in race making, for, as I noted in the Introduction to this volume, race and ethnicity are widely recognised as social and political, not economic and technical, categories. The second major problem with globalisation theory is a product of the first. As the biggest unit of social analysis – the world – globalisation's scope is awesome, but it has sacrificed detailed interpretation of the social processes in order to produce a generalised, and often overly abstract, overview of the way things work. The social processes I refer to are rather mundane forms of doing and thinking – consumption, communicating with others, moving about, keeping in touch with people, the rhythms of work and leisure, a sense of self in the world – that compose the texture of people's everyday lives. Overlooking these kinds of social processes betrays globalisation theory's lack of interest in people who, as I argued earlier, play a central part in the social processes composing race making. People and social processes are at the centre of race making as a global operation, in much the same way as they were at the centre of local spatial aspects of race making, outlined in the last chapter. I will argue that globalisation theory can be developed in ways that overcome these deficiencies and provide the basis for an analysis of race and ethnicity.

Globalisation theory's potential

It can do this because globalisation theory has great analytic potential. Globalisation theory has spatialised the story of modernity (Massey, 1999: 29), and in doing so has revealed a new set of geographies beyond Europe, exposing European claims to universality and revealing other spaces and other voices. This has obvious implications for the analysis of race. Globalisation has also spatialised the story of modernity in another way that draws attention to people's spatial practices in the living of their lives, even if it has not really effectively developed this dimension of its analysis, or applied it to understanding race. Globalisation theory has potential for telling a people-centred story. It is people who animate the processes and forms it refers to. It is people who connect places, who have a sense of what is bigger and beyond the units in which they live, who have a global sense of place in the making of our 'routinised and existential selves' (Robertson, 1995: 35).

Globalisation theory has produced some accounts of the spatial organisation of social relationships, and placed a renewed emphasis on places and the connections between them. Differences and similarities in lives are apparent in types of space, in the uses of space, and in the nature of movement between places as I suggested in the last chapter. The story of space is the story of *movement* from one place to another, not just of abstracted 'trans-societal flows' (Featherstone, Lash and Robertson, 1995: 2); it can be about all forms of *space-and-people-making-movement*. These forms of human activity are as ancient as camel routes across the Sahara, and as contemporary as the flight of refugees from the scene of the latest genocide. Some of the analytic benefits of space were set out in the last chapter where I suggested that space provides its own silent narratives: its own unspoken stories of routine human activity. Space works very well in tandem with a focus on individual activity, social relationships and subjectivity. Globalisation theory, then, makes it possible to tell stories about people and their routine activities, which would not otherwise be told. These, of course, do not just involve the trans-societal flows featured in the next chapter, but local uses of space too, for the global also operates locally as we shall see. Globalisation theory also has the potential to expose the constitution of the world order if we take a closer look at what Massey calls its 'power geometry' (1993: 43), its social relationships, its forms of movement and, what is especially significant for our purposes in this volume, the *making* and *operation* of race and ethnicity within its power geometry. Globalisation theory has unrealised potential in the analysis of race if it is properly refocused onto social processes. It can deal with divergent matters of scope and scale from neighbourhood to nation states and the connections between them, for the global is animated locally and exposes complex forms of social inequality, which have implications for the analysis of race.

Globalisation and race and ethnicity

Globalisation theories have not exactly *neglected* race and ethnicity, but they have engaged with these concepts in particular ways. This section is intended to outline these forms of engagement and, in the process, begin a critique of the race/ethnicity/globalisation interface, which opens onto a more general critical appraisal of globalisation theory, and develops further some of the criticism I have just indicated. It is important here to note disciplinary differences: anthropologists concerned with globalisation and who are centred on ethnicity rather than race have attended to micro-frames and social processes rather more than those whose disciplinary base is in sociology or cultural studies and whose attentions have settled on race. The comments that follow are primarily, but not entirely, centred on the relationship between race and globalisation, but the discussion shifts back and forth depending on the orientation of the literature reviewed. This focus moves in the next chapter to a further consideration of anthropological work on the *ethnic* dynamics of transnationalism.

The first and most ubiquitous kind of interface between race and globalisation is one in which race features in passing rather than as a central concept, where it is explicitly side-lined in the pursuit of the bigger project of setting out and defending an overview of global networks in which race is incidental. Race is acknowledged as significant; but the authors of these stories have other fish to fry and don't want to think about race or ethnicity in any detail beyond noting its 'importance'. Think of it as 'a drive by' racing en route to establishing the dawning of a new era of social formations demanding new analytic terms. The claims made on behalf of globalisation and post modernity involve a certain theoretical grandeur in which race and ethnicity could only ever have a walk on part. Featherstone, Lash and Robertson's (1995) influential *Global Modernities* is a good example of this broad-brush approach to globalisation. It briefly notes racism, but not the operation of race, in the context of a reference to the 'working class'. This, of course, taps into a vein of British scholarship – of which I was once a contributor[5] – that places the working class in a central position in relation to the generation of popular racist politics through the Labour and Trade Union Movement. This classing of race politics is often configured via the link between ultra right wing nationalist politics and social deprivation and the sense of siege that comes with it, and through attention to particular social and cultural milieu such as football's cultures of violence. There are two obvious points to be made here apart from the fact that these things can be said without reference to globalisation. In drawing attention away from more polite forms of racism, the working class have disproportionately taken the blame for something that is far more widespread than their influence, letting others off the hook. And, although this analysis did not originate in globalisation theory, in repeating these claims it endorses them while rendering them as part of the global operation of racism. Second, the local operation of racism is not connected with its possible global forms. Local/global connections are not made empirically but only abstractly in Robertson's (1995) 'glocalisation'[6]. Although this is an evocative term, we are left none the wiser about *what* the global modalities of local forms of working class racism might be. As it stands this is a *local* story embellished with largely undemonstrated global claims; a point we will return to later.

Featherstone, Lash and Robertson's (1995) passing reference to racial and ethnic dimensions of globalisation in fact lean rather more heavily on ethnicity than race. Ethnicity features implicitly and explicitly in references to 'identity', 'hybridity', 'creolisation' and 'cross over cultures'. These references to syncretic[7] social forms invoke ethnicised versions of human difference without actually exploring how these forms of difference work in making the things – like hybrid versions of ethnicity and so on – to which they refer. Suggestive though these ethnic syncrecies are, they are not pursued as references to concrete lived practices and forms of social organisation. On the contrary they are plucked from, rather than situated in, the political and social contexts in which they operate and in which they could be used to make sense of the social forms generated in trans-societal networks. These syncretic ethnic forms thus become artefacts in their own right: theorised but not investigated, they are deployed in globalisation theory's celebration of human community as tolerance and diversity. Adopting, by default, a liberal stance in which the forward march of globalisation is as inevitable as technological progress itself, this kind of account offers images of 'an immense, unstructured, free unbounded space and of a glorious, complex mixity' (Massey, 1999: 34). These carnivals of hybridity, with their free flow of bodies and messages around the globe, signal more than tacit approval. They give the distinct impression that globalisation's *social* outcomes – apart from accentuated social polarities noted as unfortunate but rarely detailed – are both positive and inevitable. Producing images of the *way things are* in terms that only just stop short of endorsement 'provides an excuse for inaction' (Massey, 1999: 36) denying the possibility of political transformation at the same time as endorsing the interests of the already powerful. Massey's (1999: 34) point – and it is a good one – is that globalisation theory lacks critical engagement with the system it defines. Globalisation theory is produced in a way that simultaneously jettisons its political potential in tandem – as we shall see later – with its analytic currency. It invites political paralysis by shifting from the more highly political category 'race' – with its connection to racism and anti-racism as ways of doing politics – to ethnicity and its carnivals of *diversity*. Racism is bad, but globalisation theory prefers not to think too long about race. Ethnic hybridity is good. Politics are boring and out. Celebrations of diversity are in. And so what?

Race and ethnicity with global wallpaper

The second type of interface between race and ethnicity and globalisation focuses more squarely on race and is exemplified in Bowser's (1995) *Race in a Global Context*. Race and ethnicity are not incidental in this text but positioned as a central consideration in an interesting and varied collection of essays. It's central question – what is racism in the context of globalisation and postmodernism? – is important, although the book fails to answer it convincingly. Its global focus settles on two dimensions of race. The first, offered by McLean (1995), is the global circulation of (raced) American popular culture through sitcoms prominently featuring African American life. McLean (1995: 105,85) notes the mediation of blackness by the myths of whiteness in these productions, and correctly identifies the importance of understanding local interpretations of circulated African American images. But because this paper doesn't actually pursue these local interpretations, but retreats instead into a more local discussion of the production of (racialised) American culture, it fails to pursue a *global* account of race through its forms of world connection. The second dimension of race in this collection consists of a multi-point reading of different nation states' engagement with race: specifically Britain, America, Europe, Brazil and the Caribbean. Its rationale for this is reasonable: racism operates uniquely in each of these locations; it is nationally and locally calibrated. But the *connections* between nation states' racial landscapes, which, had they been drawn, would have made good on the claim to be providing a global perspective, are ignored. The result is an engaging but ultimately nationally focused series of stories about race that at least (implicitly) offer scope for national comparisons. Nation states remain the basic unit for the analysis of racism despite the claim by the book's editor (Bowser, 1995: ix), that national forms have been superseded by *global* forms demanding *analytic attention*. The decline of the nation state (Featherstone, Lash and Robertson, 1995: 2) is of course one of the mantras of globalisation; and the one on which it has been most often challenged (Hirst and Thompson, 1995: 408)[8].

 In the end, Bowser's collection is undisturbed by globalisation, which is pasted over the kinds of things that have been traditionally said about race anyway as a part of nation state formation. A significant feature of globalisation theory more generally is revealed in this treatment of race: it is often written using a lexicon of spatiality and movement that is *not sustained in the analysis*. The shift in language does not bring a corresponding shift in analytic attention. The famous flow characterising globalisation – in the example in hand this is the flow of ideas about race and versions of racism and cultural products – is often poorly demonstrated and its impact improperly investigated or not at all. In these circumstances what can be known about race is undisturbed by the acclaimed shift in paradigm needed to discuss the new social order. Globalisation then operates as sociological wallpaper: as a new backdrop to existing ways of thinking and writing about race that actually manages perfectly well without it. Globalisation theory's ubiquity is both its strength and its weakness. In being about everything it can end up being about nothing (new), especially when it is used to *decorate* concepts such as race rather than re-work them.

A chronic case of globalisation as sociological wallpaper is found in the work of William Julius Wilson. Although this, like Bowser's collection, is centred on race rather than globalisation, it provides a graphic example of the processes I have been describing. Those who have, historically, concerned themselves with the place of race on the urban landscape and its operation in structures of social disadvantage, from the Chicago School on, have seen the object of their concern, urban social forms, co-opted by globalisation theorists. Accounts of racial and ethnic inequalities in residence patterns, access to housing, police protection, jobs, incomes and other facilities are still highly significant in their own right, but are now grafted onto a version of the local as the product of globalisation. What is at issue here is not the connection between the local and the global, but the manner of their being welded together and presented as the racial effects of globalisation. Wilson's (1999) concern with work/urban poverty and racialisation is a case in point. His analysis of the racial topography of American city ghettos details the impact of the disappearance of work – the result of off-shoring and re-location from urban to suburban areas, all *economic* features of globalisation – on the fortunes of a racialized underclass. Now this is an important and legitimate piece of racial analysis, not withstanding the controversial elision of 'race' with 'underclass' which we won't go in to. Wilson's argument is that poverty *in* work is different from poverty *without* work in a formal labour market sense. The disappearance of formal labour market participation, argues Wilson, has impacted on family culture and structure as well as exacerbating racial tensions between (black) welfare clients and (white) tax-payers who would like to curtail welfare spending. Undoubtedly, given the politics of the local welfare regimes in places like inner city Chicago examined by Wilson, picking up the tab on globalisation-induced poverty is a highly racialised operation, though I doubt the black tax payers would agree with his dichotomy. But it would also be useful to understand the processes composing these forms of antagonism, and some of the ways in which race actually operates within them.

Globalisation is here held responsible for two forms of racially calibrated disadvantage: the disappearance of work and the racial antagonism built into the system of welfare that partially compensates for the disappearance of work in workfare states. In other words, an existing system of racial disadvantage is shored-up by new means, to roughly the same end: further black disadvantage. None of the subtleties of globalisation's impact on the local urban scene are detailed and neither are the connections between the local and the global sketched-in, save in the broadest terms. Wilson could say these same things *without* reference to globalisation. His second link between race and globalisation is even more tenuous. At times of 'uncertainty' (the lexicon of globalisation/postmodernism with its invocations of crisis, instability & uncertainty is both tempting and highly evocative) caused by globalisation's dramatic shifts in social and economic circumstances, race becomes a 'conduit for anxiety' (Wilson, 1999: 491). Racism is here reduced to rage and prejudice – of course it *is* rage and prejudice but much more besides – a knee-jerk social reaction to shifts in macro (economic) circumstances.

Overlook for the moment the ways in which this analysis is led by economic shifts, as we will deal with this in the section following. The texture and salience of race and racism here are instantly reduced to their simplest expression in order to show the impact of globalisation's economic motor, which pervades all social forms and takes analytic priority. Race is sacrificed to the project of globalisation. Globalisation may well overlay other social forms, but the manner of its doing so needs to be properly examined. However, the global is bolted-on in this instance in a manner that sacrifices, rather than contributes to, existing understanding of race and racism. These concepts – Wilson's expressed object of investigation – are simplified, cheapened and stripped of their complexity, in the process of accommodating a version of globalisation that does nothing to deepen our understanding of them or globalisation's racial mechanisms.

Globalisation has often provided a new way of describing old things. It is able to do this because much of it operates at a high level of generality and abstraction: there are few empirical studies of globalisation in relation to race, or other aspects of social inequality. Ironically, it has jettisoned its analytic currency in order to sustain the theoretical grandeur that comes with its claims to paradigmatic status. It is not possible to speak or write as a social scientist without reference to it. It has become the framework into which everything must fit. And, the fastest and easiest way to do this is to make some minimal and abstract connection with globalisation and then carry on with business as usual. We don't learn anything new from this.

Connecting race, ethnicity and globalisation

The connections between race and ethnicity and globalisation are more clearly drawn by a number of commentators on race and globalisation. Saskia Sassen produces a more empirically worked version of the mechanisms through which globalisation operates in *The Global City* (1991) and various articles (1990, 1996a, 1996b) than we see in more abstract writing such as *Global Modernities* (Featherstone, Lash and Robertson, 1995). Detailing the operation of globalisation and its impact on the production of urban life – not understanding race – is Sassen's project, but she nevertheless extends the story of the global economy to include the *local social implications* of globalisation that have a bearing on race. Noting disparities in income generated in global economic restructuring, and especially the shift from manufacturing to services, in combination with gentrification and the intensification of homelessness, Sassen (1990) notes the racialisation and ethnicisation of poverty and homelessness in major US cities *as resulting directly from global processes.*

> ...in the 1970s and 1980s our large cities became poorer and blacker and more Hispanic. ...After 1979, white city families maintained their relative standing while black families' median income declined further and their poverty rates increased significantly. Sassen (1990: 481) based on Drennan's 1988 calculations.

Global economic restructuring through off-shoring, the fragmentation of production processes, wage polarities and the increasing significance of the service sector form the economic bedrock out of which new social realities are formed. New forms of racialised social disadvantage and poverty result from these structural shifts; producing a joined-up analysis of globalisation in which connections between the economic and the social, the supra-national and the local are clearly made. Globalisation here is an active set of processes, not wallpaper, and race is not added on, but given significance in the analysis. Sassen's argument centres on economic forms of connection, which she shows transcending nation states. She draws and demonstrates connections others take as given in constructing their own analyses.

And yet, in Sassen's argument, economic processes operate as the motor of social transformation and social and cultural processes are secondary. Massey (1999: 35) calls these approaches to globalisation 'iconic economics': the acceptance by social and cultural theorists of the stories told by economists as the starting point for their own investigations and commentaries. Social forms, analytically subsidiary, are read off from more significant and seminal changes in economic forms. The social becomes the shadow of real economic forms and the theoretical certainties of political economy are re-inscribed in new processes. When the economic is mapped onto the *social* in this way the interface between them, in which mutual forms of generation occur, is overlooked and the threads of race making operating in both domains are obscured. When the economic is mapped onto the social, so the global is mapped onto the local: and locales become the prism of global economic-read-as-social processes. Obviously the economic and the social, the global and the local are all connected, but the detailed manner of their connection is worthy of understanding, and this is precisely what is glossed over by this kind of account.

This is not social analysis but a translation of economic processes into plausible social outcomes. A *social analysis of globalisation would more fully engage racialised and ethnicised social and spatial processes, social relationships and the lives in which all of these things are animated.* Most globalisation theory is *not* social analysis. Herein lies its central problem: it has not just failed to discuss race and ethnicity adequately, but displays an analytic disinterest in all social forms. As I argued in the Introduction, social analysis is about shifting between different levels of scope and scale. Globalisation theory, with its stories of local/global connectivity, is capable of more detailed forms of social analysis than it has hitherto shown.

Connections between race and globalisation are more firmly drawn by Winant, who, non-coincidentally, also undermines the analytic primacy of economic forms. Unlike Sassen, who is concerned with the *making of globalisation*, Winant is centrally concerned with race, and its operation in the global order. The importance of race in the global order, he suggests, is that it is *the* central contemporary form of social differentiation and inequality. With the weakening of class-based politics race has become 'a fundamental organising principle of contemporary social life' (Winant, 1994b: 268–70). Additionally the global geographies of race have also made a new kind of (racial) comparative analysis possible (Winant, 1994b: 274). Going further than most others in sign-posting the route to understanding the global dynamics of race, Winant points to the legacies of slavery and decolonisation in establishing links between dispersed populations and the need to understand the diasporic versions of blackness to which these legacies give rise (Winant, 1994b: 271). Global patterns of migration produce the growth of racially defined minorities in the US, and the consequent mobilisation of white racial antagonism and flight. The internationalisation of race in global migration operates as the key to understanding the current state of US race relations: and a firm and more concrete connection is drawn between race and globalisation. Winant establishes some of the concrete conduits between the global and the local in which race is clearly marked as a central macro and micro social issue. Winant indicates potentially useful avenues of investigation in understanding the *global organisation of race* and in the *racing of globalisation*; avenues he does not, unfortunately, pursue.

A further – analytic and political – connection between race and globalisation concerns the use of race as a critical entry point into the deeper inequalities of globalisation. Most analyses of globalisation are uncritical celebrations of flow and diversity, which obscure globalisation's inequitable social relationships (Massey, 1999). Despite these celebratory and surface pronouncements Massey wants to keep globalisation as a way of approaching the contemporary social order, because it has advantages over theories of modernity. Globalisation, argues Massey (1999: 30–1) has the *capacity* to expose the 'violence, racism and oppression' of modernity. Globalisation, potentially, exposes the geography of modernity: a position from which it is possible to challenge its system of rule, the knowledge on which it is based, and the forms of representation to which it gives rise. Massey *implies* that race and ethnicity can provide an exposing critical edge, capable of cracking globalisation open and revealing its deep social inequalities.

Can race and ethnicity display some of globalisation's more inequitable aspects? Can these concepts provide a critical counterpoint to the celebration of diversity and flow? I think they can, as the case studies at the end of this chapter show. But how can we expose globalisation's racial mechanisms and outcomes, its race making? How can we uncover its racial grammar? Understanding the part played by race and ethnicity in configuring the global social order is a daunting task. What follows in this chapter can only form a modest beginning. Starting with the contributions of writers concerned with race, I will take a closer look at colonialism, at aspects of local micro globalisation, at migration and, in passing, at popular imagery, to see if these issues – which seem on the surface as though they might have something to do with race – reveal the mechanisms by which race is made, and hence reveal some of the racial grammar of globalisation. The connections made by Sassen, Winant and Massey have set us on this pathway.

Exposing the racial and ethnic grammar of globalisation: colonial connections

That the racial geography of globalisation is in part configured around the historical routes carved by empire and earlier forms of mercantilism, is a well-established connection (Winant, 1994b: 271, Hesse, 1999: 127–9). The 'distinctive political forms, transportation routes and transnational lines of communication' of empire form the 'historical conduits of modern forms of globalisation' (Hesse, 1999: 127–9). Hesse and Winant are right to make this claim, although neither draws the connection empirically. Anthropologists MacGaffey and Bazenguissa-Ganga (2000: 29–46), in their study of Congolese traders operating between Congo-Kinshasa and Brussels and Congo-Brazaville and Paris, *do* manage to make this connection more concrete. They show how the old routes between metropolitan centre and colony, are activated by new social and commercial networks and activities of traders, operating outside of mainstream legal and economic structures in a kind of secondary economy of flexible global trading. We may think of them as operating a parallel form of globalisation to that of corporations. MacGaffey and Bazenguissa-Ganga show the reconstruction of empire as new forms of global trading; and they show how the trade in clothes and food sustains resident Congolese populations in Paris and Brussels, established through the old conduits of colonialism and the denial of French/Belgian citizenship with independence. One of the forms of trade they document involved importing African clothes, music and food into Paris and Brussels to service the identities and lifestyles of local Africans; and exporting designer Parisian fashions and electrical goods back to the Congo, giving returnees and others a vicarious Parisian status (MacGaffey and Bazenguissa-Ganga, 2000: 54). Clothes and artefacts carry important social messages and have concrete circulation practices. These activities provide new forms for old colonial relationships and routes, as well as reversing the usual directions of flow in goods and bodies performing versions of cultural identities. Thus a number of connections between empire and globalisation are established in this study: connections that are frequently *asserted* in other studies but infrequently demonstrated.

Hesse doesn't draw these kinds of connections, because he is pursuing a different point. The general connection he establishes between empire and globalisation is intended to provide a way of speaking about the *racialisation of globalisation* by a circuitous route. Clearly – as I have already noted – discussing the racialisation of globalisation is an enormous and complicated task and it is therefore reasonable that Hesse should use colonialism to make his point, because its race credentials are already well established. Hesse doesn't say how, but race is transparently significant in the making of empire: in providing the texture of colonial relations and the rationale for conquest. The race/empire connection can be made in the following way, which stresses what Hesse overlooked: the race making involved in empire.

Race *was made* – it was manufactured as it manufactured empire – in the ways in which *native* populations became *subject* populations (Fanon, 1967) and in many other ways as well. Race was made in making the capacities and bearing of rulers and the administrative systems sustaining them; and race was made in the interactions between rulers and ruled. Race was made in the sea routes connecting Britain (France, Spain, Portugal) with empire, and it was made in the making of lives and subjectivities in the journeys of those traversing these routes (Knowles, 2000a). Race was made in the making of the *Black Atlantic* (Gilroy, 1993) and in the tribulations of adventurers, civil servants, empire functionaries, traders and missionaries. Empire is first and foremost a race story. Empire's racialised contours were clear, confessed, and long exposed by sociologists, anthropologists, and in all manner of post-colonial literature and race theory. This is not in contention. Empire is about race and ethnicity. But the case is rarely made for this connection in the concrete practices I have just identified. But, even setting aside this point about the making of race in empire, the race credentials of empire are not easily transposed onto globalisation. So, although we suspect that globalisation is also a race story, it is a story that needs to be uncovered and told in the present and not just borrowed from empire.

Despite this, Hesse's argument is a good one. Instead of empire serving as the political context for globalisation; globalisation serves as the political context of empire, he argues; and historical understanding is neutered, stripped of its racial content. In other words the optimism and naivete of globalisation de-politicises and rewrites history, purged of race. As globalisation rescues its empires by making them raceless, so it services 'white amnesia' in which whites are simultaneously absolved of guilt for the past, and allowed to don globalisation as a 'Western spectacle' thereby perpetuating their forgotten domination of the past. 'In the Western spectacle we find the cultural elevation of the West over the 'non-West' and the aesthetic subordination of 'non-whiteness' to 'whiteness' (Hesse, 1999: 130–2).

While there is no doubt that what Hesse says partially describes some of the racial and ethnic fault lines of contemporary globalisation; MacGaffey and Bazenguissa-Ganga's research and the case studies at the end of this chapter, suggest that things are not so clear cut; so black and white, so West versus the rest as Hesse suggests. These may be the old tectonic plates of the global order, but they do not describe its current finely etched racial and ethnic contours. Surely the point of reconnecting globalisation with its disconnected history is to expose the racial and ethnic fault lines of modernity, so as to trace their reformulated pathways into the globally configured present of high or post-modernity. Unfortunately this doesn't happen, and so we are none the wiser about the operation of race in globalisation, or the ways in which globalisation is composed through race. MacGaffey and Bazenguissa-Ganga, on the other hand, manage to give a sense of the operation of race and ethnicity in global processes while simultaneously connecting them with their past in the geographies of empire. There are important directions indicated here for uncovering the racial working of globalisation, which we will return to.

Local micro-globalisation

Local (urban) landscapes have featured prominently in the *exposure of global-isation's forms of racial inscription*. This has taken some of the forms already outlined in which globalisation is enlisted as backdrop (Wilson) or as a set of economic processes with secondary social implications (Sassen) in the organisation of local race regimes. The general idea is that the local contains the imprint of distant locales through their networks of connection, so that the city becomes the local prism of globalisation and a vantage point from which to develop a commentary on it. 'Glocalisation' (Robertson, 1995: 30) is the term coined to express these local forms of inscription of global processes, to convey the sense of a relationship between the local and the supranational without having to be very precise about it.

An example of research and writing that explores rather than assumes or simplifies the global/local connection is Eade's (1997) edited collection, *Living the Global City*. An anthropologically-oriented text, sensitive to forms of ethnicity that include local versions of whiteness as well as the racial categories applied to local Bangladeshis, the essays in this collection begin to perform the investigative work of tracing the conduits between the global and the local in people's everyday lives and activities. The fact that people exhibit a global sense of place in their social relationships, outlook and actual movements plays an important part in the re-inscription, at a local level, of aspects of globalisation. Segmented, differentiated and divergent accounts of the meaning and nature of the locale (Albrow, 1997: 52), produced through interviews in some cases, are used to challenge the salience of traditional versions of community as an account of how people currently live. Attempts to figure out the empirical social forms constituting the global order at a local level are used to re-theorise the terms of local understanding in concepts such as community. Most importantly, *Living the Global City* attempts to understand the global re-configuration of everyday lives by 'lifting of the individual's field of action from pre-given locales on the one hand, and the shaping of locales by distant social influences on the other' (Durrschmidt, 1997: 60–1, drawing on Giddens). The lives and transactions of ordinary people feature in these *particular* accounts of globalisation (Durrschmidt, 1997: 57) and this distinguishes this collection from others, where people and their lives feature only as the implied surfaces of general claims about the social impact of globalisation. This kind of 'microglobalisation' analysis aims to understand the 'stable and situated configurations of action and experience in which individuals actively generate a distinctive degree of familiarity and practical competence' (Durrschmidt, 1997: 57).

This kind of grounded understanding, which begins from people's lives, certainly points in the right direction. There is potential for developing detailed accounts of the social processes that network people and locales with bigger, global, geographies. In order to sustain the claims of local/global connection we need to understand, and be specific about, the (raced and ethnicised) nature of lives lived at the global/local interface. This kind of understanding would require a detailed racial and ethnic mapping of local lives: a re-engagement with neighbourhood, with the distribution of resources, of social capital, of opportunities, the local operation of policing, of work and so on. But this re-engagement must frame these things in terms of their bigger scenes and networks in a way that makes it possible for us to understand – at a lived and concrete level – the networks connecting the local with the global. What are the social processes composing those connections? What kinds of social transactions are they made of? These questions make a connection with the making of people and places, and people in transit between places, discussed in the last chapter. Here I suggested that we needed detailed maps of the local working of the grammar of race and ethnicity. This can then be extended by tracing local connections with global processes as some of the contributors to Eade's *Living the Global City* start to do.

The local is the bedrock of globalisation as lives are inevitably lived locally as well as extra-locally. So the local, and its in-built racial inequalities, must form the centre-point in understanding the racial secrets of globalisation. The local *is* global, it is not separate from it. The trick is to detail the local as a globally calibrated enterprise, and to understand the mechanisms through which it produces race and ethnicity, far away and close at hand. There are two ways of doing this. One is to trace an individual's position locally and to try and understand this as also the outcome of local and extra-local racial and ethnic processes. We all have our own maps of global connection and these could certainly be plotted for each of us as personal topographies. The second is to trace the connections between specific local and extra-local space: to see the character of space as produced in this combination. Both involve detailed empirical investigation in mapping exercises that foreground race and ethnicity.

Migration

Race and ethnicity are evidently key elements in *global migration*[9]. We think this because it is frequently acknowledged in (immigration and) migration literature, although the raced and ethnicised dimensions of migration are not usually discussed in any detail. It also seems that there are patterns in migration which have a relationship to disparities in wealth between regions that map, although not neatly, onto racial and ethnic differences. The racial and ethnic organisation of who goes where and why may not be immediately apparent, but many of us have long suspected that race and ethnicity are a part of these processes, even though we have not been able to be clear about how they work. Deciding *how* race and ethnicity work in global migration is a more complicated task. While this cannot be satisfactorily resolved in this section, or the next chapter in which this is dealt with directly, we can at least set out some parameters for thinking about this more clearly.

Labour market models of migration

Two basic models – from different disciplinary bases – operate in the field of global migration studies. One sustains economic and labour market-led accounts, in which people operate as mobile labour power in pursuit of economic advantage (Samuel, 1988; Kay and Miles 1992; Richmond, 1992; Ongley and Pearson, 1995). This model is dominant, and underscores British, American and European debates about asylum seekers: are they the politically persecuted in need of asylum, or economic migrants seeking material advantage? The other, more humanistic, model provides micro accounts of transplanted lives in specific locales under specific circumstances of exit and arrival (Benmayor and Skotnes, 1994). These come from oral historians and anthropologists, and are as specific as the other sort is generalised. Bridging the gap between these two models is a small anthropological literature that examines specific migrations in a broader context. Basch, Glick Schiller and Szanton Blanc's (1994) *Nations Unbound* is a good example of this, because it explores the circumstances of specific migrations while drawing broader connections.

In the migration stories of the economic and labour market model, people and their lives are transposed into the more abstract category 'labour'. Their mobility is interpreted as the pursuit of jobs and improved economic circumstances, in a unidirectional transfer from poorer to richer nations. Where the racial and ethnic dynamics of these movements are acknowledged, and mostly they are not, they are often attached to colonial histories, or to the collapse of post-colonial economies. They reconstruct the tensions of colonisation in the relations between a *core* and a *periphery*, as a set of economic exigencies mapped onto a broader set of social and political circumstances, which are not fully elaborated. Broadly speaking, these approaches rework the insights of Marxist development theorists like Gunder Frank (1969)[10]. Their advantage is that they signal the continuities of racialised colonial relations in global landscapes, although in a different way from Hesse. In doing so they flatten the complexity of the geographies of migration, a necessary precursor to exposing their racial fabric. Consequently these accounts fail to tell us why people migrate to one place rather than another; and why some people migrate while others stay put. In fact these accounts are bursting with unasked, and unanswered, questions.

Untangling the geographies of labour market migration

Economic advantage can be pursued through many different geographies of migration. Why did some Caribbean migrants move to Britain while others moved to the US or to Canada, for example? Sassen (1990) grapples with the complexities of migration geographies by looking at sources of immigrants to the US. Not all US immigrants are from poor countries on the periphery of the US. South Korea and Taiwan – neither of them poor countries in the general scheme of things – are examples of significant sending countries in the profile of US immigration. While not denying the importance of poverty, over population and economic stagnation, in creating the pressure to migrate, Sassen (1990: 373–4) suggests it is more complicated than this. Important factors are military and business links with the US, especially direct foreign investment aimed at production for export. Admittedly these are economic and technical processes; we noted earlier the lack of social content in her analysis. It is these links, argues Sassen, that 'uproot people from their traditional modes of existence' and cause intra-national rural to urban drift, which connects with international migration. Direct foreign investment by the US contributes to 'the development of economic, cultural and ideological connections with the industrialised countries' (Sassen, 1990: 376–7). Localised mini-systems operate in respect of what are called 'economic migrants' with the Middle East receiving migrants from India, Pakistan and Bangladesh (Zlotnik, 1999: 27–9), with migrations between South American countries depending on wage differentials and other inducements to relocate. Nicaraguans, for example, often move to Costa Rica because wages are higher. Similarly there are relocations between African states. In the 1980s a number of West African migrants, especially from Chad and Ghana, moved to Nigeria because, fuelled by oil wealth, it was creating jobs and paying higher wages than neighbouring countries. The wealthier countries from the Pacific Rim attract migrants from the Philippines and Thailand. This certainly points to the need for a closer examination of the geographies of migration as an important step in understanding their racial and ethnic working. This should focus on the social processes producing migration – questions about why and how people move – and not the economic and technical ones.

Sassen's analysis of the United States points to another key dimension in the analysis of the geographies of migration. The political contexts into which migrants are admitted are vitally important in calibrating racial dynamics. These are not just matters of whiteness and privilege. Different national political contexts have distinctive geographies of migration. In the US and Canada, for example, there is provision to meet skill shortages with selective recruitment, entrepreneur immigrants and domestic workers, especially from the Philippines. Filipino women form the new class of domestic servants in many middle class North American households, and this raises important questions about the complexities of gender and migration. In Britain, primary immigration, itself a selective feature of colonial presence – why did people come from certain parts of India and the Caribbean but not from Africa? – had ended by the 1970s. After the 1970s British immigration concerned a trickle of dependants, the handling of illegal entrants and asylum seekers. A shift toward the North American model of migration 'skill shortage' is now being pursued with a view to selective primary immigration privileging the highly skilled. This will allow Britain to raid Indian computer technicians and teachers in an effort to maintain a global competitive edge through lower public sector wage bills. Modern British migration, of course, has never operated as it did on the other side of the Atlantic in providing the fabric of the nation through settlement, an enterprise clearly conceived in ethnic and racial terms. A detailed geography of migration, as it is managed by nation states, yet set in the broader global political context in which migration operates, is a necessary precursor to grasping the racial and ethnic dynamics of which these processes are composed. Mapping the trajectories of human mobility and the conditions in which they are produced is an urgent task in the analysis of globalisation's racial and ethnic grammar and the race making that produced it.

Economic and labour market models of migration contain few insights into who migrates and who stays and why. We have no sense from them of the calculations – beyond an implied and undemonstrated preoccupation with jobs, income and quality of life – involved in the decision-making aspects of migration. We know little about return migration, or the routine movements back and forth between old and new countries of settlement. We know little about the social fields and social relationships migrants build across their migration points and places of exit and entry. This is because people and lives do not feature as units of analysis in the ways in which I am suggesting they should if we are to understand the operation of race and ethnicity in migration. Migration may be about the pursuit of economic advantage, but it is also about lives and families and the plethora of calculations and connections attendant upon them. To treat this as a labour allocation process is to overlook the complexities of its human dimensions, and their place in the re-imagining of lives through movement. In labour allocation stories of migration, other stories of lives-in-motion are erased so that we have little grasp of the personal, social and familial forms these movements from one place to the next take, and consequently we have no sense of the dislocation accompanying them. Labour market accounts are not *social* analysis, which needs to ask some of the questions I have just asked; indeed they are highly deficient in many respects. Labour market migration stories have also, until recently, occluded other forms of migration such as those of refugees and asylum seekers. Some of the broader, life-situated, aspects of migration are addressed in humanistic accounts, as we shall soon see. But because of the micro nature of these accounts they contain only moments in the geographies of migration, and not a grasp of the overall processes of which they are but a part.

Connecting-up micro models of migration

Micro humanistic models of global migration redress some of the deficiencies noted in economic models. Zinn's (1994) essay on Senagalese immigrants in

Bari, for example, discusses the ways in which these migrants give meaning to their migratory experiences in Italy and puts the labour migration stories that they tell about themselves into a bigger and more *social context*. Zinn shows how this is part of their daily experience and the impact of the new cultural contexts in which their lives are cast. Chamberlain's (1994) account of Barbadian migrants to Britain places what are understood as economic and job-market migrations in a broader context of family histories of social and geographic mobility. This draws connections between families historically – some families migrate while others don't and some *members* of families migrate while others don't – and differentiates forms of geographical mobility. The result is a more textured account of migration. The migration stories related by Zinn and Chamberlain show the need for more detailed pictures of migration, in order to understand the place migration occupies in the overall organisation of lives and in the social production of meaning attached to migration experiences. In the deeper texture of lives, experience and meaning, we can hope to discover the social processes composing race and ethnicity discussed in earlier chapters.

Such understanding points to the significance of the details of individual, as well as broader patterns, of circumstances. The (personal and social/political) terms on which people leave old homes and arrive in new ones are highly significant and enormously varied. The circumstances in which illegal entrants are forced to deal with those who traffic in human cargo, risk their lives in migration, and then live the rest of their lives as invisible sub-citizens in their new state, involves a highly significant blend of personal/political processes. The refugees who endure lengthy periods in camps awaiting resettlement are quite different in their circumstances from those who migrate as domestic workers with no rights of stay beyond each employment contract. The 'club class migrant' with professional, technical or managerial skills working in core sectors of the world economy is one of the dominant images of globalisation. But this migrant is outnumbered by the growing army of women who migrate to perform domestic labour in the homes of the wealthy (Brah, Hickman, Mac an Ghaill, 1999: 6), and is in a radically different position from the other types of migrant outlined above. These circumstances are the combined effects of individual and family fortune, local forms of allocation and stratification and the social and political landscapes on which all of these things are produced. In any discussion of migration finely textured enough to reveal its ethnic and racial contours we need to un-bundle these circumstances as a precursor to a more detailed understanding. A detailed mapping of social and political contexts, and the social relations, of migration would provide a starting point for a deeper understanding of race and ethnicity in these processes. Hesse, drawing on Massey, says it is important who travels, when and in what circumstances:

> ...we need to raise particular questions about the different causes of geographical mobility and variable scenes of time and place in the contemporary discourses of globalisation, as well as factoring in the experiential differences of 'race', gender, class and ethnicity. (Hesse, 1999: 136)

Dominant versions of globalisation as 'flows' responding to market conditions, easily applied to cultural products and capital, come unravelled when it is human bodies that 'flow'.

> Yet, come a debate on immigration, and they (those who applaud the fluidity of globalisation) immediately have recourse to another geographical imagination all together...in total contradiction to the vision of globalisation. [This is]...the imagination of defensible places, of the rights of 'local people' to their own 'local places' of a world divided by difference and the smack of firm boundaries, a geographical imagination of nationalism...And so in this era of globalisation we have sniffer dogs to detect people hiding in the holds of boats, people die trying to cross the Rio Grande and boat loads of people precisely trying to 'seek out the best opportunities' go down in the Mediterranean...the freedom of space on the one hand and the 'right to one's own place' on the other, works in favour of the already powerful. They can't have it both ways. (Massey, 1999: 38–9)

There *is* no 'world market' for human labour (Massey, 1999: 37) – itself a shorn-off version of lives – like there is for capital, not least because 'flows' of human labour are powerfully mediated by the political frameworks in which nation states manage immigration and refugee claims. Governments of nation states defend notions of 'belonging', and who 'fits' in tandem with the defence of the very living standards other aspects of globalisation have generated. Hirst and Thompson (1995, citing Brah, 1999: 6) contend that there are *fewer* migration opportunities today than in the past.

The economic arrangements of globalisation in which the North pursues its dominance over the South – a very rough geography of globalisation for those of us who want to understand its racial and ethnic grammar – by approximately the same and newer means 'adds to the hardships of the already poor and especially for women' (Massey, 1999: 35). This classic division articulated in development studies is a very rough guide to the racial and ethnic arrangements of globalisation. But because it fails to provide a map of what actually takes place does not mean that it should be overlooked completely in calculating the racial and ethnic dynamics of migration, as we noted earlier in response to Hesse. Zlotnik (1999: 27–8) argues that movements from the developing to the developed world account for 70–80 per cent of migrations to North America and Australia, and that the majority of the world's refugees originate in developing countries. This broad mapping, of course, lacks detail, but provides some of the contours of migration. Kushner and Knox's (1999) mapping of refugee movements since 1900 shows a close and expected correlation with political turmoil and genocide, and some of the recent flows produced by this are from the Balkans and involve white populations.

There is no straightforward way in which these processes are raced and ethnicised: (white) Eastern Europeans and those from the Balkans are as likely to be the victims of summary exclusion at British and other airports as Nigerians, Jamaicans and Sri Lankans. All are fleeing different forms of economic and political violence and adversity, and all are suspected of searching for new homes, something that frequently contextualises their tourism in the eyes of immigration officials as asylum by the back door. The ways in which these processes are raced and ethnicised is certainly not obvious and hence demands closer investigation. Britain is not alone in this, and it is anyway not one of the world's top migration magnets. Describing the US/Mexico border as a 'grim region of domination and terror' Hannerz (1997: 541) sees it as 'an exemplary instance of what borderness is all about'. Some borders are crossed with great difficulty or not at all (Hannerz, 1997: 537). It is ironic that following the dismantling of the iron curtain, the new frontiers of barbed wire and electric fences are those separating rich from poor nations. In the US/Mexico case the Rio Grande is also the border separating a brown from a white-becoming-brown nation. But this may be incidental. The Mexico/US border is defending (American versions of) global capitalism, not from communism, but from itself and its inevitable consequences in the upheaval and movement of populations.

A thorough account of the geographies of global migration is an important and outstanding task. We need an investigation that attends to the micro-realities of migrant lives, in the broader political contexts in which migrations occur. The social relationships of migration need to be placed in the political/social contexts in which they are produced, and in which they are effective in calibrating lives. The political/social tapestries of departure stories need to be reviewed in order to see their interface with individual biographies. So, too, the political tapestries of arrival, their forms of governance and the conduits through which migrants make new lives and service old ones. All of this will contain within it the texture of racial and ethnic social relationships and biographies in migration: a local/global, structural/biographical exercise in social investigation. We need to understand the conditions in which various kinds of migration are generated and maintained. We also need to know more about the social, political and individual circumstances of global movement through detailed local studies in the context of the broader social and political canvases on which these things occur. We need to track and measure people flows intra-nationally and internationally as well as understand how people handle movement in their routine lives and (stories of) selves. The micro, in other words, is usefully set within the macro systems in which it forms a detail from the bigger picture. I explore some of these things further in Chapter 5.

Popular imagery

Images of race and ethnicity as blackness – caricatured images that come nowhere near the complexity of most political landscapes – are prominent in globally transmitted forms of popular culture, while the hegemonic hold of whiteness over their production is sometimes exposed, but mostly opaque. American produced and globally transmitted images of African American rap musicians, sports celebrities and other stories of upward mobility, are routinely traded in television sitcom images showcasing versions of 'black life'

(Havens, 2000). *The Fresh Prince of Bel Air* and *The Cosby Show* popularise easy – 'lite' – versions of racial difference in which African Americans are safely re-packaged as the denziens of music, comedy and sport. These images are evidently highly selected versions of the social and political conditions they purport to convey, framed by calculations concerning the ratings and advertising revenues accompanying these forms of entertainment. Such images necessarily intersect somehow with the cultural mood, tastes and inclination, on which the production of plausible stories for mass consumption depend. These stories are not necessarily connected with the social conditions of racial inequality that persist in the racial orders producing them. Media messages do not have an obvious representational value in the transmission of social forms; they are a selective telling of social conditions removed from their broader political and social contexts. Media messages are artefacts in their own right. Social forms and their representation are two different (but connected) things, and this is no less true of race than anything else. It is important then to place forms of representation in their social/political context and to ask critical questions about the version of events and people being played for mass consumption. It is also important to think about the context in which these messages are received, both locally and globally. What *is* the status of representation in the production of social relationships? What does it matter that these images are beamed around the world? Do these things play a part in the local/national/global production of racialised social relationships? In the racialisation of space? In the distribution of income and social facilities? How do these images impact on lives? On political landscapes? On the validation of lives and understanding of difference? It is time we started joining some of these things up in our *disconnected* accounts of representation.

The social impact of representation – whether applied to racialised images or anything else – is an open question that needs to be placed in a broader social context. The key issue is not popular culture, but shared imagery. Local, globally transmitted, shared versions of what globalisation, race and ethnicity mean, may be – we don't really know – important in the ways in which people operate in the world, and it is this, rather than popular culture, that we need to understand. Shared imagery may or may not lean on popular culture. This is an unanswered question. But great care needs to be exercised over how race *plays* in popular versions of globalisation. Can race and ethnicity operate as positive attributes in images of globalisation? Can they operate as an antidote to entrenched nationalism and belonging? Can they be a way of challenging these things? If so, then globalisation theory's hopelessly optimistic version of human mixity may be worth tolerating, for its significance may be more than superficial.

But this comes with a warning. Care needs to be exercised in hollow victories in which progressive rhetoric and imagery co-exist with unchanged social and political conditions. The key issue here is the relationship between the popular and the political. This is the crucial realignment that needs to be made, and in order to do this we need to be clear about representation and the potential gap between what people see and say, what they believe to be true and what they act on. This raises many questions concerning shades of meaning and veracity.

Elements of the racial grammar of globalisation, uncovered in the social mechanisms of race making, are evident in the four issues outlined above, colonisation, local micro-globalisation, migration and popular imagery. It is by now evident that race and ethnicity appear in *no* patterned or systematic way that we are able to identify, but that when we take a close look at various situations race and ethnicity *are* apparent in the operation of bits of globalisation. The picture we get is fragmented, piecemeal and on a case-by-case basis. Information is accumulated on a local micro basis and no big picture has appeared. In the case of colonialism there are elements of patterns established such as the routes of empire, but these are reconstructed by new routes and purposes and implicate peoples who were not part of colonial calculation. Local micro-globalisation presents racialised patterns which are again fragmented and which need to be connected with extra-local processes in order to make sense of what is happening in ethnic and racial terms. The geographies of migration demand closer and more detailed attention, especially the interface between individual biography and circumstances of exit and arrival. Finally, there are the effects and calculations attendant upon the racial and ethnic aspects of popular imagery and the relationship of these things to popular culture and representation. There are questions concerning whether the celebratory imagery of globalisation can be harnessed in the service of positive images of racial and ethnic difference and whether, if this is possible, these images will be divorced from their political and social contexts and broader schemes of meaning.

Conclusion

This is all very inconclusive but points to some directions for further investigation and some of the means by which these can be achieved using approaches that foreground individual lives, subjectivities and human action in the processes of living and moving in a global context. This section on racial and ethnic grammar and the race making mechanisms producing it has attempted to aid understanding of some of the ways in which we might think of globalisation as written in, and by, human agency; as being made in the creative acts of living in the world today. Understanding race making and the racial and ethnic grammar it produces, as the forms of social practice to which race gives rise, involves a case-by-case examination in which we identify situations that involve specific aspects of globalisation, and try to identify how race and ethnicity operate in these situations. This involves examining globalisation for examples of race, both because it has been overlooked, and because we suspect it will expose globalisation's darker side. I intend to pursue a little further this review of globalisation's racial grammar with the aid of some case studies, which ground the argument and expose some of the race making involved in globalisation. Inevitably these are more suggestive than conclusive.

Case studies

The purpose of the following case studies is to highlight difficulties and ways of moving forward in uncovering the racial and ethnic grammar of globalisation. The situational character of race and ethnicity makes this an appropriate approach. The examples I have chosen convey particular sets of circumstances that can be unpacked and examined more closely to determine their forms of race making. The situations I have chosen expose different aspects of race and ethnicity. The retreat from big theory exposes complexity. Starting from particular circumstances and situations, of course, involves theoretical choices, a move away from grand theory and the hope of finding a single model that is able to explain the racial dynamics of globalisation. What follows focuses on people and bodies and movement and performance; on the personal side of globalisation, in keeping with the broad concerns of this volume.

Case study 1. Global adoption and mother substitutes

Sitting watching my children in the local park near our house in Montreal some years ago I was struck by the evidently globally organised ethnic dimensions of the forms of human interaction going on around me. Among my own and other local children – whose parents hail from all corners of the world – there are a number of small Chinese girls playing in the park. As I watch I remember that I know personally of several couples who have adopted Chinese babies, who have been vetted by local social services, and made the trip to China to pick up their new daughter. This process is punctuated by delays and anxiety provoking silences, which signal the unseen workings of complicated procedures and attendant bureaucracies. This was a process that, in the late 1990s, cost $20,000 CDN a child, and so was mostly an option for the well off. Some of these little girls were being supervised by women who could be their adoptive mothers, but others, like the local children playing in the park, were in the care of Filippino women who worked as maids and nannies and often congregated in the park to chat while supervising their tribes of little children. Filippino nannies enter Canada by means of the domestic labour quota, which makes them highly dependant on their sponsoring family. They may eventually move on to other jobs if they achieve landed immigrant status, but meanwhile they move from contract to contract, family to family. Many of these women, I knew from talking to them, had children of their own who they had left in the Philippines with their mothers or other female relatives pending their eventual return.

There are many layers to this local park's global ethnicity and race scenario. Its users were produced by many divergent departure and arrival stories; stories of families reformulated in new circumstances and in new countries. Children change hands across distant state boundaries, or stay while their mothers move on. Chinese and Filippino women have given up their children in different circumstances to service the childless and those whose household needs are so intricate in their grooming and aesthetics that they require extra labour power.

Adoption is one of the most fascinating areas of globalisation: the journeys of little bodies in diverse circumstances, a redistribution from poor to rich, countries and people. Haiti and Romania are other places sending children to Canada and anthropologists are beginning to study how this works. Romania has 100,000 children in institutions, and adoption is big business for the 109 agencies involved; children can be ordered from the internet and dropped off on the door step. America is the chief purchaser of these babies (*Sunday Times* June 24 2001). But Romania is not the world's biggest exporter of children: Russia and China send more. This flow of children from poor to rich countries and from poor to rich people within countries can be discussed in terms of its ethnic dimensions, although ethnicity is evidently only one of the factors in play in these calculations. The general point is that there are important and fascinating aspects of globalisation to study that are part of what we see happening around us. These things have a lot to do with ethnicity and race, although not in straightforward ways. In cases of global adoption, race and ethnicity operate in some fractured way in combination with locally and globally calibrated forms of poverty in concert with other circumstances. Romania, Russia and China are poor, but not the poorest, nations. They are communist and ex-communist countries, experiencing significant social upheaval. America and Canada are rich countries with high living standards
and – like China and Russia – have ethnically diverse populations. Welfare and other local brokerage systems in all of these countries facilitate the export and import of small children in response to 'market forces'. Adoption is seen as a viable solution to otherwise intractable problems of survival by mothers who give up their children for adoption or, as some reports have it, are duped out of them. Biographies and circumstances intersect with political landscape and its scattered ethnicities. Ethnicity and race are only ever circumstantially significant, they are inevitably mediated with myriad other circumstances. They are not alone significant, nor insignificant, but play a part in the working of many things that result in the situation just outlined, and which has its own forms of race and ethnicity making and its own forms of racial and ethnic grammar.

Case study 2. Trade in human organs

The second example of the global working of race and ethnicity questions the very integrity of (raced and ethnicised) bodies. The global traffic in human organs, was exposed by the American anthropologist Nancy Scheper-Hughes (2000), who asks important questions about the lives touched by organ sale for transplant surgery – 'what unrecognised sacrifices are being made?' Scheper-Hughes (2000: 192–4) argues that kidneys are a new source of capital in India: raising money for women to pay for a wedding or settle a debt through the 'organ bazaars' that operate in the slums of Bombay, Calcutta, Madras. She notes the social/political transformations attendant upon this kind of transaction:

> Transplant surgery has reconceptualised the social relations between self and other, between individual and society, and among the 'three bodies', the existential lived body ... the social representational body, and the political body. (Scheper-Hughes, 2000: 193)

Refashioning customary laws and traditional practices, which have a bearing on the body, death and social relationships, the global trade in organs reinvents the relationship between the body parts and the whole, and the treatment and disposal of the dying (Scheper-Hughes, 2000: 194). These forms of 'Bio-piracy' also rewrite the relationship between the state and its 'sub-citizens', and refashion the specific cultural practices in which they are set (Scheper-Hughes, 2000: 202).

Comparing Brazil with post-apartheid South Africa Scheper-Hughes deftly maps the connections between the human body and the body politic. Rumours of organ and 'spare baby' stealing circulating in the Brazilian favelas – among those living on the margins of the global economy – are interpreted as a 'surrogate form of political witnessing' by those who are not called upon to speak, who effectively have no voice. This takes place against a political backdrop in which the military in both countries have unfettered rights of disposal over the bodies of its sub-citizens. South African organ trading/transplanting and the 'pioneering' heart operations of Christian Barnard who 'just took the hearts we needed' (Scheper-Hughes, 2000: 204–5) are closely connected. Police surgeons had free access to the body parts of suspected 'terrorists' in apartheid South Africa. 'Donors' in this context are politically positioned as social and political 'waste' (Scheper-Hughes, 2000: 203) and the 'recipients', to whom organs are redistributed, form a local and global elite. These expressions of individual social and political worth are produced by a combination of local political circumstances and the global market in organs. Scheper-Hughes suspects these things are also produced by race, ethnicity, gender and class. Although her claim lacks a detailed analysis of the global organ trade's race, ethnic, gender and class relationships, Scheper-Hughes sketches its basic contours. Organs flow from black to brown to white, from women to men, from the poor to the rich countries and from the poor to the rich citizens within countries.

Although it is unlikely that things are as neat as Scheper-Hughes suggests, there is clearly scope for more detailed examination of the racial and ethnic grammar of the trade in human organs. Most likely this would have to be subdivided into different locations and political contexts as the claims to an overarching racial grammar spanning different contexts are not sustainable. Most importantly, Scheper-Hughes points to the significance of political context in understanding how these systems work. Bio-piracy could not operate without local sanction and brokerage: without an international market in the making of whole bodies from spare parts. And without an effective value system which posits this as acceptable. As with the global flow of small children, wealth and poverty are significant in the mediation of 'flows' and the forms of ethnicity and race it generates. The global trade in organs and the trade in 'spare' babies are clearly part of the power geometry of globalisation, part of the ways in which race is made. Micro and macro elements of this kind of trading demand further investigation so that we can map more closely exactly how race and ethnicity operate in concert with other dimensions of inequality and individual circumstance. The key question is this – in what set of global/local circumstances, and by what means, are race and ethnicity made through bio-piracy? And what forms do race and ethnicity take in these circumstances? What are the forms of social practice to which they give rise?

Case study 3. Thai sex tourism and the new slavery

Another facet of globalisation with a close relationship to race and ethnicity through the body is set out in Bales' (1999) *Disposable People* which details some of the conditions producing contemporary forms of slavery. These are part of globalisation, in that globalisation both produces it and is mimicked by it. Bales (1999: 9) conservatively estimates, using information gathered from ILO, the United Nations and various human rights organisations, the number of 'new slaves' worldwide to be 27 million. Others put it closer to 200 million. New slaves are 'bonded labour', people working off debts without pay who give themselves into slavery as security against a loan to meet a family emergency or when a debt is inherited as in India, Bangladesh, Pakistan and Nepal. Otherwise slaves are concentrated in Northern and West Africa, South East Asia and South America, although there are some slaves, usually domestic slaves, in all countries including wealthy households in Paris and London (Bales, 1999: 9). Slaves work in prostitution, brick making, mining or quarrying, gem working, jewellery making, cloth and carpet making, domestic service, forest clearance and shops. They are characterised by their deployment in pursuit of high profits, by their cheapness, their vulnerability (which is exploited), and by their disposability (Bales, 1999: 11). The effective use of violence and intimidation as a mechanism of control (Bales, 1999: 5) is shared by slaves whose circumstances otherwise differ.

Here we see differences not just in race and ethnicity but in region, regime and family fortune as well as differences in susceptibility to regimes of violence and terror and the bullies brokering them. Bales argues that, unlike old slavery which used race to justify itself, these new forms of slavery are about poverty and gullibility. This is undoubtedly so, but in fact these things are not as disconnected from race as Bales claims and rather, have a complicated and highly mediated relationship to it. New slaves, Bales argues, are local, not transported from Africa: and the new slavery is produced by a particular combinations of global circumstances. These circumstances prevail in countries where population explosion has combined with pressure on resources, creating desperation and surplus bodies. These circumstances pertain in places of rapid social and economic change and in which the elite have taken advantage of global possibilities, turning the wealth gap into a chasm. The conditions for new slavery also occur in places where the government is weak or prepared to turn a blind eye to these particular forms of exploitation (Bales, 1999: 12–14). This doesn't map onto a neat grid of ex-colonies but neither is it disconnected from the old relations of empire. It doesn't map neatly in racial and ethnic terms, but ethnicity is dissected by poverty and local social relationships, which see slavery as the solution to their problems. But this does not mean, as Bales claims, that race is not significant. The places he describes often contain race/empire connections in combination with other local political factors, as well as the ways in which these things play out in individual circumstances.

Global processes are clearly important and Bales makes this connection at a number of points, stressing that people in affluent countries are beneficiaries of cheap goods produced by modern slaves.

> Slaves in Pakistan may have made the shoes you are wearing and the carpet you stand on. Slaves in the Caribbean may have put sugar in your kitchen and toys in the hands of your children. In India they may have sewn the shirt on your back and polished the ring on your finger. They are paid nothing...your investment portfolio and your mutual fund pension own stock in companies using slave labour in the developing world. Slaves keep your costs low and return on your investment high....This is the new slavery, which focuses on big profits and cheap lives. It is not about owning people in the traditional sense of old slavery, but about controlling them completely. People become completely disposable tools for making money....not through legal ownership but through the financial authority of violence... . (Bales, 1999: 4–5)

Global dimensions of new slavery are also evident in the Thai sex tourism industry. Young Burmese and Cambodian women are trafficked into Thailand's commercial sex industry. Thai women flow out of Thailand to Japan to service a demand once catered by Japanese sex tourism to Thailand; they work in Switzerland as exotic dancers and in Germany as bar girls (Bales, 1999: 65–9). But these new forms of slavery – not all sex industry workers are slaves – are locally mediated in ways that complicate further the operation of race and ethnicity. New slavery's products are aimed at local markets. This is especially true of the local commercial sex industry in Thailand. 80–87 per cent of Thai men use prostitutes for sex and hold versions of womanhood that make these practices justified, even acceptable. The commercial sex industry is also about the flow of young women from rural to urban areas, and this is a set of processes that enlists local agents and brokers in trusted positions, as well as the complicity of the girls' families in ensuring further supplies of daughters (Bales, 1999: 45, 65). Bales doesn't say this, but the production of new slavery relies on *intimate* ties as well as local village networks and complicity at higher social and community levels too. Forms of local mediation therefore include mechanisms that tie slaves to close kin – including prostitutes to their mothers – and so make particularly effective the threats of violence and intimidation that exact compliance. This, of course, makes slaves complicit in their own exploitation and in the exploitation of others: but these are hardly circumstances in which other courses of action easily suggest themselves. These are lives and circumstances of last resort etched by desperation as much as by race and ethnicity. What *is* the racial grammar of desperation?

Images of what it means to be a Thai woman are, however, also powerfully expressed in ways that have a direct bearing on race and ethnicity as body. This is shown in the Swiss magazine 'Life Travel':

Slim, sunburnt, and sweet, they love the white man in an erotic and devoted way. They are masters of the art of making love by nature, an art that we Europeans do not know. (Bales, 1999: 76)

Bales (1999: 78) ruefully remarks that joining the global system has done wonders for Thai income and terrible things to its society. It is in the social forms produced by globalisation that we need to search through and piece together the convoluted operation of race and ethnicity, situation by situation. In the Thai sex industry race and ethnicity are part of the production of images of body and sexual submission; things which are powerfully contextualised by widespread desperation and poverty; political regimes brokering slavery at higher levels; and, most insidious of all, a web of intimate connections which are able to compel, terrorise and normalise.

Case study 4. West Central African traders

In a more privileged position than slaves, but also operating the global/empire conduits in a more obvious way are the second-economy-traders whose operations are detailed by MacGaffey and Bazenguissa-Ganga's (2000) *Congo-Paris*, discussed earlier. These traders are sophisticated, mobile, highly flexible in their business operations – if things do not work in one place they are able to shift quickly to new places exploring new openings and connections – and operate through parallel money markets offering foreign exchange and venture capital through personal contacts. MacGaffey and Bazenguissa-Ganga show how traders work their existing ethnic, community, family and friendship networks in taking advantage of global opportunities. We can see these things – as the authors do – as part of the making of individually customised and situational versions of ethnicity. The traders also, non-coincidentally, trade in goods which are about *building and maintaining* ethnicity as forms of identity and performance: clothes, music, food and so on (MacGaffey and Bazenguissa-Ganga, 2000: 59). They are Africans in Paris and Brussels, and they have European status back in Africa. They are failed students and undocumented immigrants and, like slaves, are responding to local conditions of social, economic and political breakdown and flux. They have more resources and contacts than slaves, but are responding to similarly chaotic political, social and economic circumstances. Comments by traders stress the importance of 'fending for oneself' and 'survival'. 'One must manage on one's own by whatever means one can make money and live...if you have the spirit of adventure you go for it' (MacGaffey and Bazenguissa-Ganga, 2000: 53–4). The authors comment:

> These ideas make clandestine immigration an experience of self-fulfilment in which the actor is constantly evaluating himself. '*L'aventure*' entails the use of physical and mental skills, and even sometimes putting one's life in danger... migrants do not stake assets which are exterior to them (such as title or a property). Rather, they put their own potential and power – their very selves – on the line. (MacGaffey and Bazenguissa-Ganga, 2000: 54–5)

Traders *have* to improve their lives by whatever means possible. They are the active agents of a parallel global system based on personal contact. This system runs on ingenuity and bodies, exposing its operatives to threat and violence by virtue of their position on the edge of a number of systems, familial, local communities, ethnicity and state systems in West Central Africa, Europe and the world. They are the products of local disintegration and chaos and their lives are about finding long distance ways of coping and survival. These conditions of struggle and survival, which are worse for slaves, are unimaginable for most of us.

There can be no doubt that the *selves and circumstances* producing and produced by traders are about ethnicity and race. They face racial exclusion in Paris and Brussels where they *make* highly customised versions of themselves as ethnic groups in diaspora and their routes, though flexible, are carved by empire and its racial calculations. Here, as in the other vignettes, race and ethnicity are highly contextual and operate in tandem with a plethora of other distinctions and circumstances. There are clear, reconfigured, connections to the old regimes of empire which were more straightforwardly about race. Or are they? As traders are possibly produced by the same regions and economic and political circumstances as slaves we might want to take a closer look at differences in their personal connections and circumstances, their access to capital and so on. This is to reiterate the call for more detailed research in specific sets of circumstances as an entry into understanding the racial and ethnic grammar of globalisation.

Case study conclusions

With these four case studies I have tried to set out some of the ways in which race and ethnicity operate as part of globalisation. My efforts are an attempt to sketch-in some of the contours of an expanded account of race and ethnicity making as globally organised productions. These particular aspects of globalisation were chosen because they contain clues about race and ethnicity. They also display the darker, more exploitative, side of globalisation: its power geometry in which race and ethnicity feature as forms of embodiment in a heady mix of other kinds of social relationships. In all of these cases, race and ethnicity were made in a particular set of circumstances, circumstances produced by the wide social disparities of globalisation, and in combination with other factors, some ultra micro and focused on the individual, and some macro producing the gradients of global flow from one place to the next. Race and ethnicity in global contexts, as elsewhere, work as part of a kaleidoscope of factors and circumstances and need to be reviewed in context, on a case-by-case basis. There is, in other words, no systematic way in which race and ethnicity are produced by globalisation. Its forms are as varied as globalisation itself, a handy label used to refer to a diversity of things and circumstances of connection, movement and flow. The search for race making unmasks the deeper social inequalities operating within globalisation and exposes them as targets for political action, possibly in anti-globalisation action, which is spreading in its social base and popularity, at each world economic summit. Globalisation produces race and race reveals globalisation's more exploitative side.

Summary

- Theories of globalisation have experienced difficulties in discussing race and ethnicity in an integral way. This is to do with a more fundamental problem with globalisation theory itself in its failure to properly take account of social processes, so that economic and technical processes are translated into plausible social outcomes.
- Race and ethnicity reveal some of the deep social inequalities operating in globalisation. A *social* analysis of globalisation would more fully engage racialised and ethnicised social processes, social relationships and the lives in which these things are animated.
- Race and ethnicity operate situationally and are best examined in the global contexts in which they occur. There are many of these situations and the end of this chapter suggests four examples.

Race making: The need for a materialist analysis of the production of race was set out in Chapter 1. This chapter on globalisation provided a discussion of some of the mechanisms of race making that occur in global contexts. These include colonial connections; the examination of local micro-processes which have a bearing on race; the geographies and social relationships of global migration; and popular imagery, in particular the relationship between the popular and the political.

Globalisation: The shrinking of space by time, the connections between what is far away with what is near at hand, the conduits (networks) connecting things and the flows of goods, images, money and people across the surface of the globe provide the key ingredients of what we mean by globalisation. To pursue these ideas in more detail read Giddens (1990), Held, McGrew, Goldblatt and Perraton (1999) and Massey (1993) for a critical account of globalisation.

Notes

1. I am aware of the diversity of concerns and approaches operating from different disciplines as well as within disciplines in discussions of globalisation. The thrust of the critique in this chapter is aimed at the literature that has its disciplinary base in sociology and cultural studies, as these have the most explicit concern with social forms. Good examples are Featherstone, Lash and Robertson (1995); Albrow (1996), King (1997).

2. Time/space distanciation refers to the stretching of social relations and systems across time and space arising from advances in transport and communications. This idea was taken from time geography and developed in sociology by Giddens (Jary and Jary, 1991).

3. Linked with the claims that globalisation is symptomatic of such profound social restructuring that we need new models which account for the extent of social change involved is the term postmodernity. Postmodernity has drawn intellectual sustenance from Beck's work on precariousness and risk and from accounts of globalisation as a new social order not dependant on modernity's nation states. See Turner (1994) for a discussion of postmodernity, and of Beck and Giddens' notion of 'high modernity'. See also Bauman (1992) who supports the idea that we are living in social circumstances which are so profoundly different from those of modernity that they require a new paradigm in post-modernity. Bauman (1992: 102) notes that modernity as a way of thinking about society was generated by postmodernity anyway. For the purposes of this volume this is not a particularly useful debate as we are not concerned with these issues but with the status and operation of race and ethnicity within globalisation. I do, however, take the view that globalisation is strongly connected to its earlier forms in mercantalism and empire and that there is nothing new about human mobility. These are shifts in scale aided by the technology of movement and communication. They are significant and their social forms are worthy of attention, although it matters less what these things are called. My fragmented approach to understanding race and ethnicity, however, coheres with the demise of big theory and concern with social structure, which are often identified as aspects of postmodernism.

4. Globalisation theory is self evidently distinct from globalisation. Globalisation theory is a set of metanarratives deployed to explain the things that are referred to as globalisation. Things and processes and their conceptualisation by social scientists are, I think, usefully differentiated not least because it keeps us humble by reminding us that we have a very partial and particular grasp of the things we try to understand and which happen irrespective of our noticing them or trying to understand them.

5. See for example Knowles (1992), Miles and Phizacklea (1979), Miles and Phizacklea (1980).

6. 'Glocalisation' (Robertson, 1995: 30–5) is a term used to point out that the local is not a counterpoint to the global but an integral part of it, so that the local is a micro manifestation of the global. The local is written by the imprint of global processes. This is partially developed from a discussion of world spaces by Balibar (Robertson, 1995: 39) which refers to locales as places where the world as a whole is potentially inserted.

7. Syncretic social forms are discussed by Reed (2000) in the context of young Asian mothers' approaches to health. Differences that conflict and contradict are held together in a dialogical relationship in tension and located in historical, local and personal contexts. This is a good replacement for the term hybridity, which implies that the elements combined are outside of their context and without tensions, and that they were discrete in the first place.

8. Hirst and Thompson (1995: 423) among others contest the decline of the nation state, pointing out that economies are nationally regulated and borders controlled by nation states: 'The nation state is central to this process of "structuring": the policies and practices of the state in distributing power upwards to the international level and downwards to sub-national agencies are the sutures that will hold the system of governance together'.

9. Migration is here used in a generic sense to refer to all movements which are not covered by tourism as a brief interlude. Immigration is sometimes used too as this is a term

used by the debates on which this chapter draws, but generally in this chapter and the next, I use this term to refer to them all although I stress the importance of being specific about forms of migration.

10. Very few development sociologists are also concerned with race issues. Tunde Zack Williams is an exception in combining concern with Africa, and Sierra Leone in particular, with consideration of race politics in Britain. See for example Zack Williams (1999).

Chapter Five
Migration, Displacement and Belonging

In his imagination every migrant worker is in transit. He remembers the past: he anticipates the future: his aims and his recollections make his thoughts a train between the two (John Berger and Jean Mohr, 1975: 64 *A Seventh Man*)

Mini Contents

Introduction

Belonging and displacement involve feelings and activities that are the consequence of global migration, as well as earlier forms of connectivity and mobility. Discussing the people movement side of globalisation in the last chapter, I suggested that distinguishing different forms of arrival and departure might be a way of thinking more systematically about the social circumstances and differences that work to make race and ethnicity in global terms. The globalisation case studies in the last chapter suggest that race and ethnicity are a significant part of the alchemy of social distinctions generated in supra-national forms of connectivity, even if it is difficult to discern any patterns in the way they work.

This chapter takes some of these arguments further. It takes a closer look at arrival and departure stories and so uncovers some of the threads connecting people and places, bringing space and auto/biography – biographical and geographical trajectories – together in the same analytical framework. In this chapter I argue that arrival and departure offer practical, people centred ways of thinking about different kinds of migrancy. This chapter is about different forms of mobility and the concepts used by social analysts to speak about them, and it is about the transnational organisation of lives. The people side of globalisation. Movement and displacement – whether local or global – inevitably concern belonging and home as socially organised forms of human attachment, and hence connections between biographies and places. Home is part of displacement, and involves many forms of connection. It may invoke narratives of positive association, or simply the minimisation of alienation and discomfort, or temporary refuge. Some of the meanings of home embedded in journeys of displacement – voluntary and imposed – are unpacked in this chapter and examined more closely. The scale and circumstance of mobility makes it vitally important to understand these forms of human association. These things supply some of the missing texture of social analysis, which are given a lower priority than technical and economic forms in globalisation theory, as I argued in the last chapter. In this chapter I shall untangle some of the ways in which transnational movement, belonging and displacement are matters of race and ethnicity; exposing some mechanisms of race making in this context, and with it some of the racial grammar of globalisation. Belonging and displacement are the most challenging political issues of our time. They are part of how race works deep within us. Movement brings heightened sensitivities of self and other when what we take for granted is stripped away. Belonging and displacement underscore popular and political responses to immigration and asylum; and much more besides. This chapter can only make a modest start in considering some of these complex issues, which are about the organisation of racialised and ethnicised subjectivities-in-motion on moving racialised landscapes: about forms of social organisation that are always in the process of becoming in the many journeys comprising human existence, journeys which contain some of the (racial) meanings of belonging and displacement.

Autobiographical confession

Intellectual honesty demands confession of the autobiographical elements in this chapter. Like many other people, my own life is very much organised by the rhythms of different kinds of journeys, from short bursts of travel to research field trips, to living for extended periods in other countries. These temporary and long-term forms of displacement form one of the mechanisms by which I make temporal distinctions. I think about my own life in terms of the past, present and future journeys composing it. At every opportunity I live like a tourist, my own relationship to place is a form of consumption edged by the kind of intellectual curiosity that delights in comparative sociology. A seasoned airport voyeur, I watch people meeting other people in transit as I am meeting people, or in transit myself. Fascinated by the social kaleidoscope of arrival and departure, I am quite content in transit by any method of travel except in boats. It may be that the rhythms of motion are reassuring. I am very much a (particular) product of this time, and its heightened sense of geographical mobility, and it would be dishonest of me to pretend that I stand outside of it. Inevitably this way of being bleeds into intellectual activity, so that the boundaries between research and living – carefully separated in ethics protocols[1] – are in fact blurred, as they are for many social investigators.

Drawn by the dynamic of dwelling and displacement, I am a long-time casual collector of dislocation and relocation stories, easily able to turn both close and casual encounters into an opportunity to collect dramas of displacement and homemaking. Why did you decide to come here? What was it like when you first arrived? What made you want to leave? How did that happen? Only recently, I noticed that the woman driving me at great speed in her minicab to London's Waterloo station, at the same time as she was having an animated discussion on her mobile phone, was speaking Yoruba. I don't speak Yoruba, but recognised the sound of it from living in Nigeria. I switched into the routine. By the time we got to the station we had compared the two kinds of lives that can be lived in Lagos and London. I knew why she was in London, and how she felt about it. I knew how often she moved back and forth between London and Lagos, and the key mechanisms of her connection to both places. Comparisons – *here and there stories* – are standard fare in my own, Anglo Canadian family, which shuttles back and forth servicing family, friendship and work connections in both places. I think about my own, and my children's, lives as the outcome of past (ancestral) migrations; from Ireland in the early years of this century; from Britain to the Caribbean to Canada and back to Britain 300 years later. These are some of the multiple past displacements and belongings composing mine, and my children's, lives.

There are two reasons for making this autobiographical connection, apart from placing myself within the problematic of this chapter. First, it reveals the autobiographical underpinnings of social theory, and, second, it confesses the informal, but extensive nature of some of the data that went into this chapter. I am a long-term collector of stories of displacement and have spent long periods of my own life in transit. Make of this what you will; at least you know where it comes from.

Dialogues of movement and dwelling

I suggested earlier that movement and dwelling are part of the same social processes. I want to expand on this a bit as a setting for the section following on the 'age of migrancy'. Movement and dwelling are complementary dynamics in the organisation of human existence. 'Once travelling is foregrounded as a cultural practice, then dwelling, too, needs to be reconceived – no longer simply the ground from which the travelling departs and to which it returns' (Clifford, 1994: 44). In the context of movement, dwelling takes on new social meaning. Travelling is about new and reclaimed dwelling; and dwelling is also about the journeys that presage *arrival* and *departure*. Arrival and departure, as I suggested at the beginning of this chapter, offer a useful entry point to certain kinds of social analysis. Dwelling produces travel. It produces reasons to travel and the conditions in which travel takes place, as well as the social relationships through which travel is organised and achieved. Travelling and dwelling are both ancient and modern rhythms of human existence: journeys between dwelling, and dwelling between journeys, weave the fabric of human existence; the here and there, the warp and weft of life. Dwelling and journeying raise serious social questions about the meaning, forms and terms of human displacement and connection.

These concerns inevitably lean on versions of space and biography discussed in earlier chapters. Displacement and belonging – the product of multiple forms of migrancy – centre on subjectivity, on forms of being in the world. We have in earlier chapters discussed some of the ways in which this is raced. Displacement cracks open the raw nerve of subjectivity, revealing the complexity of assimilation and marginalisation (Laws, 2000: 174), and the demands this places on people and on the formation of their subjectivity. It is the migrant's capacity for assimilation and marginalisation and the creativity of leaving and making new homes, which forges her as a person, her subjectivity and her sense of being in the world. Because, as we discussed in Chapter 1, these processes are dialogically organised, we can note too, that it is migrants' *position* and *disposition* that engages them in the prospect of moving to make new lives. Migrancy, at the very least, exposes this about the self to reflexive scrutiny, and it is this, which makes the heightened sensitivities of arrival and departure a privileged window onto subjectivity. Arrival and departure, in other words, offer an exposed vantage point from which to view the person. The subjectivities made between dwelling and travelling are, of course, particular subjectivities, particular identities, particular ways of being in the world (Minh-ha, 1994: 14), which have something to do with race and ethnicity. What these things have to do with race and ethnicity is a complicated question on which this chapter, like the last, can only make a modest attempt to answer.

These comments concerning heightened subjectivities and identities are drawn from the literature on exiles[2], and it is important to keep in mind that exiles are a particular kind of migrant. The exiled migrant carries an extra burden of marginality, which perhaps, occludes the marginality of other migrants, indeed all migrants. Despite this, the concept of exile is useful in positioning migrancy around global configurations of political circumstances, but not essential in distinguishing the effectiveness of the political dimensions of migration, which is evident in other forms of migration too. Also, we need to be mindful of the romanticism attached to exile, and avoid transforming those who actually seek a more settled life through migration into nomadic heroes (Cohen, 1998b: 15). To be on the margins, on the edge of things, is to have a heightened sense of the self as separate from others, as different, as outside, on the periphery, of the systems in which one operates. Ethnicity and race often provide a form for this. All migrants, and not just exiles, live on the edge of the unfamiliar, uncertain about their welcome and striving to understand the meaning they carry in the places to which they migrate. Breytenbach, the exiled South African writer and political activist, takes a rather broad view on the circumstances composing exile and its associated forms of social marginality:

> refugee, misfit, outcast, outsider, expatriate, squatter, renegade, drifter, a displaced person, a marginal one, the new poor, the economically weak, drop out; [are all part of a] ... new silent majority. ... The courage and perseverance, the futile quest for survival of these stowaways, wetbacks, throwbacks and other illegal humans always astonishes me...the new nomadic man of the future is being forged. (Breytenbach, 1991: 75–6)

Certainly, if we are to uncover some of the ethnic and racial dynamics of migration, we need to take an even broader approach than this in order to highlight important social differences. But Breytenbach makes an important point in including squatters, the new poor and the economically weak. Dislocation does not necessarily involve crossing international borders, and we should not assume that the apparently settled poor are outside of the migrancy problematic. Living precarious lives in tenuous circumstances always carries mobility as a threat to security. In this chapter we are concerned with those whose lives are more centrally configured by different forms of movement rather than just exile, and for that reason we shall retain the concept of migrant as a general way of describing a range of mobile people. Neither term – migrant or exile – is conceptually firm, and therein lies their utility, but migrant better suits our purpose than exile and carries no romantic claims. Versions of people (including forms of subjectivity advanced in Chapter 1) forged at the interface between people and social scenes including their administrative systems; as spatially configured, performed, embodied and as social/existential configurations in which biography intersects with broader social systems, apply to the circumstances of belonging and displacement I want to examine in this chapter. I am suggesting that the people, and their subjectivities, made by movement, are configured in particular ways. They are composed by the heightened sensitivities and awareness that comes with displacement and old and new belonging. What is taken for granted in settlement is thrown into question when its certainties are challenged by movement and estrangement. Belonging and displacement then, are forces forming people and their (raced and ethnicised) subjectivities in particular ways. Examining belonging and displacement provides us with a window onto these people because of the disruptions and uncertainties displacement produces, and which are quickly turned, through settlement, into new routines and new certainties. Unsettlement and resettlement exposes people to examination. Berger and Mohr (1975: 187), say of the impact of movement on the migrant worker that the migrant:

> sacrifices the present for the future under circumstances which continually confound his sense of continuity. Scarcely anything he experiences or witnesses confirms the value of his sacrifice. Only when he returns to redeem his

exchange-units of time will he gain acknowledgement for what he has done, or, to be more precise, for the way he has done what he was forced to do. Meanwhile he lives in a situation of almost total unacknowledgement.

The age of migrancy?

From the statistical efforts of demographers, to the literary efforts of writers in exile, the closing years of the twentieth century are characterised as one of 'untimely massive wandering' (Minh-ha, 1994: 12–13) in formulations which, like Breytenbach's account of exile, elide forms of movement that have their own conditions of production and resolution. Testing the empirical validity of this claim of massive wandering is no straightforward matter. Was the late twentieth century characterised by migrancy? Is this, as many social scientists have claimed, the great age of human mobility? Are we, in fact, seeing the unravelling of Foucault's great age of incarceration-as adjunct-to-industrial-discipline? And what might this claim of massive untimely wandering mean? Does it mean that more people travel? Or do we mean that people routinely expect to travel, that they have a globally calibrated sense of space as I argued in the last chapter? Does it mean that people who were not used to travel now expect to travel? Or does it mean that there is a proliferation of circumstances in which travel is demanded? And what do we mean by travel? Travel for resettlement purposes? Travel as tourism? What range of time-scales connecting arrival and departure are we considering? In other words is this *really* the age of migrancy, or are we simply more theoretically inclined to conceptualise it as such on account of a shift in perspective in theoretical framing from dwelling to movement? These questions and uncertainties beset the age of migrancy thesis.

Whether more people are travelling to more places, and if they are, why, are not easily answered questions. Only a handful of countries gather data showing departures and return from countries of origin. We *can* calculate the stock of international migrants present in different countries at a given time using census data on foreign-born citizens. In 1965 the 'West' – which has higher migrant populations than 'non Western'[3] countries – hosted 35.7 per cent of migrant stock; in 1990 this had risen to 42.7 per cent. At the end of the twentieth century 1 in 13 people living in the West is an international migrant (Zlotnik, 1999: 24). But this leaves out those without legal status in their countries of resettlement of which it is suspected there is a growing number. Zlotnik (1999) attempts a limited calculation of the scale of human mobility, for the 218 countries or territories comprising the world in 1985, and concludes:

>...the global number of international migrants has been growing at an increased rate since 1965. However, given the concomitant increase in the number of distinct units (countries and territories) constituting the world and the persistence of sharp economic and demographic disparities among countries and regions, coupled with the widespread prevalence of political instability

and outright conflict, the percentage of people who have left and remained outside of their countries of origin is *remarkably small and has been relatively stable* [my emphasis] for a long period oscillating between 2.1 and 2.3 per cent of the world's population during 1965–1990. (Zlotnik, 1999: 42)

Quite why we should want to *discount* the proliferation of nation states, growing political instabilities and sharp economic disparities – all of which produce the kinds of refugees we have in Southampton and elsewhere – is not clear. Zlotnik's measurement of migrancy is inevitably complicated by the continual re-drawing of the maps of sovereign territories, by the invisibility of some migrations and by fluctuations in the immigration and refugee policies and other circumstances in the countries producing and receiving refugees. The circumstances of the redrawing of the political boundaries of the former Soviet Union and former Yugoslavia have produced refugees in large numbers. In 1996 there were 525,000 refugees, 1.2 million displaced persons and 1.4m war-affected persons in need of assistance in the successor states of the former Yugoslavia (Zlotnik, 1999: 27). A number of localised mini-systems of refugee migrations operate with the movement of asylum seekers from the former Eastern bloc to Germany.

The massive untimely wanderings of the twentieth century were not all about international borders but borders between lifestyles, forms of consciousness and subjectivity. Internal migrations attendant upon industrialisation and urbanisation processes are just as much the architects of displacement and new belonging. In 1981 India alone had an estimated 200 million internal migrants. Add tourist movement. The World Tourist Organisation (1994) estimated 69 million tourist arrivals for 1960, and 454 million for 1990. Tourists involve an altogether different and more privileged (temporary) form of displacement, and not one we are particularly interested in for the purposes of this volume, beyond the fact that this dramatic rise in tourism shows that people have a global sense of place when it comes to patterns of leisure consumption. Also at the privileged end of the social scale are estimates of temporary migration. Findlay's (1988) study of skilled British migrants (with stays overseas of 1–3 years) for 1980–1985 showed a quarter of a million professional and managerial workers and 230,000 manual and clerical workers left Britain with the latter group favouring new locations in the old settler societies of the old (white) commonwealth, the USA, the Middle East and Europe. I was one of these statistics, leaving Britain for a university job in Northern Nigeria. These, of course, are 'volunteers'; lifestyle migrants who can return any time they like.

If we forget for a moment questions concerning the scale of migration to which there are no easily available answers and concentrate on its character, we may recall from the last chapter that patterns of migration are more diverse than has been supposed in the past. Twentieth century migrations are characterised by the fact that nearly all countries have become senders and receivers of international migrants. It is the character, and not just the scale, of migration that is significant. At either end of the social spectrum, the growing numbers of refugees and lifestyle migrants are kinds of migration we need to investigate. We will return to them later in the chapter, as they display the deep social inequalities in global migration.

Whether more people are moving to more places is an empirically unanswerable question, although Zlotnik's calculations are very valuable and, if we factor in refugees, her calculations show considerable levels of displacement. What we do know is that large numbers of people experience various forms of spatial and social displacement as a result of political and economic upheaval, whether or not this involves the negotiation of international boundaries. We know that people move to neighbouring states or to other places where there are structural[4] or personal connections to facilitate the move. We know that large numbers of people take holidays in other countries, although we know very little about what they make of these experiences. It is not these people we are concerned with, for these are only temporary forms of displacement. What I am concerned with is not the scale of migration, or its general character. There are certainly *enough* migrants for their social significance to be beyond question. I am not really interested in whether migrancy is of such a magnitude as to herald a new era, demanding a new model. We dealt with paradigmatic shifts in the last chapter. I am after tools not models.

What is of more interest is the impact of migrancy on a significant number of people and their lives. The concept of migrancy offers a powerful image of our time as an age of exile, not because of the *scale* of human mobility, but because it raises important social questions concerning how people negotiate and organise the forms of mobility they undertake. I am concerned with the ways in which people *make* their lives and themselves in circumstances of migration. How do they negotiate forms of displacement and belonging in getting up each morning and going to work or caring for their children. My own particular experience of (privileged, voluntary) exile in Montreal at no point raised fundamental questions concerning where in the world I wanted to live. It raised only short term mundane ones, such as what to get for breakfast or whether the children's snow boots were dry. It may well be the same for others. The homeward trudge of daily existence takes priority over fundamental questions of place. At least it does for some of us. Migrancy, as Breytenbach points out in the context of exile, is like writing or painting: it is a 'creative act'.

> ...I mean the act of using shared matter – a convention, a texture, a set of references encapsulating the codes of communication – to define or invent a history, to secrete or enshrine a viewpoint or a conduit (call it the I), and to determine a future. [In writing and living the narrative is an attempt to come to grips with chaos, to derive and bestow meaning; a structure for shaping experience]. To be an exile is to be free to imagine or to dream a past and the future of that past. To be an exile is to be written... You have acquired the knack of fitting in pretty much with any society, it can be said that you are a good impersonation of the cosmopolitan, but you probably never really penetrate beneath the surface of concerns of those around you. You are engaged with an elsewhere that cannot be reached: isn't it the defining character of exile? (Breytenbach, 1991: 71)

Living is like writing in that both make the social world in certain terms. Exiled writers, of course, write of coming to terms with their new world(s) and its relationship with old ones. Writing, like living, is a form of connection: a form of belonging that offers deep insight into social processes and a reflexive stance on lives and subjectivities in making. Bessie Head is often wielded in this capacity along with the suggestion that literary exile involves *writing home* in both senses of that term. In other ways living is not at all like writing; it marshals different kinds of activities, which are infinitely more practical and, as my example just suggested, mundane.

Past migrations

Seeing migration as a vantage point from which to review the making of lives in particular circumstances, as creative acts, applies also to past migrations. I want to frame this discussion of the meaning of migration historically so that the present is connected with the circumstances of its production, and to highlight the enduring nature – in different circumstances – of the themes of belonging and displacement, negotiated in the creative acts of making lives in new places. There is another reason for this historical preoccupation too. The age of migrancy thesis presumes a more static past. But each age has produced its own forms of mobility, its own rhythms of journey and habitation, its own forms of dislocation and belonging. Whether we are referring to the age old trade and migration routes across the Sahara; the packet ships traversing the oceans carrying people and goods to distant places; the early journeys of exploration in which the shape of the world as we know it was only beginning to fall into place; or the Jews leaving Egypt on foot: each age has its own geographies, its own trajectories, its own motives for travel, its own versions of dislocation and the making of new homes. Obviously the technologies of travel have changed: people travel faster and by different means than in the past. Also there are faster, technologically assisted, methods of maintaining contacts and relationships over distances that didn't apply in the past. The visited are now doing their share of the visiting, as the gradients of imperial domination assume new forms. The redrawing of political boundaries through war, famine and dynastic changes, of course, produced its own forms of dislocation and settlement past and present.

Nineteenth century imperial Europe produced particular kinds of travellers and geographies of exploration, conquest and exploitation. Missionaries, traders, planters, settlers, soldiers, botanists, anthropologists, explorers, civil servants and the other functionaries of imperial governance traversing the oceans, connecting tours of duty and furlough, all traded old homes for new. Men and women left Britain, France, Holland, Portugal and Spain to build new lives in new places, connecting biographically and spatially configured trajectories. The significance of travel in the making of imperial subjectivities is noted by a number of authors (Kearns, 1997), as are the practical geographies of explorers in the making of white masculinities. Victorian women travellers also wove the diasporas of white privilege in their journeys, making use of mercantile, exploration and trading routes to chart new lives in new places. The everyday social fabric of imperialism was composed of the lives of European women as well as men, many of whom had to leave home for the outposts of empire in order to pursue other versions of themselves. New lives and subjectivities were created through displacement. Two examples drawn from the late nineteenth century make this point in more concrete terms and allow me to follow up on the women travellers I mentioned in the last chapter.

Jane Waterston, a missionary and doctor in South Africa, and Mary Kingsley, traveller, explorer and political activist, both managed to remake their lives through displacement (Knowles, 2000b). Both used travel to mediate the expectations of family relationships and domestic responsibilities, which settled on Victorian women. Waterston wrote long and guilty letters to her mentor about her alienation from her family and conflicting versions of 'duty' to family and 'calling' that resulted from her absence in South Africa (Bean and van Heyningen, 1983). Letters from Waterston's father, with their reminders of family obligation, had a particularly unsettling effect on her (Bean and van Heyningen, 1983: 45). She describes the feeble models of ineffective femininity available in her parents' home, and the stifling inactivity that produced her desire to train as a doctor at a time when this was particularly difficult for women. In order to remake herself as an active professional woman, she used her experiences as a missionary in South Africa to gain medical experience, which she then used to get formal medical training in Dublin, the only place that allowed women to qualify at that time. Travel was the vehicle of her transformation. It provided a different kind of life, and she settled permanently in South Africa where she could be who she wanted to be.

Similarly Mary Kingsley – the daughter and housekeeper of George Henry Kingsley, physician, naturalist and travel writer – transformed her life through a series of short voyages around the West African Coast[5] through which she developed an interest in practical aspects of empire governance (Kearns, 1997). On her return to Britain she became a political campaigner for empire reform, and the education of the British public in the affairs of Africans. The point is that both women used dislocation as a mechanism for personal and social transformation. Biographical and geographical journeys converge. Belonging and dislocation is at the heart of lives and subjectivities. Each age and political circumstance has produced its own social relationships of 'contact' between visitor and visited; and its own lives and subjectivities generated through the rhythms of journeys and settlement composing them. The age of migrancy, if that is indeed what it is, is the product of these earlier forms of migrancy and their forms of dislocation and belonging.

Circumstances of wandering – forms of migrancy

The idea of a massive untimely wandering is evocative, but not particularly analytically useful. I argued in the last chapter that accounts of migrancy require precision concerning who goes where, why and in what circumstances, and that this is essential in unpicking its racial and ethnic grammar, and its compositional mechanisms. I suggested that circumstances of arrival and departure are a way of mapping significant social differences, which reveal the making and working of race and ethnicity. This chapter develops this concept of arrival and departure, not just as a mechanism for displaying social difference, although they certainly do that, and not only for the purposes of mapping, as suggested in the last chapter, but as a point of access to the *meaning* of dislocation and belonging. In this chapter I pursue some of these things through two completely different categories of migration, refugees and lifestyle migrants, carefully chosen so as to preserve and develop the concept of social difference as multi-layered forms of inequality textured by race and ethnicity.

Refugee departure

Nhui Mai[6], who was a child living in South Vietnam when it fell to the Communist North in 1975, describes both the practical and the political circumstances of his departure from Vietnam:

> Family after family suffered their losses, as they watched their years of hard work to earn a civilised life go down the drain. How they hated the communists! My family happened to be one of these families. My father was in prison and my mother had lost her job as a teacher in a senior school. Nothing was going our way. ...The communists continued punishing us, even though the war was over. My mother wanted us to start afresh in another country where I could grow up and have the freedom and education I had always longed for. So it was decided. We would leave Vietnam. We knew the risks, but we just had to take them, no matter how it would end. ...It was not easy to escape from Vietnam. Not only the danger of being caught and imprisoned, but also being tricked by the dishonest Chinese and losing all the money that now took so long to earn. ... Many of the Vietnamese who had lost all of their savings to the con men killed themselves and their families. Some lost their minds and died shortly afterwards. My parents made the hardest decision of their lives, to leave the country. They paid the required amount of gold to a boat owner and waited for further instructions...we lived under constant pressure. We didn't know if we could escape or whether we would end up like some of our unlucky countrymen who lost everything to the con men. ... It was a dark night. I was woken by my mother and given no time to ask questions but only told to get dressed quickly and quietly. The day we had longed for had come, but my parents looked sad...No one can be happy when they are forced to leave their own country, leaving behind their dearest relatives. In order to go, we had to accept that we would never return. ... We were disguised as Chinese [who were being expelled]...Four days we had been aboard the boat with only a few oranges to keep us going [fleeing Chinese were not allowed enough food to reach their destination]. We knew that if we didn't find land soon we would die of starvation... Everyone was too tired and weak to do anything but sit and mumble to themselves...As long as we [the family] were together we would always be happy, no matter how bad the situation was. ... It was not only the communists' [in Vietnam] fault. The boat owner had turned greedy and took over

500 people more than the limit of just 200 people. How could a boat only four meters wide and 20 metres long carry over 700 people. [By this time everyone on board knew the boat was going to sink and everything heavy was thrown overboard]. … The boat was quiet and still. All we could hear was the beating of the waves against the side of the boat and the murmur of people praying.

The refugee boat is rescued by a larger ship on its way to Hong Kong. There Nhui Mai and family were interned in a refugee camp, and later taken to Britain. The arrival story is not told, but the departure is most dramatic. It displays the practical, emotional and political difficulties of leaving: the balancing of attachment with the erosion of freedom to earn a living and receive an education. It shows two versions of family: one to be rescued to live a better life, the other to be permanently abandoned. The family risked ruin and death in order to build another life, much like those who attach themselves to the underside of trains crossing the channel from France to Britain and end up in Southampton.

Lifestyle migrant departure

I used the term 'lifestyle migrant' earlier without saying what I meant by it. I am using it to refer to those who weave together bits of what they 'need' or demand in life from different places, and who use this form of bricolage to think about belonging as the satisfaction of needs. Lifestyle migrants include those who move to upgrade their general life circumstances. They have no real need to leave home, although of course, the idea of 'need' is problematic. We could say that the Vietnamese family did not 'need' to leave Vietnam: plenty of other similarly placed Vietnamese stayed. Some people suffer and die rather than move, and other people move to avoid these things. These are matters of auto/biography. The 'needs' of lifestyle migrants, however, are obviously of quite a different order from those of refugees. Europeans who move to the US, to Canada, to Australia and New Zealand are a part of this category. They are people of varying circumstances who move from one rich country to another in pursuit of better jobs, higher incomes, higher disposable incomes, leisure opportunities, sun, beaches or open country. British people who retire to Portugal, Spain, Greece or France are lifestyle migrants. Lifestyle migrants move to particular places. They do not move to Nicaragua or Bangladesh as the one-time functionaries and beneficiaries of empires might have done. This is a vague formulation covering widely different social and economic circumstances. They are neither rich nor poor, and in fact they may be both at different times. What characterises them is their interest in the prospect of new beginnings and complex forms of upward social and lifestyle mobility.

My knowledge of British lifestyle migrants comes from the many conversations I had with other expatriates living in Canada about the circumstances of their departure and arrival. More systematic than this are some of the interview data I collected with British expatriates living in Hong Kong as part of a research project on Britishness. These are an interesting and varied group of people with different reasons for being there and staying on after independence in 1997. It is this data – backed up by the Canadian conversations – which provides the example of a lifestyle migrant. The departure stories of lifestyle migrants are obviously not as compelling or graphic as those of the Vietnamese refugee. Departure is easy. Allow me to offer the banal inventory of my own most recent departure from Montreal as an example. Household things were packed in boxes and moved into a large metal container; house keys were handed over to the new owners; an easy drive to the airport, an overnight flight to London, and the next morning brought a new (old) life in Britain. The practical ease of departure, of course, contrasts strongly with the refugee experience. We could easily have stayed, and we did not risk our lives in leaving. But the simplicity of departure also masks its emotional complexity and the feelings of dislocation, which persisted throughout the year ahead. The departure stories of lifestyle migrants are marked by choice rather than urgency or compulsion. They are episodic rosters of disappointment cast in the certainty that there is an elsewhere where things are better. Here is John's story, which also stands for other stories I have been told in Hong Kong and in Canada.

John is a second-generation lifestyle migrant. He grew up in New Zealand between the ages of five and 17, when his family returned to Britain. Now his mid thirties he has lived in Hong Kong for ten years and sees it as 'my home. I have no particular desire to go back to Britain at all'. I can report that for John and the others, New Zealand and Australia, but rarely Britain, were favoured retirement spots.

> I came on holiday and stayed! Life was so much easier then if you were British, whereas now they've quite rightly made the immigration status the same as for any other national. … I arrived to see my then girlfriend. I'd just folded up my light engineering business in Britain, and I was at a loose end and she always said 'Come to Hong Kong, come to Hong Kong' and I came with the intention of staying two weeks, a month or so…and I never went back, basically…wandering up and down the little back alleys [was what made him want to stay]…people were making it happen [His admiration for this unfettered enterprise is clear and linked with the red tape which stifled his business in Britain. His departure was about]…all the violence and unpleasantness in Britain. I mean Britain is the only place where I've ever been badly beaten up for no reason…you don't see graffiti [in Hong Kong] you don't see cars that are vandalised, petty crime virtually doesn't exist and that's due to police on the streets. And the police don't have the 'them' and 'us' mentality that's certainly been growing up in Britain over the last thirty odd years. Where they feel besieged so the police then tend to cleave to themselves…it's one of the marked differences is the attitude towards the police here and their attitude to the public. [He gives a 'classic' example of public order policing Hong Kong style in the handling of protest during the hand over ceremonies in 1997 in which the police drown out the protest with loud Beethoven played on the public address system rather than arrest the protestors in front of the world's TV cameras. He moves on to reflect on examples of the British Government's handling of empire.]…a lot of it has been shockingly inept, shockingly isolationist and in a lot of cases, spineless. If you make a decision,

stick with it. That was one of the reasons why I was quite fond of Margaret Thatcher because, right or wrong, she'd make a decision...Britain saddens me. Because I see so much potential, that is just getting lost. Wasted...that now you are reaching a different culture of haves and have-nots, based on education. In a lot of cases the state schools are shockingly inefficient; and it's a case of dumbing-down, which is not good. Man was meant to look up, not down. It's got man where he is today: the ability to look at the stars and wonder. You have to set standards and this is why my sister has struggled to put her kids through private schools [which are good at standards and]...discipline. [Would he live in Britain again?] Not unless you undo forty odd years of social engineering. You've got a very slow breakdown in society from the point of view of education and the bureaucracy that is supposedly there, for the people, in law and order. I mean one of the few blessings still in Britain is that the common law system is basically intact. And the judiciary is politically independent [Ironically he is drowned out by a police siren outside! But this gives him time to pause and feel superior to Americans]...I have more attachment here. Here is my home...(John, from an interview at his office in Hong Kong, December 2000.)

John, like other lifestyle migrants, sees Britain as sliding into a social and political abyss of disintegration and decline from which he has escaped. The formulation of this, if not its content, he shares with the refugee who also had (temporary) asylum in Hong Kong, but was relieved to move to the country John was so keen to leave. John is a fierce social critic. He wants, expects, things to basically operate for his personal convenience and betterment. His life and his requirements are the vantage point from which the world is judged. He is able to compare other countries and other lifestyles and make choices: he is a knit-your-own-world global citizen and his actions are a form of global individualism. John belongs, not in a country, but in a set of circumstances that promote, or at least do not impede, the things he wants to have and do: things he regards as entitlements. He and his wife have bought an apartment on an island off Hong Kong and it is a good life. What he wants from his life is about those forms of private pleasure that come from living a certain way, and he seeks a political and social context in which this can take place. Ironically – given his right wing libertarian political views on democracy and fears of social disintegration – he finds his particular brand of freedom and the good life in a bubble off the shores of Communist China. Hong Kong, of course, occupies an interesting position on the global stage. A strategic part of the global economy, it was also the most recent remaining bit of empire to be returned.

Circumstances of arrival are a combination of personal and political situations. John the lifestyle migrant does not encounter any difficulties in moving to Hong Kong. He records instead his admiration for the kinds of human enterprise he finds in the back streets. As a British citizen, at that time he had no immigration problems. He simply gets on a plane, arrives and soon gets a job. He is still able to live there: his lifestyle is not threatened although Hong Kong is a Special Administrative Region of China and he does not speak Cantonese, but he can get by because so many Hong Kong Chinese speak English. He can go back to Britain when he likes for weddings and family reunions, although generally he chooses not to.

In contrast, refugees have to negotiate difficult political and legal circumstances in order to remain in their new countries of settlement. They are not necessarily welcomed and may experience formal and informal local hostility. 1999 saw anti asylum seeker protests in the British port of Dover, at hostels and detention centres, where refugees are held while awaiting determination of their case and which often attract hostile curiosity from local residents. Britain's current dispersal policy applied to asylum seekers has created many local tensions. Firsat Yildiz, the Turkish campaigner for a Kurdish homeland who came to Britain to escape torture and imprisonment at the hands of the Turkish Government, was knifed on the streets of Glasgow in August 2001, one of 70 recent racist attacks on the Glasgow Sighthill estate. Glasgow has hosted 3,500 asylum seekers with families who have been sent to live in empty council flats on that estate amidst growing local hostility and the sort of racial tension that makes refugees afraid to leave their homes for fear of attack (*Guardian* 7 August 2001). These hostile conditions of arrival operate in a part of Glasgow marked by high levels of poverty and hopelessness and where refugees are seen as adding an unwanted burden not backed by entitlement. The day after Yildiz was killed, an Iraqi asylum seeker was badly injured in an attack by locals. The report on Radio Four news quoted him as saying that he wanted to go back to Iraq, as there he would be killed for his beliefs, not for being nothing.

Arrival for refugees must feel, not just temporary and tenuous, but dangerous in these circumstances. Should they be allowed to stay after lengthy proceedings their exile must be permanent, given the costs and political difficulties of returning to visit family. This is quite different from the easy back and forth of John's voluntary exile. Another Vietnamese refugee who settled in Bath in the 1970s had this to say about arrival:

> My first impression of England was when I went to the Sopley Reception Centre. They took us by coach from Heathrow airport. We stopped at some service station and I looked around...the weather was very, very cold, we didn't have the right clothes. When we had boarded the plane to come to England we had nothing. Some people didn't even have shoes! ... There are 360 Vietnamese in the Bristol area. They are all working too hard to feel isolated. ... I am a devout Buddhist but there is no temple... Mai Van Thong, 1998, *Origins*

Refugees belong in forms of survival, not in lifestyles, although in practice the boundaries between these two things are blurred: all lives and choices are circumscribed by circumstances, but some more than others. Stories of arrival and departure reveal personal and political circumstances. They can be used to address questions concerning who goes where, why and in what circumstances, questions developed by Lefebvre and used by Massey to get at some of the power geometry of globalisation.

Diasporas and transnationals

Considering diasporas and transnationals involves a shift to two of the more abstract concepts used by social scientists to discuss forms of migrancy. These two concepts are chosen because of their central relevance to travel and dwelling and attendant forms of displacement and belonging; and because both are strongly linked with race and ethnicity. Despite operating at a more abstract level than the concepts we have just been concerned with in the arrivals and departures of refugees and lifestyle migrants, thinking about diasporas and transnationals allow us to continue to explore circumstances of arrival and departure slightly differently, connecting and differentiating some of the lives and circumstances of migrants running through this chapter. The first thing to say about diasporas and transnationals is that the two concepts are not distinct, but bleed into each other in describing similar sets of people, circumstances and social processes. Bhachu (1996) explicitly connects them in her account of the wedding practices of Asian women who have migrated from India to East Africa to Britain, and then on to North America, and who connect all of these places through the circulation of gifts and clothes. Her point is that the Asian diaspora is also a set of culturally highly articulate transnationals. Generally, transnationalism and diaspora have different functions in social analysis, and so are usefully considered together in order for their differences and similarities to become apparent.

Anthropologists with patience for micro social forms and processes have paid more attention to transnationalism than social and cultural theorists[7]. Consideration of transnationalism grew out of the recognition that migrants did not necessarily substitute old homes for new in a straightforward transfer, but built active social fields – involving various forms of movement, communication and long distance participation – across national boundaries connecting any number of places of successive migration and potential return. Margolis (1998: 120) concludes in her study of Brazilians living in New York City that 'Immigration in the jet age is more circular than linear'. Basch, Glick Schiller and Szanton Blanc's (1994) *Nations Unbound* was one of the first high profile empirical investigations of the social processes composing transnationalism, and moreover, one which grapples with *race* in the routines of displacement and settlement.

Nations Unbound was concerned with the circulation of populations between place of origin and host societies, and drew attention to the networks, activities, patterns of living and ideologies through which transmigrants connect their societies of origin and new settlement across two, or more, nation states (Basch, Glick Schiller and Szanton Blanc, 1994: 4,7). *Nations Unbound* suggests that transmigration brings its own forms of subjectivity forged in these social processes of movement and multiple belonging. These subjectivities, grounded in their specific geographies in the threading together of place, produce new forms of connection and home. Unusually, *Nations Unbound* is grounded in the details of everyday (transmigrant) life, the social networks and relationships through which the social fields spanning nation states are built. 'In their daily activities transmigrants connect nation-states, and then live in a world shaped by the interconnections that they themselves have forged' (Basch, Glick Schiller and Szanton Blanc, 1994: 8). And yet it acknowledges the regulatory power of the boundaries crossed. Based on a series of case studies drawn from a number of postcolonial transmigrant source countries – St Vincent, Greneda, Haiti and the Philippines – *Nations Unbound* distinguishes itself by considering the operation of race in these circumstances: 'For Caribbean and Filipino women, the ability to live transnationally is an accommodation both to the forces of global capitalism, and to their place within the global racial order' (Basch, Glick Schiller and Szanton Blanc, 1994: 29). What they mean by the 'global racial order' in practice is the rather restricted tapestry of race-making the transmigrants enter in the United States. But at least they consider race. We return to these issues later because they have a direct bearing on the circumstances of arrival and departure and the social organisation of home and belonging: issues which are both subtly and not so subtly raced.

Margolis' (1998: 2–3) study of New York based Brazilian transnationals includes the undocumented and temporary 'sojourners not settlers' who are often ignored and whom she also describes as economic, not political, refugees who are unable to live a middle class life in Brazil's chaotic economic and political circumstances. There are elements of lifestyle migration here, which underscore its softness as a category as a way of grouping people and circumstances. Governader Valadares, the area of Brazil sourcing most of the American axis of transmigration, has a 'culture of out migration' and receives half a million dollars a month in remittance money. The transmigrants say of themselves: 'our heads are in two places' (Margolis, 1998: 114). The term transnational was intended to convey this sense of concrete conduits of connection and circularity, in which local effects operate across long distances. Brazilian arrivals in New York are brokered by the Catholic Church, which provides an important social network along with family and friends. Unlike transnationals from the Caribbean and the Philippines who 'fit' in a particular way in the American racial landscape, Brazilians are politically and geographically invisible in the polarised American calibration of race as blackness and whiteness. Brazilians therefore have an ambiguous place in the racial scheme of things because, not being Hispanic but Portuguese speaking, they do not fit standard American racial categories and so are spoken of instead as having complex – transnationally generated – ethnic identities. We will return to the racial politics of home in a later section. This shows ethnicity being used to provide a more subtle picture of social texture than race does.

The term transnational covers a wide range of migrant circumstances and experiences as well as time scales of potential return from immediate to long term. The Brazilians and the transnationals from the Caribbean and the Philippines have quite different circumstances of departure. Most of the Filippinos, and many of the Caribbean, migrants who moved to North America and to Britain were women who had to leave children at home. Elaine King (1998)[8] tells what this feels like as a child joining her mother in Britain from Jamaica:

> I've always felt like a parcel. I can hear you asking why? Well, you see when I was nine, my mother sent for me. I came in the June and I was ten the

following February. I remember I wore a blue suit which was two sizes too big for me...I remember walking across the tarmac when I left Jamaica. I never looked back. I was so thin, I felt so lonely, I was leaving all I ever knew. I sat next to a white boy who was going to school, he tried to make me eat, but I couldn't eat a single thing. I was leaving Mum, Auntie Nita, Sister Virgi, Mamie, Mackie, Paulette and Marie, Baby G, my brother Frank, Laurent and Black Boy, Uncle Herman, Uncle Hosea, Miss Florence, Bev and Jimmy. I arrived in England. Funny, I knew my mother straight away, only from her photograph. I couldn't call her Mum, I called her Auntie Birdie. Why? Because the only mother I ever knew was left behind in J.A. It was a long drive to Bristol. When I reached Grosvenor Road I thought the houses were factories... I was head in my last year at school, only the second black girl to be so. I was brilliant at commerce. My teacher told me to get a job in banking and insurance. Alas, I couldn't get in. Only NatWest offered me a chance, but only if I was willing to move to London...I've always felt like a parcel and now I want to be posted back. (Elaine King, 1998)

King's story raises many issues, not least concerning the position of children in transnational migration, and combines impressions of arrival and departure with reflections on many years spent in a Britain as a new home. One of the issues it raises concerns length of stay and whether only those who move more frequently are covered by the term transnational. This is one of the many places where this concept is fuzzy and bleeds into others. Elaine King's situation is not quite the same as the New York Brazilians. She's stayed longer and possibly goes back less. Apart from being a child migrant she is telling her story 32 years later. But her final comment shows that, 32 years not withstanding, return is not ruled out. It is likely that she has been back for visits and maintains contact with the people she was so sorry to leave in Jamaica, thus building social fields across what for her may be two versions of home, for her length of stay in Britain is an implied belonging, even if it is qualified by her feelings about Jamaica and the forms of discrimination she encountered in Britain. Decisions about length of sojourn are interesting: another aspect of the biographical unfolding of a life, recollected from the vantage point of later life. Staying may just mean a failure to return so far, and it is likely that this is something that happens rather than something that is planned. It may even happen despite plans to the contrary.

Feroze Ahmed[9] who came to Britain from Pakistan over 35 years ago and opened one of the first 'Indian' restaurants in Bristol describes how staying 'happens':

I came to Bristol in 1959 when there were few Pakistani people in the West country...Indian food started as far as this country was concerned in the early 1950s, but there was no Indian restaurant in the West Country. British ex-army officers who had been in India were more or less the only ones who would eat curries. A few Indian restaurants opened and people realised what they were missing. ... We used to go to London to get the spices...Now after 30 years every corner has a curry house. ... Customers were always English, and they still are...Pakistanis eat at home with their families...and we didn't open the restaurant for Pakistanis! We opened it for local people [during this time also the political map of home changes dramatically and he is no longer

Pakistani]... I started a Bangladeshi Committee in 1971 to support the Bangladeshi Freedom fighters...Life has changed. At that time curry was half water and half spice. Now everyone knows curry, what is good, what is bad...People know what is good food. ... When I came to England I didn't come here to live for ever, for always. I was a student first, and then I started work. When I first came here, I weighed only seven stones, I used to run and play football...eventually I had a massive heart attack. I have full respect for England because I have spent 40 years here, but now because I have not been well for 20 years, and have had 20 years of not being active, what can I do? One part of my life has gone – work. Now I feel that all my children have been educated and can live anywhere in the world, that's OK. But I don't want someone to insist that I stay in England. My heart is in Bangladesh. (Feroze Ahmed, 1998)

One of the advantages of looking at circumstances of arrival and departure is that they are amenable to detail. They can incorporate the social and political circumstances of a place, as well as collective and individual lives. They are vividly recalled and are most effectively told as auto/biographical stories. These stories display something of the texture and complexity beneath the surface of social categories like transnationalism with its fuzzy boundaries of time, place and circumstances. Are all migrants in fact transnationals? Or only some? And if so what are the circumstances composing this concept? Feroze Ahmed possibly always intended to return to East Pakistan, which became Bangladesh, a set of circumstances to which he responded with local forms of long distance political action. If staying and going are about daily life then what are the circumstances that disrupt the routines of staying, and replace them with the routines of departure for other places? We know little of these issues beneath the surface of transnationalism. Urgent investigation of returnees as well as those who stay could settle some of these issues. Transnational is a useful concept for stressing continuing forms of connection through social relationships and other factors and the impact of distant social fields upon each other. But empirically, as my examples show, it is fuzzy and covers up a diversity of circumstances that could usefully be disentangled. It can be used to understand and map connections across social fields, and the meaning people attach to their journeys and dwelling. But it does not offer these insights easily, and it is eminently capable of ignoring them. The concept transnational can be put to work by the social researcher but it does not work on its own either as an explanatory or investigative device.

'At the heart of the notion of diaspora is the image of a journey' (Brah, 1996: 182): it is a 'travelling term' in 'changing global conditions' (Clifford, 1994: 302). Diaspora captures, in its imagery and meaning, the intention of this chapter and its concern with the rhythms of movement and dwelling, of belonging and displacement woven around a complex texture of arrivals and departures. Like transnationalism, from which it is not clearly distinguished, diaspora disrupts the binaries of rooting and displacement, so that even the most locally rooted 'maintain structured travel circuits, linking members "at home" and "away".' (Clifford, 1994: 309). Diaspora then, is part of a more general theoretical claim about the nature of human life and community as *mobile*. Most significantly this mobility disrupts the old horticultural metaphors used in the nineteenth, and most of the twentieth, century to discuss the racialised association between peoples and nation states as *roots*. Most accounts of diaspora are aimed at the doctrine of fixed origins (Brah, 1996: 180) and serve, as we saw in the last chapter (Hesse, 1996), as beacons of hope and liberation; offering forms of hybridity which defy essentialist accounts of racial identity, origins and belonging. Accounts of diaspora – like belonging – are finely textured by race in ways that disrupt the certainties of their connection. Diaspora, in other words, plays a significant part in challenging racist politics. It insists that people can live anywhere, making new homes away from home: that there is no primordial connection between race and place. This is a highly significant political claim, and marks the utility of this concept. The purpose of diaspora then, in the literature in which it is developed, is theoretical and political. And yet its image of the journey is closely aligned with the structure of individual biographies: the life stories of the human agents without which theoretical and political categories are impotent. Diaspora blends the image of personal topography with political claims about arrival and new forms of dwelling-in-displacement. It also offers a theoretical realignment that settles on dwelling in the context of its dialogues with movement, rather than as an undisrupted and natural state of human community.

'Yet not every journey can be understood as diaspora' (Brah, 1996: 182). Which journeys are significant in establishing the meaning of diaspora? Clifford (1994: 305), an anthropologist who is curious about the intellectual and political meaning of diaspora, notes that Safran uses the term to refer to those who have a history of dispersal; to whom myths and memories of homeland are important; who suffer alienation in their place of new belonging; who sustain the desire for eventual return to a homeland; and who have a collective identity which is defined by this relationship. In this list of defining characteristics we catch glimpses of ethnicity and race as providing the substance of some of these characteristics. Clifford (1994: 305) notes that while diaspora in the sense in which it is staked out by Safran is distinctive, it bleeds into other kinds of dispersal with adjacent maps and histories like immigrants, expatriates, refugees, guest workers, exiled communities, overseas communities, ethnic communities: so that diaspora ... is the domain of shared and discrepant meaning, adjacent maps and histories (Clifford, 1994: 303). Moreover, older forms of travel for religious and spiritual purposes from pilgrimage to crusades are replaced by newer ones, so that:

> In the late twentieth century all, or most communities have diasporic dimensions (moments, tactics, practices, articulations)...[so that it is] not possible to define diaspora sharply...[although it is] possible to perceive a loosely coherent, adaptive constellation of responses to dwelling-in-displacement. (Clifford, 1994: 310)

Diasporas then are about maps and, we can add, experiences of displacement and (dis)connection. Quite different from travel: diaspora is a blend of 'roots' and 'routes' (Clifford, 1994: 308). Not simply about forms of transnationality and movement, 'but of political struggles to define the local, as a distinctive community, in historical contexts of displacement' (Clifford, 1994: 308). Diasporas 'thus mediate, in lived tension, the experiences of separation and entanglement, of living here and remembering/desiring another place' (Clifford, 1994: 311). It is then, in Clifford's rather useful formulation, precisely, the tension between the *lived* and the *desired* that makes and fuels diasporas: the selective amalgam of traditions attendant upon body and food and their deployment in blended social patterns and networks of ongoing connections, of 'collision and dialogue' (Clifford, 1994: 314–19). It is this that produces the 'different histories and maps of travelling and dwelling [and telling]' (Clifford, 1994: 320). Diaspora as Clifford positions it, is about particular forms of lived politics: the building of a personal 'here and there' in the context of a collective one, and in this formulation its forms are researchable, as well as being an important political claim. The rationale for maintaining a sense of collective displacement is inevitably political; otherwise diasporic people would simply melt, if they were allowed to, into their new landscapes. This aspect of diaspora has two ingredients: a historic grievance over displacement and a reason for this to be maintained because of current grievances of discrimination or some form of disadvantageous social marginality. These struggles inevitably define forms of association and collective action, both political and social. The concept of diaspora places these tensions and political differences at the forefront of our consideration and research agendas.

Jews are the archetypal diaspora whose claims to homeland are mediated by contemporary and historical forms of anti-semitism. The other is the African diaspora of Gilroy's *Black Atlantic* in which a 'counter history of modernity is crucially defined by the still-open wound of slavery and racial subordination' (Clifford, 1994: 320; Mercer, 1994: 2). Racially and ethnically calibrated forms of subordination are crucially important in sustaining the concept of diaspora. Diasporas are constrained by nation state structures and global histories, but at the same time exceed and criticise them: nation and nation state are not identical (Clifford, 1994: 307). Nations form in exile in the hope and prospect of eventual return. Their homeland in the Middle East, about which many Jewish people are deeply ambivalent, is a good example of how this works and shows the inevitable fragmentation that occurs in versions of what it means to be Jewish. Diasporas are about myths and dreams and personal and collective journeys: the collision of personal and collective/political topographies.

Beyond these archetypal cases how does the term stand up? The stories of Feroze Ahmed and Elaine King contain elements of diaspora experiences. Their stories display the still open wound of discrimination in Britain; the tension between the lived and the desired; they hint at how living in one place and dreaming about another actually works. Their stories show the desire for eventual return to a 'homeland' as a place where the racially and ethnically defined alterity of migration dissolves, and where their right to 'be' is not placed in question, not scrutinised by others, and not the subject of political calculation. Feroze Ahmed's political participation at a distance in the formation of Bangladesh, speaks of a collective, political dimension to his being in exile, while he feeds the returned empire functionaries who helped cause the problem in the first place in his West Country restaurant. Both Ahmed and King have recognisably biographical connections with this concept of diaspora, something which, along with its political intelligence, supports its utility, despite the fuzziness at the boundaries. We can see that diaspora applies to their lives in ways in which it doesn't work for John. John's new life in Hong Kong has no myth of return, no desire to return to Britain. He is not systematically disadvantaged in his life in Hong Kong; in fact, quite the contrary, as the individual remnant of an imperial presence, he is reasonably well treated and sometimes respected, allowed to stay without feeling he is unwelcome. For John and other lifestyle migrants to be considered a diaspora the term would have to be repositioned so as to incorporate the mobile networks and habits attendant upon privilege. I earlier suggested that white British people's journeys wove the diasporas of privilege: but this presumes that it is worth extending this concept, so as to reveal the other side of the political circumstances of disadvantage and persecution in the beneficiaries of privilege. As it is, diaspora is a useful concept for speaking about difference in migration and in foregrounding its racial and ethnic grammar and the political contexts in which that has meaning. Extending it to include discussion of the privileged would draw attention to these differences. Diaspora reveals some important distinctions (and conceals others) but it reveals enough to establish its theoretical, empirical and political utility in speaking about migration and race making.

Diaspora misses things too. It does not come close to revealing the complex rhythms of melting and distinctiveness of the people whose lives it describes, although its cognisance of political circumstances opens a space for this. Melting and distinctiveness are about public ownership of diasporic categories, issues in which some people, rather than others, have options. These are matters of political and personal circumstance and generation: diasporic identities are intricately etched by time. Marian Liebmann (1998)[10] expresses this when she talks about being a second generation Jewish refugee in Britain:

I was born in Cambridge in 1942. ... I had a fairly ordinary British upbringing, except for the awareness that my family was a bit different – my parents were Jewish refugees from Nazi Germany, having escaped to England in 1937. This 'differentness' exhibited itself in several ways. My parents had foreign accents and mispronounced a few words from time to time. Occasionally visitors with much thicker accents came and talked German with them, and we were very bored as we did not understand. My parents mostly refused to speak German at home and we were brought up speaking only English. ... My parents tried as hard as they could to assimilate into their new haven and country of asylum. ... I was at university when Enoch Powell made his pronouncements about sending immigrants, including second generation immigrants, 'back home'...I realised that this would apply to me, too. I would be sent 'back' to Germany, a country I hardly thought of as mine after what happened. Until then I had seen myself as 'ordinary British', not a 'second generation immigrant', an experience parallel to that of many black people. ... My parents never went back and also took pains to avoid Germany whenever they travelled to Europe, even if it meant taking a longer route.

Here we see diaspora as a series of personal memories. We see how a shift in political climate activates a set of dislocations, which were not otherwise felt. We also see open questions about the ways in which diasporic experience reverberated down through generations. This woman grows up hardly realising she is a member of a category once marked for annihilation: such is the reconstruction of lives affected by place, time and political circumstance. She is reconnected with these deadly forms of distinction by shifts in the political climate in Britain, in which the unwanted are forced to take stock of their immigrant origins. Her mother, who escaped the holocaust, was equally shocked by the revelation of her Jewishness in Berlin in the 1930s:

We considered ourselves first German and only second Jewish; we were very patriotic. After all Jews had lived in Germany for many generations. So the Nazis' persecution of Jews came as a big shock to most Jews. (Marian Liebmann, 1998, relating some of her mother's memories recorded in her diary)

Race is sometimes *made* through diasporic experience, as well as producing and underwriting it.

Arrival: a note on administrative circumstances

A few comments on the administrative organisation of circumstances of arrival usefully form a bridge between our consideration of displacement migrations and our consideration of home. Home, with its racialised landscapes and implied and explicit possibilities of joining and belonging, operates in particular administrative conditions which are applied to the arrivals of those people covered by the terms diaspora, transnational, refugee and other categories of arrival including tourists (especially those from destinations producing refugees and economic migrants). It is here – in administrative circumstances – that we see the distinctions manifest around the wanted and the unwanted: those whose claims to entry are not so closely scrutinised and those whose claims are. All nation states have their own conditions and cultures of entry. Reflect on John's comments on the ease with which he arrived in Hong Kong, then a British colony. Contrast this with what Miles (1999) has to say about British airports and the ways in which the British state manages its arrival points and the 'social differentiation and exclusion' that operate in them. Airports, Miles suggests, play a significant role in 'the confirmation and transcendence of nationalism' while managing the global flows of human bodies in transit. Airports remind people of their national identity. Edward Said's (1999) biography *Out of Place* comments powerfully on reactions at airports to his mother's Palestinian travel document. Passports contain our 'juridical status in the international order' (Miles, 1999: 162); and airports are where the business of deciding 'who may pass across that frontier and on what conditions' (Miles, 1999: 162) occurs. Miles' 'political economy of migration control' notes the immigration service's focus on the movements of non EU nationals in respect of whom the decision to grant leave of entry is made quickly and 'instinctively'; guided by the 'instinctive racism' of immigration service personnel. We know almost nothing about illegal migrants and Miles (1999: 171) sensibly suggests that research would expose their poverty and their vulnerability. The Audit Office acknowledges that strict immigration control is impossible.

Most illegal immigrants are not picked up by the immigration service but by chance: they are reported by the public or discovered by the police investigating unrelated offences (Miles, 1999: 175–6). In line with other forms of privatisation, British immigration control is offloaded onto the private sector by the Immigration (carriers Liability) Act 1987, which allows a system of fines imposed on airlines carrying those without proper entry papers. The fining and imprisonment of truck drivers at seaports in an effort to cut down on trafficking in human cargo, is another aspect of offloading from state to private sector management in migration. The circumstances of arrival described by Miles certainly suggest that immigration to Britain is difficult to control – and this sustains new popular fears of swamping and being taken advantage of – shifted into private hands and often subject to individual ill-informed and summary judgement at the point of entry.

Although those arriving will interpret these processes in many ways, it is very unlikely that these circumstances create a *favourable* or *welcoming impression* of Britain, or convey any of the locally more positive interpretations of what it means to be a migrant. Whatever the varied circumstances of departure, the circumstances of arrival – in Britain and elsewhere– are highly disadvantageous to migrants and tourists from certain regions. The precise ways in which these processes involve race and ethnicity, the ways in which they play a part in race making, certainly need investigation. Britain is not alone in this, and is not one of the world's top migration magnets anyway. The administrative arrangements for arrival throughout the receiving countries of the world – and all countries are to some extent receiving countries as Zlotnik points out – is certainly an obvious target for further investigation.

Home

Where and what is home in the late twentieth century? (Robertson, 1995). This question is prompted by the heightened sense of movement and displacement defining this period, in which new forms of dwelling are forged, raising questions of belonging. The intricate connections between movement, displacement and dwelling, glimpsed at in the stories in this chapter, produce new belongings, which are usefully conceptualised as threads connecting people with the social and physical environments with which their lives intersect. This may, but need not, produce connections to place, although all lives are spatially configured. These connecting threads are conceived as forms of belonging and are, popularly and intellectually, referred to as *home*. What *are* the forms of belonging invoked by the concept of home? And why are we concerned with them?

The meaning of home settles on primordial connection in some of the literature concerned with it. Rykwert (1991: 51) contends that home does not need a fabric, only a fire, the mark of human culture and settlement. Home in this formulation attains its simplest form; it is at the centre of all human settlement, a basic ingredient of survival, providing warmth, food and human association. At the other end of the (theoretical) scale of things, Rapport (1995) suggests that people can belong in the routines of movement: home *without* settlement or fire. This suggests two significant general properties of home, which have a bearing on questions of meaning. The first is that home is comprised of various forms of connection between people and the social and physical environments in which their lives are cast: the filaments of connection accumulate to the string of belonging. This is a useful way of thinking about belonging and home rather than as settlement. Although connections routinely emanate from, and produce, settlement they do not require it. The capacity, the need, for connection with others is at the centre of the human condition: a property of human existence and subjectivity; a point established in Chapter 1. Home is thus constitutive of being in the world, and need not have a primordial connection to human 'need'. We are so socially wired. This is not a matter of innate properties of human nature, it is something we act on in making ourselves and our lives. Home is a part of human anchorage to the social world: an anchorage that takes multiple forms in social and political relationships, relationships to routines, places and so on. It is part of what it mans to be a person. ' ...being a person entails being able to be at home in the world at large and, by extension, a successively narrowing set of loci' (Hollander, 1991: 46). This brings us to the second general property of home. Breytenbach (1991) captures this when he says that home is both that which the exile *cannot let go of* and the *creative acts of resilience* composing new belongings in difficult circumstances. Home is made in the imagination and practical accomplishment of human agency. It is a testament to human capacity to go on making and remaking lives, even in the most adverse circumstances.

The point that homes are made in connections – as conscious and unconscious accomplishments – is very important. This means that new homes can always – are always – being made and remade. Anyone can make a home anywhere: although these forms of belonging are mediated by circumstances of arrival and departure, and the administrative actions of nation states in defining their new citizens and territories. Nothing fundamental connects anyone of any nationality or ethnicity to any particular part of the planet. Connections are made in circumstances belonging to broader political landscapes: and belonging is negotiated, more easily by some than by others. Home connections are an open question: they are made by people. Their circumstances are personal and political agendas. This way of seeing things is quite different from conceptualising home in ways that prioritise myths of return: Home is 'not the destiny of our journeys but the place from which we set out and to which we return, at least in spirit' (Hobsbawm, 1991: 65). In this cradle/grave formulation more definite and essential connections are drawn between people and places: and there are hints in some of the stories in this chapter that this works for *some* people but not for others. In this formulation too, home is always a place, and is always dissected by time, and in this sense of home there is no return. Indeed, this is the tragedy of the exile. These are landscapes of memory – discussed earlier – and they settle on home, but are not what is essential to it. In its broadest sense then, home is about being in the world, a property of existence and a capacity of human agency.

Why should we be concerned with home? For some of the reasons just outlined. It is important to people and their lives and it shows in the stories they tell about themselves. And because of its popular, political and intellectual casting in arguments about race and ethnicity. I am concerned with how the forms of connection composing home make race and ethnicity. Home is a part of the bigger questions and social scenes through which race and ethnicity are made. Home, like race and ethnicity, is manufactured as I have suggested. What we need to understand is how they are manufactured in relation to each other.

Home, as forms of connection between self and others, is an enormous subject. Here I can only point to *some* of its features, selecting those that are raised in the case study material of this and the last chapter, and which co-operate with the overall themes around which this volume is organised. The emotional dimensions of home are evident in the stories repeated in this chapter, and I want to say a bit more about this. The routine everyday nature of home is also apparent in refugee stories, so, second, I want to say something about routine homes and lifestyle. Third, I want to say something about landscapes of home. Landscape has many dimensions: personal, environmental and political. There are things to note about the personal and environmental – imagining and arrangement of space – but mostly I want to consider the politics of landscape, as this has an obvious and direct bearing on the making of race and ethnicity. These, I think, are some of the crucial pressure points in the calculation of belonging as forms of connection. Most important are the political landscapes on which belonging is cast.

Home as emotional connection

Brah's (1996: 180) account of the 'homing desire' as distinct from desire for a 'homeland' marks the emotional valance of home. The literature on exile (Breytenbach) speaks about home in terms that refer to 'longing' and 'desire': the need to be in the place you cannot be, the place that is so etched by memory and loss. It is at an emotional level in people's lives that the here and there of being in one place and desiring another is played out as nostalgia and longing. In fact emotional connection need not settle on nostalgia, although it often does, as new emotional connections are made all the time, and form the backdrop against which old ones are evaluated. Put in this way, the business of emotional connection sounds very open and very simple. It is nothing of the sort. Making new homes and processing the significance of old ones – these things are inevitably connected – emotionally is deceptively problematic and inaccessible. Of course this claim depends on what I mean by emotional.

A Polish refugee I had regular 'here and there' conversations with in Montreal, confessed that her twenty-year relocation process actually took years of psychotherapy. Her relocation wasn't about being able to operate in French, or being visibly part of the local Anglophone/Francophone and East European émigré communities and rearing visibly Canadian children. Beneath the layers of practical accomplishment is human consciousness: a place where things are anything but straightforward and tangled with all sorts of baggage and feelings of personal security and connection. My own migration proffers another example of the power of emotional attachment. Living in Montreal I had contrived to live also in Britain through the mechanisms of work – research projects and conferences – maintaining the same set of highly localised, London-based – research interests and family and friendship networks, which question what it means to move at all. Emotionally and intellectually I continued to live in London although my possessions, household and other version of family were in Montreal. I managed to hold all of these things together. It was when I returned to Britain that things fell apart. Moving back after eight years in Canada, the move I had worked to accomplish, practically very simple as I described it earlier, in fact brought a protracted period of disorientation, stress and related illness, which raised unanswered questions about the nature of emotional connections, some of which settled on a highly localised version of place, and some of which settled on social relationships. Clearly a significant element of connection is about *feelings of attachment*.

We can gather clues about the emotional dimensions of Elaine King's version of Jamaica, or the Bangladesh that was East Pakistan and where Feroze Ahmed's 'heart' still lives. They don't speak about Britain with the same nostalgia, memory and longing, but it is clear from their respective stories that their home in Britain has an emotional landscape of connection too. Longing, the imaginary, and memory, feature large on emotional landscapes, and hence play a significant part in the connections making homes. Certainly the experience of home is as much about the psychological as the social geography of space and neighbourhood and networks of significant others. Psychological geographies of home allow intimacy even in moments of intense alienation (Brah, 1996: 4), and here we learn something important about the nature of emotional connection. Intimacy and alienation speak loudly in the experiences of those with immigrant biographies in their homes of recent settlement *particularly when specific kinds of racial landscapes are in play*. The psychological properties of ease and alienation have social concomitants in political landscape and the salience of race and ethnicity in those landscapes. These are issues to which we will return. The emotional is *work* too, but it is not like the practical work of settlement and resettlement: and it is to this aspect of home that we now turn.

Routine homes

The routines of everyday life form a strong connection between people and their social environments. In the same routines in which subjectivities are made, so belonging connections are also forged. Conduits of belonging are everyday practical activities: composed of practical action reflected upon and not reflected upon but ingrained in kinetics, the routines of work and leisure; social relationships; and the use of neighbourhood and bigger spaces. At this level Feroze Ahmed belongs in the running of his local restaurant as well as the activities involved in his campaign for Bangladesh; his relationships with his neighbours, friends, children and grandchildren. He belongs in his health and in his capacity to work: and losing these things loosened his connection with Bangladesh. He belongs in the streets he traverses and the places he visits, the post office, the mosque, the café on the corner where he pauses to speak with his friends. His routine has a configuration in place, but would just as easily translate into another place. Should he move back to Bangladesh he would do much the same. The post office would feature in his transplanted life, so would the mosque and the café on the corner. He would maintain, at a distance, his relationship with his children and grand children. He would have new friends and keep up with some of his old ones. He would spend his day in similar routines, but in a different place with a different setting, a different set of social relationships and in a different political context. Routines of everyday life are both highly specific, located in place and highly mobile, and this ambiguity is its attractiveness. Home is both firmly rooted and infinitely mobile in this sense of it as everyday activity.

These everyday activities are the building blocks of lifestyle. Everyday activities are the templates, the formulas, by which life is conducted as a series of connections. Lifestyles are their extension, their embellishment or their retrenchment, their aesthetic trappings. Lifestyle is as mobile as the everyday routines of which they form a part. This is what is significant about them – they form a mobile connection or home in which place is a secondary consideration. Lifestyle is about appearance or style, not substance. It may involve the idealised casting of daily routines: the differences made by having more money, more time, more opportunities to follow one activity or another. Equally it can involve less of all of the above. John's daily routines are probably much the same in Hong Kong as in Britain. Only in Hong Kong his work is less hampered by government regulation; he has more leisure opportunities afforded by a higher disposable income and a tropical climate which makes his time off feel like being on holiday, and makes exotic holidays a routine affair; he eats out more and there are other people he can socialise with doing the same, ever ready for a party or a weekend on a 'junk' in the South China Sea. He would have leisure activities in Britain, but not the same ones; and he would not eat out so often, or have someone to clean his house and take care of his kids; he would go on holiday but not three times a year to Thailand or the Philippines. Through a 'lifestyle' people 'instinctively and mutely declare their will and aspirations' (Rykwert, 1991: 54–5): these things are neither trivial nor inconsequential. Those in a position to enact their will and aspirations live more in a lifestyle than in a place: their attachment is to the *aesthetic* and specific content of daily routine.

These things have ethnic significance as part and parcel of the making of ethnicity in style and food and daily conduct in ways stipulated in situational models of ethnicity. They are also matters of racial landscape. Feroze struggled with a quite different racial landscape than John. Feroze lives on a landscape in which his alterity has negative, rather than (grudgingly) positive, associations. Lifestyle migrants can choose where to live and grace us with their presence: immigrants from poorer countries drain our resources and our patience. Here again we see the muted operation of arrival and departure as significant in the making of home.

Landscapes of home – 'safe in my own skin' (Dido)

Landscapes of home connection have a number of dimensions. There is the emotional landscape referred to earlier; there is the scenery of particular places, which often feature in narratives of connection involving place; and there is political landscape. The scenery of particular places features prominently in memories and nostalgia, as well as in reorientation to 'new' places in which newness is especially vivid. The greenness of 'England' is a cliché steeped in nationalist claims to distinctiveness and grandeur, but it always struck me most vividly when I returned from the winter landscape of Quebec with its silent monochromes. Reading Hanif Kureshi's *Black Album* with its evocative descriptions of the London in which I was *not* living would paint the landscape of home, only to disappear, mirage like, as I actually returned to it on my frequent trips. Leaving Quebec I missed the *feeling* of the trees lining the street where we lived, rather than the house or the neighbourhood itself. Intimacy and familiarity with landscape are highly significant connections:

> I started buying a few things and got to know the shops and know that this road went here and that road went there, and I won't get lost. I used to carry my address with me so that if I did get lost, I could show it to someone. (Anon, Barton Hill Asian Women's Group, 1998)[11]

New landscapes are negotiated and learned. Old ones remembered and re-encountered. They are of course not incidental to, but intricately connected with, our everyday routines: past and present.

Political landscape is the most salient feature of landscape because it is connection with race and ethnicity. All arrivals in a new country and even their descendants – because this is how they are seen, as *arrived* and not otherwise there – negotiate the political landscape with which they must deal with publicly recognised and repeatedly validated versions of who they are, and what it means to be them. They also have to deal with dominant conceptions of what it is that is being displaced or joined with their arrival. Both of these aspects of arrival and homemaking forge connections that are highly racialised and ethnicised, in different ways in different places. This of course recalls an earlier chapter on the racing of space. We will focus on Britain in developing these dimensions of the political landscapes of home.

Political landscape establishes the terms of welcome on arrival and the conditions of stay. It is connected with administrative practices of immigration control referred to earlier, but it is also more than that. Cohen (1993: 11) notes that home operates as an implicit anchorage in racialist argument: and it is these politically calibrated notions of home that produce the *sense* of political landscape I refer to, with its versions of belonging and entitlement (Cohen, 1993: 6). In this sense home is a particular form of connection:

> ...a place of birth which is also a politico-legal entity based on some invented tradition of exclusive ethnic origin, a locus of jus soi. The other sense belongs to a discourse in which race functions as a primordial way of being at home in one's own body while making Others feel uncomfortable in theirs...jus sanguinis as an imagined community of kith and kin. (Cohen, 1993: 5)

This is the sense of home, which is mobilised by anti-refugee agitation and which carries significant messages about the collusion between race and ethnicity and belonging. Cohen says (1993:5) that domestic images of home operate as some of the 'more intimate registers through which imagined communities of "race" and "nation" are articulated in everyday life' in arguments for exclusion; in which boundaries of state and nation are pinned to neighbourhood and family. This is what makes these notions of home connection so insidious: the very familiarity and intimacy involved in nailing together two versions of home as domestic space and as nation space. The familiar distinction between family and outsiders gets recycled over the nation as a bigger connection, a bigger form of belonging and its attendant forms of entitlement.

Race and ethnicity are also made and encoded in political landscapes in another sense: a sense in which *all* landscape is political. The elision of landscape with national character – a short step from racial character – clearly makes this political connection. Again we draw on Britain for this example. 'The [British, wartime] countryside was a homology of the people's own idea of themselves – devoid of extravagance, unromantic, understated, moderate, enduring' (Schama, 1991: 11). The ruling paradigm for patriotic topography in Britain was pastoral.

> The claim that landscape and people are morphologically akin, constructed, as it were, from common clay, and that they constitute in some primal cultural sense the nature of each other – the land and homeland may be interchangeable – is now a familiar commonplace. (Schama, 1991: 11)

The defence of the countryside ravaged by animal disease at the beginning of the twenty first century, conducted against the accusation that is a way of life belonging to a previous era and hence doomed to disappear, is a part of this popular and political landscapeism: a Constable painting of *Englishness*. Cohen (1998a: 16) argues that landscape is not closed, but open in offering incomers terms on which it can be joined, occupied. He says that the British

Isles have an *archipelagic* identity also forged by some open conceptions of home as a rite of passage across the sea. Hence the island 'constitutes a particular kind of travelling story...creating the island as a place of ideal beginnings and happy endings outside time' (Cohen, 1998a: 18). The island landscape was created out of the patriotic labour of painters and poets, and its story is founded on a paradox:

> Here is an English nation continually being founded from outside itself, by the advent of strangers from continents overseas. The island story is never not an account of invasion and settlement. How then is it possible to impose a pattern of insular meaning on this constant rupture, and give the nation a singular overarching narrative identity? (Cohen, 1998a: 19–20)

The rights of sea passage transform invaders into kith and kin: a mechanism for nation making out of the diverse material making its way to the British shores. We considered this in the last chapter. Home connection in this sense is about the story told – or as I would prefer to put it – the meaning and mechanisms of belonging, the plausible rendering of connection. Exposing some of the mechanisms of race making, this lays open the formerly closed political question of home-making connection through different meanings of landscape.

Home making connections are always selective. John taught us this in his inventory of what was wrong (and all right) with Britain. The political conditions described by Cohen, and to which his alternate rendering of the island story is an astute political response, foreground my own ambivalence, also shared by others with similar political allegiances, about what is involved in home connection with Britain and the very selective way we might want to negotiate this. When your own sense of connection settles on a landscape which denies others this right of settlement connection; a landscape that is built and imagined in the mire of racial oppression; then home connection turns on the casting of political allegiances. These deliberated acts of alignment and critique, which are the only way of being comfortable in your own skin if you are white British: by protesting that others are *not* safe in their own skins and by tackling the political conditions in which these dangers are cast.

Concluding comments

There is no overarching sense in which race and ethnicity feature in migration displacement and belonging, indeed we suspected this from our account of the racial grammar of globalisation in Chapter 4. Instead we have a number of points at which we can see that race is being made in the context of rhythms of movement and settlement. Arrival and departure offered a window onto some of these processes. They allowed us to think about the political conditions in which people move, and the political circumstances governing where they can stay, on what terms and how they are made to feel about being there. All of these things are amenable to systematic investigation. Arrival and departure allowed us to think about biography and place and the ways in which people attach themselves to places and other versions of home. It provided a way into the uncertain racial politics of transnationalism and diaspora, and allowed us to unpack some of the stark polarities of refugees at one end of the mobility scale, and lifestyle migrants at the other. We saw that notions of belonging settle on home. We looked at the emotional, routine and political landscapes of home and saw that home, race and ethnicity are made together in a complex alchemy of attachment. These elements of race making are reinforced by what I set out in earlier chapters in relation to race making through auto/biography and place. Much of what I said about race making and the forms of racial grammar it exposes also works in this chapter when attempting to think about race making through its rhythms of movement and settlement.

Summary

- Migration takes many different forms and concerns basic issues of dwelling and displacement and modes of belonging that come with these rhythms of human life.
- Migration is the explicitly 'people' side of globalisation. Tracing the circumstances in which arrivals and departure occur allows us to identify forms of social difference and inequalities which are partly (but not entirely) drawn around race and ethnicity.
- Arrival and departure stories reveal both personal and political circumstances simultaneously.
- Forms of belonging are woven in different kinds of personal and political circumstances around emotional and routine factors in which landscape (physical and political) is a salient issue.

Transnationals: Transnational migrants build social fields comprising relationships, visits, communications and, sometimes, long distance participation, across two or more nation state boundaries. Their movements are about multiple belonging.

Diasporas: Diasporas are not clearly distinguished from transnationals or from other sorts of migrants. They are part of a political claim which asserts that any one can belong anywhere, that it is routes not roots that are significant, and that there is no primordial connection between race and place. They are also part of a claim about marginality and displacement that is enduring over time. Jews are the archetypal diaspora: their historic displacement is continued in a present set of circumstances flecked with anti-semitism.

Home: Home need not involve settlement but various forms of connection between people and social and physical environments. Home involves forms of anchorage and are part of what it means to be human, to be social. It is a practical accomplishment of human agency and, although connections are often made with race and ethnicity, these are just political claims and attempts to exclude others. Important elements of home include emotional connections, connections to (political and physical) landscape and daily routines.

Notes

1. The British Sociological Association code of ethical practice, in common with others, clearly distinguishes research from non-research contexts.

2. There is a useful account of exile in a series of papers presented at the New School for Social Research, New York and published in *Social Research* Vol. 58, No.1 Spring 1991.

3. The terms West and non-West are of course problematic and reinsert the kinds of distinctions this account of globalisation and migration this volume is trying to get away from. There are the terms of Zlotnik's (1999) rather useful calculation on the gradients of global migration.

4. Sassen (1990), as noted in Chapter 4, provides a useful discussion of some of the bridges connecting the US with places like Korea in migration terms.

5. Mary Kingsley's (1982) *Travels in West Africa* details her 1893 and 1894 journeys around the West Africa coast.

6. Nhui Mai's story is in *Origins: Personal stories of crossing the sea to settle in Britain* (1998: 24–9)

7. See Hannerz (1998) and Bhachu (1996).

8. Elaine King's story is in *Origins: Personal stories of crossing the sea to settle in Britain* (1998: 40).

9. Feroze Ahmed's story is in *Origins: Personal stories of crossing the sea to settle in Britain* (1998: 104–6).

10. Marian Liebermann's story is in *Origins: Personal stories of crossing the sea to settle in Britain* (1998: 32–8).

11. Anon, *Origins: Personal stories of crossing the sea to settle in Britain* (1998: 131).

Chapter Six
The Unbearable Whiteness of Being

[with apologies to Milan Kundera]

Mini Contents:

Introduction

In world demographic terms whiteness is insignificant. In terms of the racial grammar of globalisation and multi-racial societies, it is anything but. Whiteness involves diverse personal and political circumstances, from an East European asylum seeker to a wealthy global elite. We can see that being black or brown or Hispanic carries the same kind of diversity, but it doesn't do so in the same way as whiteness. In crude terms there are more rich white people and more poor black people, if we take a global, or even a local, view of things. We have a more complex sense of this from Chapters 4 and 5 from looking at who goes where, why and on what terms. In global terms whiteness is a badge of privilege, which is not the same as claiming that all whites are privileged, which would clearly be ridiculous. Understanding racial privilege is the other side of racial disadvantage: the two are connected. It was whites who *named* blacks 'black' in historical circumstances of racial oppression, and who, in turn, were named 'white'. This was a short way of referring to the operation of privilege and the complex forms of power[1], exploitation and violence on which it is based. An analysis of race that has nothing to say about whiteness is incomplete: missing half the problem. More than half of the problem for racism, as we have seen in the preceding chapters, plays a significant part in race making, and racism is a white problem, to which black people have been forced to respond.

Because this volume is *all* about race making, we already have a good idea about the mechanisms making whiteness. Whiteness, like blackness and other forms of ethnicity, is made in the operation of people in space. It is made in racial geographies, which produce 'white areas'. In the mobile habits and local movements of white people. It is made in comportment and dress, in grooming, eating and all manner of habits. Whiteness is made in the power geometry of globalisation, in who goes where, how and why. We caught a fleeting glimpse of it in John the lifestyle migrant in Hong Kong, in the travels of Mary Kingsley and Jane Waterston, and in the returned colonials discussing dinner placements in Budleigh Salterton teashops. There are, however, some mechanisms we need to pursue a little further, which are centred on the generation of particular forms of whiteness, and not race making in general.

In this chapter I look at some historical examples of social boundary making in which whiteness is differentiated from non-whiteness. I revisit performance and everyday life because these are relevant in the context of a growing literature on whiteness, which this chapter also examines, and because these mechanisms display the open texture of whiteness. Most importantly, and turning to specific forms of whiteness, I examine the arguments advanced in white and cultural studies regarding the status of empire in the making of white Britishness. I propose that empire is *one* of the mechanisms producing white Britishness, and suggest some of the more material ways in which this mechanism operates. For this chapter I have chosen critical moments in the making of whiteness that display connections between places, across time, and that display the connections between political landscapes: between the past and the present, and between the dialogues in which the boundaries of whiteness are made and challenged. In pursuing these issues, this chapter will show how whiteness is central in the making of (certain) regimes and its subjects; central in understanding the world in which we live and its recent past. Understanding how whiteness is made is a first step in its remaking. This chapter then, is a people-centred political story of the making of whiteness as a badge of racial privilege.

Adopting a critical stance on whiteness

We can only make sense of whiteness in the context of its political landscapes and at particular intersections of time and space. Whiteness entered the lexicon of the social and cultural sciences in the late twentieth century as 'critical white studies'. Dyer (1997) in *White* argues that the effectiveness of whiteness lies in it occupying a central, yet undeclared and unmarked, position from which the world is known and judged. To be white, says Dyer, is to be just human, and there is no more powerful position than being just human. Whites speak about nothing *but* whites but pretend that they are talking about people in general (Dyer, 1997). Racial imagery is central to the organisation of the modern world, and its regimes in which whites are privileged.

> ...at what cost regions and countries export their goods, whose voices are listened to at international gatherings, who bombs and who is bombed, who gets what jobs, housing, access to health care and education, what cultural activities are subsidised and sold, in what terms are they validated – these are all largely inextricable from racial imagery. (Dyer, 1997: 1)

In critical white studies whiteness is named, marked and located as one privileged position among others, thereby unmasking it as an undeclared central position from which the world is judged. It is, of course, important to note that whiteness does not involve a single position, but a matrix of related positions, as this chapter will suggest. It is *unmasking* and *naming* that characterises the present attention to whiteness. In critical white studies whiteness carries an admission of racial guilt and culpability, a reckoning with history, and recognition that anti-racism requires whites to transcend their racial significance (Cohen, 1997: 245–6). Cohen effectively characterises this new mood. This version of whiteness is self-conscious and self-critical, not taken for granted and disavowed. It is:

> ...the visible focus of open conflict and debate, not the silent support of an invisible consensus of power...a source of guilt and anxiety rather than comfort and pride....it issues from a perspective that privileges a certain black experience of racism and insists that racism is primarily a white, not a black, problem. In this story; whiteness is the new white man's (and woman's) burden; their first task is to recognise and then to help lift its oppressive yoke by acknowledging its function as a badge of racial exclusion and privilege. (Cohen, 1997: 245–6)

Critical whiteness thus issues from a particular political stance and operates in a dialogue with taken for granted versions of whiteness as unquestioned superiority. This is what makes it *critical*.

What is being critiqued?

The whiteness of critical white studies is the descendant of the forms of whiteness being challenged, and is most usefully placed in this context of dialogue. What are the forms of whiteness being contested in white studies? These are difficult to characterise briefly without over generalising or exaggerating their coherence, and overlooking the challenges levelled against them. It is important to say at the outset that although I am characterising the ancestor of critical whiteness as the whiteness of unexamined superiority, it *was* constantly examined and challenged, as this chapter will reveal. The motor driving its examination and eventual transformation into critical whiteness, was black struggle. Whiteness, in its different historical forms – from unexamined superiority to its present appearance as critical whiteness – is *produced by the political agency of black people* in struggle with the political agency of white people. Blackness then, is the motor of white (and black) history. The treaties of whiteness as unexamined superiority formed a significant framework in European thought from the eighteenth Century and surfaced in a number of places. I will mention just one or two of them as illustration, and to establish the terms of its dialogue with critical whiteness, and its engagement with the political agency of blackness.

Whiteness as taken for granted superiority surfaced in eugenics, for example, with its class based biology of breeding habits in which the forging of white nations was tied into the project of international competition *between* white nations for industrial and economic advantage. It surfaced in many ways in the social practices, administrative apparatuses and racial assumptions of empire-building: in the global conquest and control of space by western Europeans. It surfaced in the Orientalist cannon, criticised by Said (1978), as the detailed systems of expertise in which western enthusiasts encountered and classified the rest as objects of knowledge. And it surfaced in social anthropology's ordering and rendering of the other in frameworks organised by racial hierarchies and deployed in the service of colonial administration. All of these practices, processes and discourses were challenged by those they placed as the racialised other. The histories of empire and slavery are peppered with revolt and insurrection. They were challenged from other, internal, sources too.

White crises and black struggles

Whiteness also suffered its own crises. Unravelling the certainty of white global superiority occurred through a number of processes and events in the early years of the twentieth century. Bonnett (2000: 39) suggests that 'the legend of white superiority was shattered' in the Japanese defeat of Russia in 1905; by the turning of whites against themselves in the First World War in which colonial subjects were enlisted as allies; and the anxieties surfacing around the sexual behaviour of white women travelling and living in the colonies, shown in Henry Champly's (1936) salacious travel book, *White Women, Coloured Men*. Bonnett (2000: 38) suggests that the literature of 'white crisis' of 'anger' and 'burnt pride' at the precariousness and fragility of the position of whites in the global order was a reflection of their extraordinary claims to superiority. A 'fabulously exceptional human type', they, we, were never simply just another ethnic group, as Hall astutely asserts, thereby putting us whites in our place. In fact the making of whiteness into *just another ethnic group* took another set of social and political processes, which spanned the second half of the twentieth century, and which were bound up with other forms of black assertion. What Bonnett points to is the precariousness and fragility of whiteness; fears that turned on its making, its defence and differentiation from non-whiteness. These are enduring themes in the making of whiteness as a series of racial categories. Crises of self-confidence are evidently a significant part of unexamined white racial superiority.

Black movements for colonial freedom, starting with demands for Indian independence from the British empire in the early years of the twentieth century and continuing into the 1960s with the decolonisation of Africa and the Caribbean, drove assumptions about white racial superiority into the open and confronted them head on. Pan-Africanist Movements put European colonial authorities on the defensive, and in America the Civil Rights movement built a new moral topography around recognition of the racialisation of rights and the racial ordering of lives. Anti-racist struggles forged the immediate political and social circumstances of critical white studies, and its appraisal of the meaning and benefits accruing to whiteness. As connections between forms of black oppression were made and contested, so blackness was consolidated as a political category with global significance. This, in turn, produced the oppressor – whites – in similarly overarching global terms. If blackness was produced by oppression then whiteness was produced by culpability for racial oppression. It was blacks' (opposition to white oppression) that made whites white. The new moral topographies of the late twentieth century produced white critical reflexiveness and brought apologies for the past. On this topography the European Union struggles over the form of its apology for the transatlantic slave trade (*Guardian*, September 3 2001), and reparations are demanded as compensation for the enslavement of African Americans. It is on this topography that critical white studies became significant, squeezed between its relationship with earlier – fragile – forms of white superiority on the one hand, and the politics of black self-assertion on the other. Contemporary white studies are situated by this political and historical dynamic, and so our consideration of it necessarily begins from this starting point.

Political landscapes and their connections

A number of transnational connections between political landscapes are implicated in the comments above, and it is in this bigger context that we note that the meanings and strategies of whiteness (and blackness with which they are intimately connected) are macro/micro matters of political landscape[2]. Rooted in local specifics of political configuration, whiteness has travelled between political contexts publicising its conditions of production as paradigms, and taking on new meanings and strategies in the political contexts to which it is applied. It is some of these local and transcendent aspects of whiteness that this chapter seeks to explore. Transcendent in the sense of when things move out of place to new places and accrue other meanings and strategies. Specifically, as with other aspects of race addressed in this volume, this chapter plots some of the dialogues concerned with whiteness that took place between Britain and the United States, already suggested earlier in the travelling of civil rights politics producing particular forms of black self-assertion in Britain. If we go back far enough in time the connections between these dialogues are clear: they can be characterised as the dialogues of empire versions of what Gilroy (1993) called the *Black Atlantic*.

Versions of whiteness and its strategies of conquest and settlement circulated the British Empire of which America was once a part. Versions of whiteness, its meaning and significance circulated with the migration of people back and forth, and with popular representation at home of what was going on in the colonies. Popular renditions of empire and its versions of whiteness entered the domestic imagery of British popular thought (McClintock, 1995), and Empire by this route is accorded a special place in the making of whiteness. These are issues we will examine more critically later. Our focus here is less the histories of empire than their *reworking as systems of movement and circulation to expose* the situatedness of whiteness, by understanding the mechanisms by which it is made. Our purpose here then, is to understand how versions of whiteness were made as micro matters of political landscape within broader (empire) contexts of movement and transcendence. This is an extension of Bonnett's (2000) project, which involves the critical exposure of whiteness, through a reckoning with the past in which he warns of the dangers of US domination of accounts of whiteness. These are, for Bonnett (1996: 150), a travelling of the local: a transposition of American versions of whiteness onto other political landscapes. His warning is duly heeded, and he is right to suggest that in understanding whiteness as Britishness we need to think more closely about the crucibles of empire, but the development of the stories and trajectories of whiteness involved precisely this circulation of ideas and bodies across divergent political landscapes, past and present. Hence the rationale for approaching things in this way: not in place but in movement from place to place. Whiteness, as we noted earlier, is both locally placed and transcendent and needs to be addressed as such. This is less an analytical than a practical and pragmatic point. We can trace the actual conduits of bodies and ideas as they move from place to place.

Within this, the articulation of whiteness also had its micro-climates, its details, its infinite variation. Forms of whiteness are significantly calibrated by nation states and the racial micro-climates of which they are composed. Being white Californian, white American, white British, white English, white Canadian and white Australian are all categories which make appearances in critical white studies and provide the material for this chapter. I use the term British rather than English here because it offers a broader canvas on which to work, and because it acknowledges the contribution of the Scots, Irish and Welsh in the British Empire. I am, of course, aware that Celts were only latterly drawn into the category white, that in the nineteenth century the Irish in particular were regarded as separate race from Anglo Saxons. Hickman and Walter (1995) discuss British racism in the context of the Irish, showing, as I have suggested elsewhere in this volume, the fractured nature of whiteness. Drawing selectively on these different sources should not be confused with their conflation. Their local circumstances of production are specific, but the social forms and narratives they produced have not remained in place but travelled.

This concludes our preliminary consideration of political landscapes and the connections between them in the making of whiteness as a series of connected racial categories. We return to it later because political landscape, of course, is one of the mechanisms producing whiteness, rather than just the backdrop against which it is made.

Some mechanisms making whiteness

This chapter charts the appearance of whiteness at a number of significant moments in the racial making of political landscapes. These are discussed as a means of understanding how whiteness is made. This chapter rehearses some of the stories of the making and remaking of racial categories as a means of getting at their social mechanisms. It focuses on the following themes in the making of whiteness as a way of identifying a limited number of social mechanisms that can be dealt with in this preliminary analysis. These are social boundaries, performance, everyday experience, empire and consciousness and subjectivity. Whiteness, always unstable, like other racial categories, for this is in the nature of racial categories, unravels even as it is being made as Bonnett's (2000) examples from the early twentieth century show. Whiteness maintenance requires constant work, constant effort, on the part of people and systems. We want to understand what that work consists of, and the mechanisms identified above are a means of doing so and adding to what we already know about race making from earlier chapters. Like other racial categories, whiteness is *manufactured* through a series of overlapping social processes on the shifting sands of political landscape – itself also an important mechanism – through the efforts of people. This is evident from the review of whiteness that follows. What are the social processes that operate as conductors of whiteness? And what part do we white folk play in their manufacture and maintenance? It seems to me that these questions make a contribution to the development of critical white studies in a grounded way. This modifies my earlier claim that the social and political agency of black people was responsible for the production of whiteness. In fact race making is necessarily a collaborative activity involving both the *people it includes* and the *people it excludes*. My point about black agency was about the mobilisation of racial categories in political struggles. In their constant calling into question of whiteness as privilege and domination, and in building transnational movements to contest this privilege and in the process remaking the moral topography of the late twentieth century, the political agency of blackness was a crucial factor in forging whiteness in the first place, and later in transforming it through critical white studies. The foundation of any prospect of white humanity and ethical conduct, we owe to black challenges to the privileges we took, and still take, for granted.

Social boundary mechanisms

Inevitably one of the characteristics of race making concerns establishing its own boundaries, its own parameters, ways of distinguishing itself from others. Whiteness is made in its social boundary activities: not alone, but in concert with other social markers. There are places where whiteness works harder than others. Whiteness' production and association with over 300 years worth of privilege makes it, as Dyer (1997) suggests, a good category to get in to. We might reasonably expect that whiteness *works* particularly strenuously at the points at which it intersects with other racial and ethnic categories. It works particularly hard in what Primo Levi (2000) calls the 'grey zone'. This, for our purposes in this volume and not the sense in which Levi intends it, is the zone in which whiteness must be distinguished from not-whiteness, because of the edifice of entitlement it sustains. Levi, of course, did not use it in this way to speak about whiteness, although he does use it to talk about the drawing of ambiguous racialised social boundaries in very difficult circumstances. There are things to be learned from examining the ways in which critical white studies interrogated this murky grey boundary between whiteness and blackness, say, in the South of the United States in the last century in the context of formal segregation. But the grey zone is also applicable in another sense, and this is the sense in which Levi used it, as a zone of indeterminacy in which the *practices* composing racial categories come to the fore. As we noted in Chapter 1 the grey zone is made by the functionaries who serve, and the regimes that *make and act on, racial distinctions* (Levi, 2000: 50). This highlights some of the social processes composing the arbitrary and the everyday: the interstices of biography and social structure, between people's lives and social relationships and the regimes in which their lives are set. The outcomes of these race-making activities, as I suggested in Chapter 1, are often crucial matters of life and death. On a lower scale of lethalness, the same is true of the regimes of formal segregation in the United States in the nineteenth century. Being accepted as white in the grey zone carried an edifice of rights, the prospect of not being lynched or facing summary execution. American blacks fled north well into the twentieth century in order to avoid that lethal brand of politically organised whiteness, the Klan and other formal and informal regimes of racial violence as we saw in Chapter 2.

Enforcing the boundaries of whiteness: some practical examples

Nothing better displays the social mechanisms of whiteness in the setting of social boundaries, than the practicalities of defining and defending whiteness itself. Examining this gives some insights into the composition of whiteness in certain circumstances. Race making is always and inevitably circumstantial as we noted earlier. Societies legally operating forms of racial classification, whether for purposes of segregation, the calculation of entitlement, or summary death, are inevitably drawn into establishing the boundaries of whiteness (or forms of whiteness such as Aryanness), in a variety of circumstances. British colonial regimes in Africa and the Caribbean dealt with colonial subjects through forms of racial categorisation; 'coloured', 'European' and so on, were recorded on birth certificates. In quite different political circumstances, the Canadian Federal Government today operates biological (blood-line) definitions of race in order to accord special status and racially-construed rights (in place of citizenship and meeting land claims) to Natives, administered by the Department of Native Affairs. Regimes operate racial classifications for different reasons as well as in different circumstances. The difficulties of doing so reveal the arbitrary, unstable and contingent nature of racial classification and the social mechanisms composing these classifications. We can investigate them in order to reveal these.

The vast and complex systems of slavery and segregation operating to structure American society from the eighteenth century demanded operational versions of white, in demarcating a category of human subjects with rights. No straightforward matter, the operational definitions of white were repeatedly subjected to juridical scrutiny as states struggled to impose the neat black and white binaries of racial classification, over the chaotic affairs of its misceginated and multiply-origined immigrant population. Lives interface with administrative priorities! Braman's (1999) account of the late nineteenth and early twentieth centuries makes this point about the difficulties involved in defining and maintaining whiteness in the cauldron of American race segregation. Divergent versions of whiteness prevailed in the different states. North Carolina's 'one drop' of African blood rule was balanced by Ohio's version in which European blood (calculated genealogically) of more than 50 per cent qualified as white (Braman, 1999: 1396). Differences between states, suggests Braman, were about making themselves attractive to potential residents so as to boost population and meet labour needs. Miscegenation of course, at different times the object of legal, social policy and popular action, muddied the establishment and operation of whiteness as a privileged racial category. Differences between state classifications were further complicated by forms of internal migration and travel as transit between states became easier. By the 1890s segregation on trains crossing state lines was forbidden (Braman, 1999: 1397). Murky and divergent versions of whiteness were tested in court, as in the case of Homer Plessy, the light skinned man with one great grandparent from Africa, counted as white in some states but not in others, who was arrested for violating Louisiana state laws by sitting in a section of a first class train carriage reserved for whites (Braman, 1999: 1397), which was mentioned in Chapter 1 in the context of arguing that people matter. Cases such as these show the flexibility and ubiquity of race in American lives at the turn of the nineteenth century. Other examples of testing the outer contours of whiteness are offered in respect of nation-building immigration to the US in the 1920s. I will return to this later. For now it is sufficient to note that whiteness was, and is, both circumstantial and negotiated by people. Hence claims about its instability.

Hale (1998) suggests that the train – significant as a means of moving people and things from one place to another – was important in the maintenance of American racial structures on which whiteness depended. In place of a more settled life in plantations with their forms of racial ascription and definite, differential juridical status, came the mis-identifiable stranger and anonymity of urban space[3]. She argues that the Jim Crow signs 'for whites' 'for coloureds' that sprouted in the context of mobility and urbanisation were designed to 'reproduce a white supremacy that had become detached from the personalised relations of local power' (cited in Nightingale, 1999: 143). She shows how difficult it was for Jim Crow to work in stores, on transport, in towns where commercial values clashed with racial divides, which were increasingly difficult to maintain and operate. Her argument is that urbanisation, industrialisation, mass society and consumer culture worked against the practical accomplishment of segregation in the daily lives of American citizens[4]. Hale (1998) suggests that Jim Crow – as a legal system effecting racial separation – should be seen as a culture: as memory, identity, values, taboos, daily life, ritual and spectacle. But as a system, it was more fluid, contradictory, ambiguous and violent than we know (Nightingale, 1999: 140). Hale's study of narrative, folklore and visual imagery shows that they were rich in codes of white male honour and vulnerable, if tenacious, white womanhood (Nightingale, 1999: 141).

Here we see a cultural analysis of whiteness – a major theme in critical white studies' accounts of whiteness – implicitly displacing more politicallyworked analyses. However, if we think of imagery, folklore, identity and so on in ordinary everyday life terms, rather than as simply matters of representation, then there is a space for thinking of race making through human agency in this kind of analysis, even if the author intends industrial capitalism to serve as a central explanation for the erosion of segregation. Anyway these things didn't move against segregation, but provided it with new modern forms, which were less formally inscribed in legal processes, but more firmly entrenched in the everyday social practices composing the kinds of lives that could be lived within these chaotic urban regimes. The role of human agency is no less pertinent in the demise of segregation because of industrial capitalism. People were an active force in this too.

Whiteness and other social boundaries

Whiteness is also made in the composition of *other* social boundaries only alluded to above such as class, masculinites and femininities (reviewed in Chapter 5 in the lives of nineteenth century women travellers) and not just in the making of racial distinctions. Racial distinctions always take other forms from which they are not separable. Roediger (1992) traces the significance of whiteness in the making of American blue-collar workers, and here we see the intersections of some of the things we refer to as race, gender and class. Hartigan's (1999) study of the class modality in the construction of

Detroit versions of whiteness is an ethnographic comparison of two communities, and shows the interconnectedness of gender and class with race. The white working class, at least in Britain and, implicitly in the United States in accounts like Roediger's and Hartigan's, has provided the iconography of racism through a focus on football hooligans, ultra right-wing groups and studies that focus on poor areas, fears of displacement and labour and trade union politics (Miles and Phizacklea, 1979; Knowles, 1979, 1992). Cohen, (1997: 254–5) working in East London, the heartland of white racism, puts these associations between the working class, masculinity and race on a different footing. He writes of the whiteness of the not very privileged, whose whiteness has transcended the work habitus of the old labour aristocracy. Freed from this social anchorage of work, and work as site of white masculine privilege; whiteness takes on a 'tactical essentialism' in 'Nationalisms of the neighbourhood'. The difference is that:

> The whiteness of the new 'postmodern' racism starts much closer to home…it is based on the fetishism of certain 'ideal types' of manual labour and their abstraction into displaced images of the body politic. (Cohen, 1997: 256)

Nationalism of the neighbourhood has a broader social base and, from our point of view, a different set of social mechanisms worthy of investigation. In the contemporary making of white masculinities we need to acknowledge significant shifts, as boys grow up to become hairdressers and waiters rather than steel workers, and what Cohen refers to as the tactical posturing of whiteness makes itself with the new material of different social boundaries and accompanying subjectivities. Even slight privileges are worth maintaining and their racialised anchors and forms of entitlement – in nationalisms of the neighbourhood, which lay claim to the local in similar terms to the nation state – require new forms of social understanding. In this formulation, the mechanisms of place are transcendent over work, in making the bonds of belonging and entitlement in racially white exclusive, but actually quite plastic, terms. The mechanisms composing and combining social boundaries are an ever-shifting set of considerations and circumstances, which can only be known through investigation of the sort Cohen pursues in East London. Cohen's research strongly supports the need to transcend the iconography of blue-collar masculinity in the making of whiteness. Class position and gender play a vital part in making racial categories, and whiteness is no exception.

Performance mechanisms

We looked at performance in Chapters 1 and 3, but not specifically as whiteness. Whiteness, too, is made in performance. Examples of performances of whiteness are codified in social etiquette and rituals as in my earlier example of the dining rituals and manners of British ex-colonial returnees. Of more interest are the performances *undermining* social boundaries and racial categories of which Schueller (1999) provides an example. Performance is about comportment and bearing, it is about the ways in which bodies move in space and conduct themselves in social relationships. Performance is about personal versions of the self and its dialogues with forms of social recognition and the edifices of expectation on which they are premised. Performance works across different kinds of social distance. It can put the finishing touches to unfinished racial categories, literally providing the moving flesh to fix otherwise ambiguous circumstances, or contract the messages of skin and hair. The light skinned black attaches himself, through performance to whiteness, because it is ambiguous, unstable, always at the point of unravelling even when it is also a legal category. Schueller (1999) tells the story of the light skinned slave in antebellum America. A 'New Orleans mulatto' who didn't fit the local/national black/white official binary, Dorr, the slave, travelled to Europe with his master. His story, published as *A Colored Man Around the World* (1858) shows how, even in the circumstances of slavery and its apparently categorical versions of race, the permeability of the colour line and the working of performance in undermining it. Dorr's story draws upon the meaning of European travel for white cultured Americans. He performs the consumption of leisure in Europe as a trope of class in a way that questions the gentility of Southern American whites (Schueller, 1999: 244). Being in Europe, Dorr is liberated from the social relationships of slavery: he is in a place where his existence has an alternate set of meanings which can be mobilised in repositioning himself and in questioning the social order organising his positioning. He rewrites the text of slavery by objectifying his white master, and at the same time avoids the traditional slave narrative of Southern suffering sponsored by the abolitionists. His performance of whiteness undermines the racial contours of the political landscape on which he was produced. The performance of travel, to social contexts racialised by other means, is the mechanism by which he demonstrates the instability and ambiguity of whiteness and condemns the social system sustaining and giving it meaning. This is just one account of performance working against the boundaries of racial categories. It stresses the significance, not of skin, but skin in motion around social practices and relationships and places that carry alternative racial meaning. The performance of whiteness is not confined to whites.

On a more contemporary note, the performances making whiteness are those we noted in relation to blackness in Chapter 3. White performances are about the people and activities characterising places through bodies and their posture, movement, attitudes and habits. They are about the ways in which bodies eat, sleep, move, wash, groom, dress and eat. These social mechanisms making whiteness are about the mundane and the ritual, the conscious and the unconscious ways we have of being in the world. The most important thing about these performances and the spaces they mark is whether they are open and inclusive, or hostile zones of exclusion in which others are made to feel discomfort. Dorr's example suggests that they are potentially open and inclusive, in that performances of whiteness do not demand unambiguously white skin. Ideally performances of whiteness in multiracial societies in which whites form a majority, are part of a culture which is open to, and welcoming of, those who bring other performances. It is not the performances that matter, but their social and political context. It is the forms of social and political meaning and judgement, which are brought to bear on manners and comportment that matter and not their content. In countries like Britain and France, for example, ways of eating, moving and forms of conversation are producers and indicators of complex forms of social positioning, which include much more than race and ethnicity. These are antithetical to a spirit of openness and tolerance. The central issue is not just how whiteness is made, but how it operates in being made as part of a broader social and political context. What matters are the terms in which it is made and the social and political meaning it carries. Politically, whites need to address these issues of their performance and its impact on others.

Mechanisms of everyday experience

We have already considered the contribution of everyday life in race making. I mention it specifically in relation to whiteness as a way of thinking a bit further about some of the literature on whiteness. This raises important issues concerning empirical research with white people. Whiteness is made in everyday experience and its emotional and relational landscapes in Ruth Frankenberg's study of white women in California. Bonnett is critical of this, as we noted in Chapter 1, because he thinks that race cannot be both an arbitrary social invention and refer to a category of people and their lives. He notes (1996: 17) that the US engagement with whiteness follows two paths. In one whiteness is the agent of the history of class struggle: the modality of class formation, as in Roediger's (1992) and Hartigan's (1999) studies. In the other it is the diverse experience from which the race-privileged approach the world, as in Frankenberg's (1993) work in which the landscapes of social identity are viewed through the window of experience (Bonnett, 1996: 147). Both are clearly gendered, the former operates primarily as an account of masculinities, the latter redresses this gender imbalance in its focus on white women.

Frankenberg's (1993) empirical study of whiteness is an account of experience voiced from California, but also concerning other aspects of the American racial landscape as Californians come from any number of places. Frankenberg's study is an attempt to note the ways in which racial structuring operates in people's lives, experience and reflexivity. She is unusual in providing an everyday life focus for a study of whiteness. She (1993: 2) identifies the 'discursive repertoires of whiteness': what do the 30 women interviewed draw on in making sense of their lives as racialised experience? This is a mapping of women's daily lives onto broader – raced – social processes (1993: 6). Frankenberg details the women's childhood race landscapes, gets them to think about how race operates in contexts concerned with sex and intimacy, and establishes something of the spatial dynamic involved in the ways in which selves and racialised social environments are plotted. In some cases this involves reviewing the landscapes left by desegregation and the ways in which white women operate through these landscapes. This is an account that skilfully slips between racial micro-climates and broader land-scapes. Women are both entrapped by, and grapple with reinventing, the racial discourses and practices with which their lives are entangled. Frankenberg's portrait of white selves positioned on particular racial land-scapes draws some of the connections between the intimate and the political, as overlapping landscapes producing and sustaining each other.

Bonnett (1996: 151) takes this work (on class and experience) to task for its essentialism and for having it both ways. 'They [whites] are, at one and the same time, deconstructed as a slippery, "Other-dependent", category – a cate-gory constantly in danger of "leaking" and "failing" – and addressed as a dis-tinct community that needs to be re-educated and take its place in an anti-racist dialogue with "other races".' Whiteness, he says, cannot be both a discourse and a set of people. Of course by now we know that it can, that it must be both, or it will lack the volition of human agency and be inert. Bonnett (1996: 153) claims that these texts are unreflexively embedded in one specific history of racial oppression, and obsessively centred on whiteness and white people as the principal actors in American history. Bonnett is right to say that you have to say more about whiteness than that it is an unstable racial category. We need to know how racial categories are made and what makes them unstable. The way that people organise themselves so as to live, give meaning to, and embody, the narratives of whiteness are worthy of understanding. How do people make sense of and live these things? People are not removed from these categories, they interface with them and make practical decisions about them.

Of course there is a problem here, which researchers of whiteness who are interested in everyday life such as Frankenberg encounter when they try to do empirical research on whiteness, and that is that the category 'white' does not necessarily have a meaning for the people to whom it is applied. The narra-tives of whiteness are not always explicit, and are often disavowed because of their association with racism. Frankenberg discusses this disjunction between narratives of whiteness and the whiteness embedded in lives. Whiteness is embedded in the lives of those whom she interviews and hence taken for granted, and for that reason not discussed. In this case you can't interview people about it directly. Or, it is associated with racism and disavowed, inad-missible as part of modern liberal conceptions of the subject, which defaults to a position of race blindness as part of a conception of social progress, of a moving forward from a history of racial oppression. That those whom we investigate do not inevitably share our terms of analysis is a common issue in social research. In fact whiteness, as we discussed at the beginning of this chapter, is a term of critique and hence only has an explicit meaning for those who at some level engage with it critically and reflexively. Alternatively, it presumably has a meaning for race supremacists. But outside of these two functions of whiteness we might expect that few people actually see them-selves as white, it is, as Dyer (1997) noted, a taken for granted central position of privilege from which the world is viewed, something which may or may not occur to those to whom it applies.

As well as referring to a category of lives and people, whiteness is a category of social analysis and engages a political perspective. It has been made into a category of political engagement by the politics of racism as we noted earlier. It is about the naming of blacks as black by whites who, while not naming themselves, became the refracted target of counter racism. It was, as we noted earlier, by this route that whites became white. Whiteness is the logical outcome of our own racism as well as a badge of privilege. Bonnett (1996) correctly notes that this ignores the symbolic role and political presence of those who lie between these polarities of black and white like Latinos, Asian Americans and the rest. Dialogues of whiteness and blackness in which these stark polarities – widely acknowledged to belie the complexity of the racial landscape and the identities of which it is composed – are mutually constituted out of political necessity in an interpersonal dynamic.

Mapping the spatial aspects of everyday life for whites in countries like Britain, Canada and the US would produce some stark data on the racial grammar of these societies. Plotting who occupies which places and on what terms would offer graphic illustration of white domination, of the social relationships and circumstances texturing whiteness.

The mechanisms of empire and beyond

That empire is somehow a part of the making of European whiteness is a well-worn claim. *Exactly* how empire works in the making of whiteness has not been much considered. Empire is assumed to be the crucible of British whiteness, its defining moment, in cultural studies and in critical white studies. In this section we will take a closer look at some of these claims to see what they involve and whether they are sustained. Cultural studies[5] has done a good job – at the level of representation and popular culture – of explaining how versions of the experience of those few who lived and worked in the empire reverberated through the lives of the many back at home. What did we learn from their accounts of the popularisation of empire?

The domestication of empire thesis in which the 'intricate filaments among imperialism, domesticity and money' form a nexus of empire, domestic space and market (McClintock, 1995: 16) invokes multiple, but loosely specified, connections between Britain and Empire. Domesticity and commodity racism operated in the Pears' soap connection of cleanliness and the white man's burden in the civilising mission (McClintock, 1995: 31–2). The argument here is that commodities commonly used in Britain carried a vocabulary of racialised images, which operated in race making (although this term isn't used), in making whiteness in some broader sense a part of empire. Goswami (1996) pursues a similar argument using the image vocabulary of Indian monuments. She writes of the popularisation of empire in the 'mutiny tours' of India and the monumentalisation of sites of rebellions overcome by the forces of empire. Here popularisation, and the vocabulary of images in which it is achieved, acts as a conduit for race making, as the history of empire is 'narrated as the biography of the English race.' (Goswami, 1996: 58). Dyer offers a different vocabulary of images. Versions of whiteness, which he doesn't separate from each other, reverberate with empire. Historically, argues Dyer (1997: 18–19), whiteness is made through expansiveness and political effectivity: enterprise, 'spirit' and 'will' (Dyer, 1997: 30–33) manifest in the conquest and control of space by white European men. Culturally significant images of white masculinity, depicted in the western movies, pushed the frontier westward across America. This is a carefully selected set of images – as in all stories about representation – and quite different from Lesy's (1973) *Wisconsin Death Trip*, which depicts the precariousness of life and immanent death and chaotic nature of the western front as also being about the lives of women and children.

As accounts of the popularisation of empire at home through a vocabulary of images, these accounts make reasonable claims. Their implied claims to have grasped the mechanisms of race making, however, are not sustained by the type of analysis they provide which is about imagery and representation. Rutherford (1997: 8) claims 'Imperialism was a central element in the making of modern Englishness'; Goswami (1996: 55) insists that empire contains the 'generative conditions of "Englishness" as a world-historical identity'. Even if they are right, and this claim too, I think, is exaggerated, then their arguments have not adequately shown the *mechanisms of white British race making*. Images and popular thinking are doubtless important facets of whiteness. But these accounts omit the more material aspects of the manufacture of race as whiteness I refer to in the introduction of this volume. The domestication and popularisation of empire has formed the broad and uncertain nexus of race making; a connection often implied rather than explicitly made. Exactly how does British/English whiteness reverberate with empire?

There are other problems too. The framing of race in representation arguments, in which the wide appeal of the experiences of a minority of empire functionaries had to be explained in the making of whiteness for the masses, overlooked something rather more narrowly defined and obvious. Ordinary, and not so ordinary, British people lived and worked in the empire: their daily lives forming part of its fabric. How did this work? What parts of this experience formed who they were, and how they operated in the world? And what was the impact of this on Britain? Another problem with these accounts is the assumption that the historical conditions of the production of whiteness are somehow still present or relevant to today. 'Yet the ways in which white people were once racially talked about still inform the ways we are now imagined ... not least because the cultural production of the past few centuries still provides much of the image vocabulary of the present' (Dyer, 1997: 18). I am questioning how a *vocabulary of images* makes *race past or present*, and I am questioning the linkages that are made, in the vaguest of terms, between the past and the present manufacture of whiteness. Said (1994: 1) puts it better, despite offering admittedly a rather general connection between past and present:

What animates such appeals is not only disagreement about what happened in the past and what the past was, but uncertainty about whether the past really is the past, over and concluded, or whether it continues, albeit in different forms, perhaps.

'Perhaps'! If the past lives on in the present – and this is a perfectly reasonable argument – it most certainly does so in *new* social forms. How could it possibly live in the same forms? Old forms of subjugation are inevitably substituted for new: the political landscapes on which they operate have radically changed. A present of racial subjugation inevitably irritates its past. But they *are new* forms of subjugation, and will have newly formulated connections to the past. We should be able to say what these new forms might be, and what their connection to the past consists of.

What would a less evocative and vague analysis of empire and its connection with the making of contemporary whiteness look like? First this question needs to be posed in specific terms. There is no whiteness in general but only specific – if connected – forms. Although few would actually disagree with this statement, Dyer's *White* does rather conflate what needs to be distinguished and explored. I want to focus on British whiteness, and the nexus of settler nationalisms with which it is, through the *mechanisms* of empire and post imperial landscape, connected. This begs at least two big questions. What do I mean by Britishness? And what do I mean by empire, if not the grammar of images and popular representations that cultural studies analysts have offered?

Britishness is as problematic and unstable a concept as whiteness. Colley (1992: ix) details the making of Britishness between 1707 and 1837 as a 'surprisingly rapid and always partial invention' built around various 'incitements': 'Protestantism, empire, recurrent, successful wars, and a complacent sense of superior constitutional freedoms ...' (Colley, 1992: xi). She attributes this invention of Britishness on the one hand, with mass allegiance and on the other to the succession of wars between Britain and France. But whatever the cause, it is significant that she traces some of the ways in which Britishness had a meaning in the lives of ordinary people. Significantly she says that:

> The evolution of Britishness as I understand it cannot, in fact be understood without reference to both European and world history...the British are not an insular people in the conventional sense – far from it. For most of their early modern and modern history, they have had more contact with more parts of the world than almost any other nation – it is just that this contact has regularly taken the form of aggressive military and commercial enterprise ... this is a culture that is used to fighting and has largely defined itself through fighting ... (Colley, 1992: 9)

She concludes hopefully that: 'if Britishness survives (and it may not), it will in the future find a more pragmatic and more generous form' (Colley, 1992: 9). I hope that this optimistic assessment can be realised. It will hopefully take a more openly multiracial form, which extends beyond formal incorporation of those with migrant biographies through the technicalities of citizenship.

Colley also makes two other very important points about Britishness. Even the white British are not insular – although this worldliness has taken unacceptable aggressive forms in the conquest and control of other people's space – and this is, perhaps, one of the only positive outcomes of empire. Part of being British – then and now – may be precisely this preparedness to pick up and live other lives in other places although admittedly on restricted terms. Second, Colley lists empire among other incitements to Britishness thereby implicitly challenging its place as a defining moment in the making of whiteness. This usurps the claims of cultural studies accounts, which are almost unanimous in their view that empire occupies a privileged place in race making activities producing whiteness. My own position lies closer to Colley's than cultural studies versions of empire. Empire is a highly significant mechanism in the making of white Britishness, but it is less a defining moment than part of a series of processes in which the construction of post imperial landscapes were at least as important as mechanisms making whiteness. I have elsewhere argued (Knowles, 1999) that in looking to empire for the roots of racism we need to understand that, in certain cases and particularly India, the terms of decolonisation did at least as much damage as 200 years of empire. In other words the terms and political forms of decolonisation contained their own versions of black/white superiority/inferiority. The form in which India was awarded independence, for example, underscored its second-class status as a chaotic, conflict ridden and highly divided nation (Knowles, 1992). Not just empire, but the resolution of empire, significantly shaped the post war global political landscape.

Empire and ex-empire nation states form a critical complex in which whiteness is made in ways that display some of its mechanisms. Not a cultural or symbolic connection; but a political one. British, American, Canadian and, Australian versions of whiteness are forged in the crucible of empire, and post-imperial arrangements in which these nations marched off in different directions and *made their own versions of whiteness* in some kind of relationship to empire, but not in a way that was reducible to it. It is this nexus that the version of empire I advance explores. Empire then, is not a vocabulary of images: it may also be this, but it is much more. Empire, and what replaced it, is a political landscape with a series of significant connections, which played a part in the making of white Britishness. Rather than a vocabulary of images, I prefer to think of empire as composing forms of travel and sojourn, rhythms of movement of bodies in space, in particular spaces in fact; as being about the texture of lives lived in different places, lives composed of routines and social practices and forms of local and distant social relationships; ways of being a person with forms of consciousness and subjectivity and performance. This doesn't dismiss the significance of imagery, but retains it as *one* among many other social processes. There are many processes and mechanisms working within the large mechanism of empire and the political forms to which it gave rise. What remains of this chapter discusses some of these processes and mechanisms, and then turns to cut the forms of consciousness and subjectivity underwriting empire and the white settler nationalisms to which empire gave way. White Britishness then, spawned other, connected, forms of whiteness.

Three sets of race making mechanisms were at work in making whiteness in empire and post empire situations. These mechanisms concern the social distinctions composing empire; bodies, effort and will; and citizenship. Empire and after were historically significant in the making of whiteness, but not a watershed or defining moment, but rather part of an ongoing set of processes with specifiable relationships with the present.

Empire's social distinctions

We want to know what part empire played in the fashioning of human fabric, the production of racialised (white) subjectivities and social relationships. In contradiction to the popularisation of empire thesis, Bonnett points out that the whiteness of the imperial race – the human fabric of empire – was far from assured. Below the surface of empire were serious questions concerning the social boundaries and distinctions marshalled around whiteness. Whiteness was made in the empire through the modality of class (hinted at above), and in the dialogues between empire and home, which are not *just* about the domestication and popularisation of empire. Nineteenth century versions of whiteness were construed around their extraordinary claims to superiority: a 'fabulously exceptional human type' (Bonnett, 2000: 38) noted earlier. These claims on behalf of whiteness were themselves part of the development of racial categorisation, as a practical strategy of colonial governance. The categories 'white' and 'European' were employed in the sixteenth century to legally and economically structure colonial and settler societies in South and Central America, and in North America from the seventeenth century (Bonnett, 1998: 319). Racial distinctions between coloniser and colonised rebounded on the coloniser in the colonial context, reifying racial distinctions which were then applied to the British at home in the context of some of the dialogues between Britain and empire. As the production of whiteness in the empire rebounded on domestic racial configuration in Britain, Bonnett (1998: 316–18) claims that the Miles and Phizacklea[6] type of idea that the white British working class was an unproblematic category is unfounded; arguing that while the British working class was white in colonial settings it was: 'sometimes less than, or other to, white in the context of Britain's internal social hierarchy … most whites, at least within Britain, were unworthy of whiteness'. The working class in the nineteenth century was marginal to whiteness: yet later came to actively employ it 'as if it was significant – or, indeed, central – to their own sense of self, nation and community' (Bonnett, 1998: 316).

The historical/political circumstances of this process of *becoming* white, are hence flagged as highly significant, but not really documented. It is not clear exactly what the race making processes Bonnett refers to actually are? Bonnett ties this shift in the racialisation of the white British working class with the development of welfare capitalism, which they were incorporated into as the projects of the nation and its empire: a big theory connection. He explains *why* they became white, in a hasty retreat from social to economic processes, but not *how*. Bonnett offers the view that the meaning of whiteness shifted to accommodate this connection from extraordinariness to ordinariness; and this fits snugly with the domestication of empire thesis as another big theory connection. The micro-elements of the making of British whiteness at home out of the 'ordinary person' are not tackled. Bonnett (1998: 322) does, however, raise the connection between whiteness and rural environment, affirming the position of the English countryside as the authentic place of racial production. The urban milieu, on the other hand, is the locale of immigrant Irish and Jewish labour; people whose whiteness was placed in question (Bonnett, 1998: 327). The urban landscape of the English city was the site of racial degeneration, just as the countryside was a site of authentic and healthy racial production.

While I doubt Bonnett's thesis that the new politics of whiteness was the product of welfare rights, I agree that whiteness is a problematic, dynamic and multiply constituted category, and I further suggest that its meaning and forms of inclusion/exclusion travelled between Britain and the empire in a dialogue of 'making'. What Bonnett offers, is an account of the instability of whiteness: a claim that stops short of empirical demonstration, and which pins its production on the contours of grand theory, instead of a close up examination of the actual social processes involved.

Empire's bodies, work and effort

One of the ways in which whiteness is made through empire, it seems to me, concerns the deployment of white human labour and its relationship with non-white human labour. Dyer argues that will and effort are integral to the making of whiteness: and what is it that will is exercised over? Others whose will is, by definition, less potent, and over the environment and the other conditions in which conquest is possible. An interesting take on the relationship between white bodies and effort, surfaced in tropical medicine. 'There is no mistaking tropical medicine as part of the military and colonial enterprise' (Bashford, 2000: 252). If black bodies were environmentally honed to operate, though ineffectively as the argument goes, in tropical climates, then how would white ones fare in the same circumstances? There was extensive research on the British in India, which became the paradigmatic colonial situation in the management of living in hot climates. 'The tropics' itself is an idea that stands for hot spaces and also colonial spaces, where 'white man' does not quite fit, but over which white man and white culture desires control' (Bashford, 2000: 253). Serious questions were raised over the permanent operation of white people in hot colonial spaces. In India this was managed by two mechanisms; the annual migration into the hill stations of the Himalayas in the hottest parts of the year; and through the *indirect* manner in which will and effort, conquest and control were managed. Whiteness as the exertion of effort was mediated through the directed physical exertion of Indians, activities the colonial class *supervised,* but did not themselves *perform.*

The obverse was the case in white settler societies where white bodies provided the effort and will themselves. The interface between environment and white effort took a quite different turn in the case of tropical Northern Australia, where aboriginal settlement was displaced rather than enslaved in the colonial project, and the white British (working class) provided the bodies necessary to exert the physical effort involved in white settlement. Bashford (2000: 250) details the measurements anxiously taken of white bodies labouring in the Australian tropics, heart rate, excretions and the rest. He describes how tropical medicine became a vocabulary, not of images this time but, of *modern citizenship* in its biological processing of the effort and will sustained as part of the making of whiteness. 'Is white Australia possible?' became a political question to be addressed by measuring the effort of which white people were capable, using the tools provided by tropical medicine, in the early years of the twentieth century. This repeated the environmentalist concerns applied to North America in terms of favouring whites over non-whites as nation building material. Only in Australia did the arguments about race and environment have to be reversed. The viability of white settlement in tropical Australia involved the investigation of the physical constitution of white, working class men, who, unlike in other tropical spaces, provided the effort on which prosperity was to be built (Bashford, 2000: 260–62). This was no class of colonial overseers. In Cilento's (cited in Bashford, 2000: 263) calculation, whiteness adapted to manual labour in the tropics was lightly misceginated – 97 per cent British, 2 per cent foreign white and 0.8 per cent coloured (and 0.2 per cent missing). The routines stipulated for women in settler colonies – clearly the object of eugenic concern in the first quarter of the twentieth century – were highly regulatory in their intent, and centred on the conduct of daily life and its routines of strenuous effort. The flexibility accorded to whiteness in operating in unfamiliar climates and environments was not extended to non-whites as the history of immigration to the white settler colonies of North America shows.

Empire's citizens

Arguments about the fit between racial biology – indexed in labouring bodies – and environment were often wheeled out in defence of the white project in Australia and in Canada. Because these are issues of nation building we will continue this discussion under the heading of citizenship, which is one of the *political mechanisms* operating in the making of whiteness. What is interesting about the white Australia and the white Canada policies is that both made the body/environment connection in opposite ways. Canada, anxious to maintain its status in the Commonwealth as a white country prioritised white

European migration as the appropriate material for providing the human fabric of nation-building. Ward's (1990) *White Canada for Ever*, a study of anti-orientalism in British Columbia, from the mid-nineteenth to the mid-twentieth century, shows how Asians were only considered suitable to operate as indentured labour used to build the Canadian Pacific railway. They were not suited to Canadian citizenship, which they were systematically denied. The 1884 Royal Commission on Chinese Immigration begins the move towards alien exclusion through formal immigration restriction (Ward, 1990: 38). Canadian nation building material, at least as it was articulated in the Federal Parliamentary debates of the 1920s, originated in the cold climates of Northern Europe and the capacity to turn 'empty' land into agricultural produce. The farm, racialised through particular versions of whiteness – white people – as the agent of transformation through agricultural enterprise, was the moral centre of Canadian life, and at the heart of the nation-building project. White skin and cold climates: vigorous people and harsh cold Northern environments tamed by the exertion of effort in pursuit of cultivation, were ideally suited to each other.

The Canadian and Australian examples show that whiteness is made in the making of nation states in the decolonisation process, as much as in the making of empire (Knowles, 1999). The earlier exits to nationhood from empire came from the white settler nations. The British North America Act (1867) established the dominion of Canada – America seized independence in the war of independence – but India had to wait until 1947. This indicates some of the highly racialised contours of decolonisation, which were steeped in political debates about the potential capacities of people for citizenship. Whiteness itself, in the racial hierarchies and classifications of the time, operated as the visible demonstration of racial capacity, despite its instability and its contested boundaries and meaning. This rationale for independence was sustained in the various nation-building processes. America, Australia and Canada attended to this in their different ways through immigration restriction: a set of processes requiring the demarcation of whiteness from non-whiteness, of nation building material from the rest. The building of white populations through selective immigration – policies that were only formally abandoned in the 1960s – structured immigration policy in all three nations. Arguments leaning on the biology of white race-ness were pursued through concerns with raced bodies and environment as in the case of Australian tropical medicine referred to earlier.

The US offers an example of the strategic operation of whiteness in this context too, and in the process shows some of the difficulties involved in sustaining versions of whiteness through immigration policies. As Roediger (1994: 182) points out, the 'legal and social history of immigration turned on the question "who was white" ...'. And deciding who was white, as in the problem of the maintenance of segregation, was no simple matter. The Naturalisation Act of 1790 allowed to be admitted to American citizenship 'any alien being a free white person' (Braman, 1999: 1401). Only in 1870 was this extended to include those of African nativity and descent. Definitions of whiteness embedded in the Naturalisation Act, were tested by Ozawa, a Japanese immigrant resident in Haiti. Tapping into anti-Chinese sentiment and distinguishing him through his *Japanese* origins, his counsel argued a combination of popular and biological versions of whiteness, but lost the case. The court decreed that whiteness was not just a matter of skin but popular knowledge and assessment of racial status. Ozawa was Mongolic – yellow – not white (Braman, 1999: 1402–3). Courts defining whiteness in this case operated social distinctions derived by a reading of the popular imaginary. In practice the popular imaginary must have been at least as varied as the boundaries drawn in each state referred to earlier, and yet was wielded as authoritative enough to be the basis of legal definition. Roediger's (1994: 190) account of American race making supports this account of juridical intervention. His 'not yet' and 'not quite' ethnics – Irish, Italians, Greeks, Jews and Poles – *became* white in a particular alchemy of social and political circumstances.

Consciousness and subjectivities

What claims of the significance of empire in the making of whiteness imply, but never set out and confront head on, is the implicit smug superiority of white British people themselves. This sense of superiority is wielded over non-whites, but also over other whites – the Canadians, Americans, New Zealanders and Australians – to whom we feel, in different ways, superior. The internalisation of British (and French) superiority is discreetly embedded in many facets of Canadian life; and in Australia this is called the 'cultural cringe' (Dalziell, 1999: 22). Consciousness is a way of discussing this sense of superiority, often used as a link between past and present, which is a continuation of our discussion of empire and an aspect of subjectivity, the focus of Chapter 1. Specifically we can think about consciousness as a part of subjectivity, as distinct but not separate from, other more embodied and performance aspects of subjectivity. Consciousness here means a consciousness of self: it is what lies beneath the grammar of everyday life, surfacing in a narrative of self, but a chaotic, disorganised narrative, not the sort told in biographical/autobiographical accounts of the self. It is this consciousness of self that articulates, selects and processes versions of the self: the idea of a continuous narrative of self-reflexivity composing the core of human being. But consciousness is also beneath and beyond narrative; manifest in practical action along with the habitual. What I want to discuss here, briefly, are some of the interior aspects of subjectivity, which cohere around whiteness and which are raised by Fanon's critical, psychoanalytic approach to colonial dynamics which was, of course, applied to the making of black subjectivities.

Fanon (1986: 97) probes the 'inner relationship between consciousness and the social context'. The making of blackness in the social context of colonialism – note the significant interface here between consciousness and political context – produced dependency and inferiority. Fanon's position on this is well known. In the colonial encounter new forms of uncertainty are created. Speaking of the Malagasy 'he has been led to ask himself whether he is, indeed, a man, it is because his reality as a man has been challenged' (1986: 97). But it is not the making of black colonial subjectivities that we are here concerned with, but white ones. Fanon, of course, points us to the other side of the colonial dialogue. The generation of inferiority arises in the dialogues with a European sense of superiority:

> The feeling of inferiority of the colonised is the correlative of the European's feeling of superiority. ... It is the racist who creates his inferior. ... It is [quoting Satre] the anti-semite who *makes* the Jew ... (Fanon, 1986: 93).

White senses of superiority, then, are not entirely separate from the inferiority of which Fanon writes. We might think of it, in the light of the accounts of subjectivity aired in Chapter 1 as part of a dialogue, as part of the interface between people, and between people and the mechanisms through which they are dealt with. But to claim that the anti-semite *makes* the Jew, is to deny the Jew her sense of agency, her existential version of the self with which she processes the mechanisms dealing with her. Back to the grey zone, in which the negotiations about who we are in racial terms occur in specific transactions, and on the vicissitudes of political landscapes.

Barthes, in *Mythologies* (Sandoval, 1997: 86), attempts to untangle the interior superiority-consciousness of the privileged. He provides an inventory of the psychosocial forms around which consciousness 'becomes constituted as "white", middle class, and above all else supremacist... a rhetoric of supremacy' (Sandoval, 1997: 86). Like Fanon, Barthes attempts to unpick racialised consciousness into what he calls its (constituent) poses: the equivalent of Fanon's masks. In summary these racial poses composing white consciousness are as follows. Western identity secures itself against invasion by difference. In estrangement from cultural context there is an evasion of responsibility for the way things are. All difference is equated with the self thus avoiding the abyss of absolute difference through identification. There are various ways of legitimating what is; a guise of neutrality; and ways of asserting the colonial version of reality as fact (Sandoval, 1997: 89–96).

Barthes has, I think made a start in identifying some of the tactics of colonial human agency and its present legacy. This goes well beyond consciousness, and appropriately so. These are political matters too. There is also the question of the composition of the colonial unconscious, which we have not even discussed. Barthes' project was the unravelling of white racialised consciousness: its transformation into something else, new ways of being human, beyond supremacy. While Barthes notes that these consciousness forms are white, he believes them to be a social location, which can be occupied by any form of social agency: they are masquerades of identity (Sandoval, 1997: 96). Ultimately, in the Barthian scheme of things, the masks are forms of colonial, middle class, consumption and production: so that the real self is profoundly alienated; socially corrupted and imprisoned within the social structures defining it.

While this is problematic as an account of subjectivities, it is an attempt to unpick the substance and production of a warped subjectivity; and Barthes does propose a method for disclosing the rhetoric of middle class white western consciousness. The rhetoric of colonising consciousness and its forms of speech fasten those who are different to an, 'effigy of themselves' (Sandoval, 1997: 97) and in the process *enslaves the coloniser* too. As Sandoval (1997: 98) points, out this opens up the question of the re-composition of the self as an ongoing process of mutation, something that needs new psychic terrain. 'The categories by which the human becomes human must be reformed' (Sandoval, 1997: 100).

Both Fanon and Barthes, because Fanon too was interested in the racial consciousness of the coloniser, 'agitate these categories by revealing them as constructs of the white imaginary, as a set of mythologies ...' (Sandoval, 1997: 102): theirs is an exposé of the 'rhetorics of being'. This work draws attention to 'the permeable boundary between psyche and the rhetoric of dominant citizenship ... between coloured skins and figurations of "white masks",' (Sandoval, 1997: 103). It is through this 'vulnerable borderland' that we find the 'ability to tell another story' (Sandoval, 1997: 103). And tell another story we must, for this one is profoundly antithetical to a modern spirit of human equality. This is easily addressed legislatively and at the level of public pronouncements. It is less easily addressed in the way people *feel* deep down inside themselves.

Concluding comments

Whiteness is a concept activated through the social practices and thinking of white people. In this chapter I have identified what some of these social practices and forms of consciousness are. I have identified some of the social processes that operate as conductors of whiteness, past and present. I have looked at political landscape, the drawing of boundaries, everyday life and performance. Paying particular attention to the production of the present, I have carefully examined the mechanisms composing the British empire, as made by the effort of labouring bodies, journeys and lives (Chapter 5) and the calculation of citizenship. I have presented whiteness as a nexus of local and transcendent meaning, a racial category dissected by ethnicity and nation, and held together in motion around the British Empire. Obviously I have only discussed a segment of whiteness. But in this analysis, empire is at least a series of social processes to be investigated and understood in material detail, and not just a mass of representations with a grammar of images. I have shown that through the nexus of empire, related forms of whiteness are made through definite social practices. Through this approach some of the mechanisms composing racial categories come to the fore. Using Fanon, I have considered the dynamic of consciousness between coloniser and colonised: between senses of superiority and inferiority and the continuation of these things in white British appraisal of foreigners including other whites in ex-empire nations. There is a strong suspicion, from a number of quarters, that this persists in the present making of whiteness. What is it that makes this part of the present? It couldn't just hang around like a bad smell left over from empire.

Barthes' assessment of what he calls western whiteness, that it secures itself against invasion, that it avoids the abyss of absolute difference, and that it evades responsibility for the way things are, points to something most significant that has a bearing on these issues. Political landscapes are very important in the making of whiteness, as we have noted a number of times. Multi-racial Britain provides a political landscape in which the conditions that Barthes points to, in fact operate. We most certainly secure ourselves against invasion, avoid the abyss of absolute difference and responsibility for the way things are. These are the political conditions in which we reinvent and sustain our sense of superiority, giving it new forms and new political salience. It is this that sustains the significance of empire in the present. Whiteness is made problematic in this regard. White people, as the social and political agency of whiteness, are problematic in this context. The interface between white people and the regimes that allow us to feel justified in our sense of superiority and ways of dealing with the racialised other, to be white in the ways in which we are, are deeply problematic. The regimes in which whiteness is able to operate as a badge of privilege are problematic. The people who accept these privileges need to think about them more critically, and campaign for their ending. The fact that whiteness is made through our own racism is problematic. It is necessary for us to make sure that this racism sustaining our whiteness, ends. If these things are attended to then the performances of whiteness, dress, manners, habits and the rest become inconsequential. The racial geographies of our towns and cities can be taken on as targets for political action for they are part of racism, and the global grammar of race can, with enormous effort, be taken on as a political target. Here we begin to see a particular aspect of the racial grammar we have centred on, difficult questions of culpability surrounding the making of whiteness. The need to make amends, not just for the past, but for the present. Is whiteness capable of being more open, of turning its empire experience into a form of cosmopolitanism based on principles of human equality that involve relinquishing the privileges accruing to whiteness? What are the prospects for re-making white subjectivities and regimes in more open and inclusive terms, which do not inevitably invoke current and past fault lines of racialised privilege and disadvantage? We have seen that whiteness is an unstable category. Perhaps it is possible to popularise the thinking behind critical white studies? There is hope. But it will take political will to unwind whiteness and make it a suitable partner for multi-racial co-existence.

Summary

- Whiteness is made in the operation of people in space: in the racial geometries of globalisation, in comportment, dress and habits, in forms of consciousness, in social relationships and in political contexts supporting racial inequalities. These are some of the social mechanisms making whiteness.
- Race making – and the production of whiteness is only one kind of race making – is a collaborative activity involving dialogue between those who are included as well as those who are excluded by forms of racial classification. Race and ethnicity are always negotiated in specific political contexts.
- Claims that empire is significant in making white Britishness need closer scrutiny in order to establish the contemporary significance of empire in making whiteness.

Critical whiteness: This is a matter of making a political stand. Critical whiteness means challenging the privileges accruing to whiteness, and seeing it as a set of racially located positions among others, and not as a 'norm'.

Notes

1. The discussion throughout this volume of racial grammar conveys what I mean by a sense of racialised power. This is a blend of Foucauldian notions of power as disciplinary networks but with a more effective sense of human agency as in Goffman's work.

2. Micro/macro distinctions as I said in the Introduction are not particularly helpful because they are always connected. I use this term merely as a shorthand way of referring to differences in scale and not to imply that these are firm conceptual distinctions.

3. It is difficult to know whether this was a more settled racial past or whether Hale simply describes it as such in order to mark the contrast of what she wants to think of as a later age of heightened mobility.

4. I refer to this and other works on whiteness as cultural analysis because it is focused on images, which are very important, but neglect to examine schools, jobs etc. Cultural studies or cultural analysis also alights on a commodity approach to whiteness (Nightingale, 1999: 146). But they do challenge the totally political versions of whiteness of Omi and Winant by insisting that we take culture into account. They are quite right to insist on this, my key objection is that they often do only this, and hence become over reliant on commodities and vocabularies of images to make the argument at the expense of a more materialist approach of the sort I propose.

5. Rutherford's (1997) *Forever England* draws some of the contours connecting masculinity and empire in an interesting way, situating empire as a central element in the making of Englishness. In the process he makes the point that dealing with Englishness in this way disavows 'our troubles preoccupation with our origins' (Rutherford, 1997: 6). McClintock (1995) is another very useful cultural studies account of empire, which stresses the popularisation and domestication of empire thesis through commodities.

6. Bonnett's reference to the Miles and Phizacklea kind of argument on the whiteness of the working class is exemplified in their (1979) *Racism and Political Action in Britain*, to which I was a contributor. The basic thrust of this kind of argument was to situate racism in working class institutions as a way of explaining the rise of ultra right-wing political parties and racist actions and policies among the trade unions and in the Labour Party. Whiteness was treated as unproblematic and unfractured, except by class.

Concluding Comments

This is a beginning rather than an end. *Race and Social Analysis* gathers some conceptual tools for thinking about how the world works in racial and ethnic terms. A set of tools that reach beneath the surface and beyond the way things seem; and make connections between big and small circumstances, that can look up close and into the distance. A set of tools that can be used to make sense of what goes on outside of your window and on the buses of Los Angeles and, of course, the other places where race matters. It offers ways of thinking about why race matters, where it comes from, how it is made. If we return now to the beginning of our journey, to Southampton and to Los Angeles, there are many things we would want to know. We would want to know about how race is made and maintained in each of these places, and about the connections between them. We would want to know about the circumstances bringing asylum seekers to Southampton, and Hispanic and Chinese people to California. We would want to know about the edifice of entitlements, exclusions and other conditions that make the woman in the short skirt, who travels by bus, white, and the others Hispanic or Chinese. We would want to know the mechanisms connecting these people to these places, and the pathways they tread in forming these connections. Global migrations and the multiracial societies they produce are socially, politically and biographically made; they are simultaneously micro/macro matters, and we would want to know about the mechanisms by which they work.

Materialism

The analytical tools discussed in this volume are used in a way that supports a materialist analysis, although they are not always used in this way in other places, where many of them operate in more abstract accounts. By material-ist I simply mean an analysis that sustains examination of concrete social practices, of forms of social interaction, of the production of the social and political landscapes of which we are a part, of bodies in motion, in space.

I have taken a fragmented and pragmatic stance that stressed the importance of connections between the social world and our means of thinking about and analysing it. This is a materialism that disrupts the analytical primacy of representation and the love affair with discourse and narrative as ways of knowing the world that are not sufficiently grounded in social practices and action. It doesn't dismiss narrative, discourse and representation but looks at the practical outcomes of these things. This text is also an attempt to reinstate the physical and the visceral into social analysis, into the analysis of race. Social analysis, as I said at the beginning, is about lives and deaths; about the ways in which we live and the manner in which we die. This book is a modest attempt to think about the operation of race and ethnicity in the organisation of lives and deaths and their spatial contexts.

What is race? What is ethnicity?

This is a good point to return to fundamental questions flagged in the beginning. What is race? What is ethnicity? Throughout this volume the reader will have seen all sorts of circumstances in which the intersections between race and ethnicity are apparent. As I pointed out earlier, these concepts often operate in tandem and yet they are not the same, they have different intellectual and political histories, but they can have similarly dramatic consequences in shaping lives and deaths. Throughout this volume you, the reader, have been confronted with pragmatic, situational, answers to these questions about the nature of race and ethnicity. You have been shown how these concepts with such dramatic consequences work in particular circumstances and locations and in particular lives. The answer to these questions always needs to be investigated in the circumstances of operation. The things race and ethnicity share, as general characteristics, are that they are *compositional, positional and personal*. By compositional I of course mean that they are made or produced in a given set of circumstances. By positional I mean that race and ethnicity act as social locators, positioning people among others, and that they work in tandem with other factors that also act to position, factors like biography, fragments of class, gender, the ways in which people interface with social agencies and so on. Politics is also a significant aspect of position that interfaces with the social positioning elements just listed. The politics of race and ethnicity in any particular time and place are highly important in race and ethnicity making. The personal has been extensively covered in this volume, and this is about the ways in which race and ethnicity operate in individual lives. These three factors, the compositional, the positional and the personal are most significant in shaping race and ethnicity and are discussed in more detail below.

Race and ethnicity making – composition

This book is centrally concerned with the social mechanisms and processes of race making, with the production of race (and ethnicity) as a set of spatially located, people centred activities. This deconstructionist approach, in which race making mechanisms are identified, provides us with what I have been calling racial grammar. This is the underlying web of social practices to which race gives rise. Race and ethnicity are the sum of their compositional mechanisms and the social effects to which they give rise. They take quite different forms and are (micro) contextually specific. They can be mapped, as I have suggested, as constellations of social practices and other mechanisms. Many of these compositional elements, from people's reactions to the drawing of political landscapes, are things that we refer to as racism. Indeed, as I have suggested throughout, racism is a key compositional element in race making. Racism is embedded in our minds and in the details of our social and political landscapes. We see these processes at work, for instance, in the discussion of migrant arrival, in the race maps of urban occupation and territory. Because of its routine everyday character, racism can only be identified by paying attention to the details of race composition. Other compositional elements of race, take for example comportment, corporeality, consciousness, the ethnic aesthetics of space, notions of white British entitlement, co-operate with the compositional mechanisms of race that we associate with racism. Neither works without the other. One provides the substance for the other to operate. As we saw in the chapters on people and auto/biography, on space, globalisation and migration, these micro-compositional elements making race are as personal as they are about large-scale transnational processes. As I said at the outset the micro mechanisms of race operate in the deep texture of our subjectivity, in who we are as people, and in the regimes – from the small-scale organisational to national and global political landscapes – with which are lives are bound up. To understand racial grammar, then, we need to be able to think about its compositional mechanisms at all levels of magnitude.

The Positional

The positional is as important as the compositional in my analysis. Position works in a number of ways in the analysis. It is a way of establishing the core units, in people terms, contextually invoked by the concepts race and ethnicity, and of establishing significant social differences between these units. These will bear a resemblance to categories of public recognition – who counts as British Jamaican, Vietnamese and so on – but categories of public recognition are blunt and insensitive instruments. They obscure the finer kinds of social distinctions we need to make between racial and ethnic categories. Position acknowledges the social production of racial and ethnic categories in a way that takes account of, acknowledges and maps, their mechanisms of production. This approach draws fine social distinctions between and within groups, distinctions that account for, but which are not solely dependant on, identities. This volume suggests a number of axes of mapping from the character and directions of global movement, to the tenor and content of a multitude of social and bureaucratic relationships within a given locale. Regimes are good at making racial and ethnic distinction in subtle, and not so subtle, ways that can be mapped and which better reflect the social distinctions to which race gives rise than approaches reliant on identities and categories of public recognition. The approach I suggest places race (and ethnicity) as one of a range of social distinctions, AND as the outcome of social distinctions and differences. This does not remove race as an axis of difference by collapsing it into bigger social maps, rather it underscores its ubiquity and its centrality in understanding the social morphology of our time. Race in other words is made from all manner and arrangement of social distinctions. And this works for forms of whiteness, just as for non-white forms of ethnicity.

Other aspects of positionality in the treatment of race in this volume include more obviously spatial aspects of the analysis. Position, of course, is a spatial concept. We saw in relation to global migration and city residence that we need to understand race and ethnicity distributively, in space. Plotting who moves from one place to another, who lives or operates where in geographical terms, will provide sophisticated and detailed distinctions not made by other means. The relationship between these things and other positionally derived distinctions will, of course, provide additional information on the texture of the racial fabric in any given place.

Between the compositional and the positional we can develop detailed versions of race and ethnicity that go beyond skin and other physical markers, and which go beyond the blunt categories of public recognition and the political categories collapsed together as black and white. We should be able to trace and identify some fine social distinctions and constellations of social differences which have a practical, material, force in people's lives, and which are highly sensitive to macro and micro geographical and social contexts. This takes us beyond the mantra of race and ethnicity as social categories, to an understanding of how those social categories are produced and some of the differences that operate within them.

The personal

The third element in this conceptual schema – the compositional and the positional being the first two – is the personal. This involves recognition that people, volition, auto/biography and the existential are highly significant elements in race making. Of course the personal is also an aspect of composition and position, but worth mentioning in its own right in order to draw attention to its significance. Of particular significance is the relationship between the people and regimes, whether at the level of small scale local, municipal, organisations or the nation state. These are the interfaces of race in action, and again what we call racism is highly significant here. Understanding these interfaces requires a detailed drawing of biographies and close attention to the micro/macro operation of regimes: a grasp of the dialogues of mutual composition in which regimes and their citizens are made, in racial terms.

Research agendas

This conceptual schema involving the personal, the compositional and the positional, suggests research agendas and approaches for developing our understanding of race making and operation. It is, of course, important to operate circumstantially. Deconstruct regimes into their largest and their smallest units and examine these and all that lies in between. Note the social processes operating at all levels and the connections between levels. Note how regimes operate around individual people. Note how people respond to these circumstances. Map the distribution of people in terms of these social processes. What patterns does it produce? Repeat this mapping geographically. Work locally and globally in establishing personal topographies. Look for patterns. Document the circumstances of movement, the character of arrival and departure. Note the mechanisms of movement. By what means is it achieved? Globally, who goes where, why, and in what circumstances? What is the social character of local/global space? Differentiate types of migration. What are the diasporas of privilege? What are the mechanisms attaching people to space? Map these things and see what patterns, if any, emerge? All of this requires detailed empirical work, working and drawing connections between different levels. If you work with micro processes, check what you find against bigger processes, and look for the connections. If you work on a macro level check your findings against the micro, the personal, the small-scale situation. Note the interface between people and social processes. Place people at the centre of the frame. Check abstraction against social practice and process. Note how people contribute to/disrupt the priorities of regimes. What is the scope here for individual/collective action, volition? Pay attention to whiteness, its composition and positionality. What are its fault lines and how are they made? Pay particular attention to its interface with regimes. Whiteness involves an edifice of unevenly distributed privileges and invisible support.

Beneath this analysis of the very ordinary, banal, nature of race and racism, for as I present it, it is clearly nothing special and part of everything, lie some big, unanswered, questions. We will end by indicating two of them. They are connected. They are the status of race histories in the present, and the related issue of personal and collective culpability. Both of these things are also connected to issues of social transformation, for what is the point of all this detailed mapping if it does not produce targets for transformation of the sort that reduces the significance of race and ethnicity in the mapping of social position, and, ideally, removes/reduces all forms of social differentiation as a basis for social inequality. Detailed maps open the possibility of pragmatic adjustment in the regimes of race, but, because this makes demands on human volition and individual will, it is a complicated set of processes in which there must be a will for change as well as an understanding of what might constitute progressive reform in any particular set of circumstances.

Living with the past

Whether we acknowledge and understand it or not, the present operates as a multitude of pragmatic accommodations with a past that may be unacknowledged. When it comes to our *racial and ethnic* pasts this is a most sensitive point. In a different context, Zizek (1996:74) remarked that humanity lives off its past catastrophes. How we live, honourably, with the past catastrophes of race is a vexed question '...what we fear is our own eternal past' (Zizek, 1996: 74)? How *do* we come to terms with our eternal past of racially organised brutality and face the future? These are not just matters of living with white liberal guilt, but of acknowledging responsibility for the past, a reckoning with the past, as part of an understanding of the present. White Britons have an unresolved relationship to empire, which, like the slave bones in the Quebec cornfield, keeps surfacing in the present when we least want to see it. The same can be said about the American relationship to slavery and segregation, and the Canadian relationship to nation building, slavery and empire. Nations in which white people form the majority have an unmastered relationship to the historical processes producing their whiteness. Is this resolvable? What might resolve it? The past is neither the past in the sense of being over, nor insignificant in the calculations of the present. For the British the present significance of empire is a murky and unresolved issue. But it would not be so difficult, as I suggested in an earlier chapter, to think about its current social forms and practices, to elaborate its current significance. What is the contemporary significance of empire? What would it take to resolve it?

White culpability

Whatever this is lies in the present and plays an important part in resolving the race politics of the past. 'The outcome of the struggle for freedom will determine the meaning of the past itself' (Zizek, 1996: 67). Freedom, in this context, involves both personal and political transformation for, as we have learned, they are part of the same process. It is not just regimes that need to change but the lives and selves composing them. This is bound to be a difficult and painful process, involving as it inevitably will, personal and emotional investment in who and what we are in the world, and squaring forms of political assertion with feelings. White culpability for the past is tied to our responsibility for the way things are in the present. Our subjectivity, our being in the world, is inseparable from its social and political regimes, our very being is always already political whether or not we choose to engage with this fact of our existence directly. Who we are is part of the regimes in which we operate, its racial politics, its forms of categorisation, its meaning, its systems of allocation, of privilege and disadvantage. And, as I have argued, we need to take a closer look at how this works. In doing this we cannot afford a complete collapse into individualism – the Winfrey and McBride biographies show this clearly – we need the constellations resulting from our mapping exercises as a basis for building collective action in the context of personal change. Race making will no longer matter when the political and social landscapes on which they matter are transformed in the lives and thinking and actions of people. White folk have the most to give up and a great deal of the past for which to make amends. But it is not until we acknowledge this and do something about it in practical and material, rather than rhetorical, terms that the present can be transformed and we can begin a reckoning with the past. Black and ethnic minorities have been telling us this for years. It is time we listened and acted.

Bibliography

Ahmed, Feroze (1998) 'Opening Soon', in *Origins: Personal Stories of Crossing the Seas to Settle in Britain*. Bristol: The Kumba Project, pp. 104–6.

Albrow, Martin (1997) 'Travelling Beyond Local Cultures in Socioscapes in a Global City' in, Eade, John (ed.) *Living the Global City*. London: Routledge, pp. 47–70.

Alexander, Claire (2000) *The Asian Gang. Ethnicity, Identity and Masculinity*. Oxford: Berg.

Alexander, Claire (1996) *The Art of Being Black. The Creation of Black British Youth Identities*. Oxford: Clarendon Press.

Alibhai-Brown, Yasmin (1997) *No Place Like Home*. London: Virago.

Amit-Talai, Vered (1996) 'The Minority Circuit: Identity Politics and the Professionalization of Ethnic Activism', in Amit-Talai, Vered and Knowles, Caroline (eds) *Resituating Identities: the Politics of Race, Ethnicity and Culture*. Peterborough: Broadview Press, pp. 89–114.

Anderson, Kay J. (1991) *Vancouver's China Town*. Kingston: McGill-Queens University Press.

Anon, Barton Hill Asian Women's Group (1998), 'First Impressions' in *Origins: Personal Stories of Crossing the Seas to Settle in Britain*. Bristol: The Kumba Project, p. 131.

Annual Reports of the All India Congress Committee (1931–32). Oral History Archives at the Nehru Memorial Library, Delhi.

Anthias, Floya and Yuval-Davis, Nira (1992) *Racialized Boundaries*. London: Routledge.

Back, Les and Solomos, John (2000) (eds) *Theories of Race and Racism*. London: Routledge.

Bales, Kevin (1999) *Disposable People*. Berkeley: University of California Press.

Barber, Benjamin R. (2001) *Jihad vs McWorld*. New York: Ballantine Books.

Barthes, Fredrik (1994) 'Enduring and Emerging Issues in the Analysis of Ethnicity', Vermeulen, Hans and Govers, Cora (eds) *The Anthropology of Ethnicity. Beyond Ethnic Groups and Boundaries*. Amstedam: Het Spinhuis, pp. 11–32.

Barthes, Fredrik (1969) (ed.), *Ethnic Groups and Boundaries*. Oslo: University Press.

Basch, Linda, Glick Schiller, Nina and Szanton Blanc, Christian (1994) *Nations Unbound*. New York: Gordon and Breach.

Bashford, Alison (2000) 'Is White Australia Possible?' Race, Colonialism and Tropical Medicine', *Ethnic and Racial Studies* 23 (2): 248–71.

Bauman, Zygmunt (1999) *Modernity and the Holocaust*. Ithaca, New York: Cornell University Press.

Bauman, Zygmunt (1992) *Intimations of Postmodernity*. London: Routledge.

Bean, Lucy and van Heyningen, Elizabeth (1983) (eds) *The Letters of Jane Elizabeth Waterston 1866–1905*. Cape Town: Van Ribeeck Society.

Belluomo, Nina (1998) 'In Principio', in *Origins: Personal Stories of Crossing the Seas to Settle in Britain*. Bristol: The Kumba Project, p. 39.

Benewick, Robert (1972), *Fascist Movement in Britain*. London: Allen Lane.

Benmayor, Rina and Scotness, Andor (1994) *Migration and Identity*. Oxford: Oxford University Press.

Berger, John and Mohr, Jean (1975) *A Seventh Man*. Harmondsworth: Penguin.

Bertaux, Daniel (1981) 'Introduction' in *Biography and Society*. Berverley Hills: Sage.

Bly, Nellie (1993) *Oprah. Up Close and Down Home*. New York: Zebra Books.

Bhachu, Parminder (1996) 'The Multiple Landscapes of Transnational Asian Women in the Diaspora' in Amit-Talai, Vered and Knowles, Caroline (eds) *Resituating Identities: the Politics of Race, Ethnicity and Culture* Peterborough: Broadview Press, pp. 283–303.

Bonnett, Alistair (2000) 'Whiteness in Crisis', *History Today*, December 2000, pp. 39–40.

Bonnett, Alistair (1998) 'How the British Working Class Became White: The Symbolic (Re)formation of Racialized Capitalism', *Journal Of Historical Sociology*, 11 (3): 316–40.

Bonnett, Alistair (1996) '"White Studies". The Problems and Project of a New Research Agenda', *Theory, Culture and Society* 13 (2): 145–155.

Bowser, Benjamin (1995) (ed.) *Racism and Anti-Racism in World Perspective*. Thousand Oaks: Sage.

Box, Mark (2000) 'Warlords, Priests and the Politics of Ethnic Cleansing: A Case-study from Rural Bosnia Hercegovinia', *Ethnic and Racial Studies, 23:16–36*.

Bracey, Ernest Norton (1999) 'The Legacy of General Daniel "Chappie" James' in Conyers, James L. (ed.) *Black Lives: Essays in African American Biography*. Armonk, New York: M.E. Sharpe.

Brah, Avtar (1996) *Cartographies of Diaspora*. London: Routledge.

Braman (1999) 'Of Race and Immutability', *UCLA Law Review*, 46: 1375–1463.

Breytenbach, Breyten (1991) 'The Long March from Hearth to Home' *Social Research, 58* (1): 69–87.

Burgess, Ernest (1967) 'The Growth of the City: An Introduction to a Research Project', in Park, Robert E., Burgess, Morris and McKenzie, Roderick D. (eds) *The City*. Chicago: University of Chicago Press (originally published 1925), pp. 47–62.

Butler, Judith (1997) *Psychic Life of Power*. Stanford: Stanford University Press.

Cambridge, Alrick X. (1996) 'The Beauty of Valuing Black Cultures' in Amit-Talai, Vered and Knowles, Caroline (eds) *Resituating Identities: The Politics of Race, Ethnicity and Culture*. Peterborough: Broadview Books, pp. 161–183.

Cambridge, Alrick X. and Feuchtwang, Stephan (1992) *Where You Belong*. Aldershot: Avebury.

Caygill, Howard (1997) 'The Futures of Berlin's Potsdamer Platz', in Scott, Alan (ed.) *The Limits of Globalization*. London: Routledge, pp. 25–54.

Chamberlain, Mary (1994) 'Family and Identity: Barbadian Migrants to Britain' in Benmayor, Rina and Scotness, Andor (1994) *Migration and Identity*. Oxford: Oxford University Press, pp. 119–136.

Chamberlayne, Prue and King, Annette (2000) *Cultures of Care. Biographies of Carers in Britain and the Two Germanies*. Bristol: Policy 2000.

Clifford, James (1994) 'Diasporas', *Cultural Anthropology* 9 (3): 302–38.

Cohen, Anthony (1994a) 'Boundaries of Consciousness and Consciousness of Boundaries', Vermeulen, Hans and Govers, Cora (eds) *The Anthropology of Ethnicity. Beyond Ethnic Groups and Boundaries*. Amsterdam: Het Spinhuis pp. 59–80.

Cohen, Anthony (1994b) *Self Consciousness. An Alternative Anthropology of Identity*. London: Routledge.

Cohen, Philip (1998a) *The Last Island*. London: Centre for New Ethnicities Research.

Cohen, Philip (1998b) 'Who Needs an Island', *New Formations* 33: 11–37.

Cohen, Philip (1997) 'Labouring Under Whiteness', in Frankenberg, Ruth (ed.) *Displacing Whiteness*. Durham, North Carolina: Duke University Press, pp. 244–82.

Cohen, Philip (1996) 'All White on the Night? Narratives of Nativism on the Isle of Dogs', in Butler, Tim and Rustin, Michael (eds) *Rising in the East*. London: Lawrence and Wishart, pp. 170–214.

Cohen, Philip (1993) *Home Rules. Some Reflections on Racism and Nationalism in Everyday Life*. London: New Ethnicities Unit, University of East London.

Colley, Linda (1992) *Britons*. London: Vintage.

Conyers, James L. (1999a) 'Maulana Karenga Kawaida and Phenomenology. An Intellectual Study' in Conyers, James (ed.) *Black Lives: Essays in African American Biography*. Armonk, New York: M.E. Sharpe, pp. 3–17.

Conyers, James L. (1999b) (ed.) *Black Lives: Essays in African American Biography*. Armonk, New York: M.E. Sharpe.

Cross, Malcolm and Keith, Michael (1993) (eds). 'Racism and the Post Modern City', in Cross, Malcolm and Keith, Michael *Racism, the City and the State*. London: Routledge, pp. 1–30.

Crossley, Nick (1994) *The Politics of Subjectivity*. Aldershot: Avebury.

Dahya, Badr (1974) 'The Nature of Pakistani Ethnicity in Industrial Cities in Britain' in Cohen, A. (ed.) *Urban Ethnicity*. London: Tavistock. pp. 77–118.

Dallmayr, Fred R. (1981) *Twilight of Subjectivity: Contributions to a Post-Individualist Theory of Politics*. Amhearst: University of Massachusetts Press.

Dalziell, Rosamund (1999) *Shameful Autobiographies: Shame in Contemporary Australian Autobiographies and Culture*. Victoria: Melbourne University Press.

Davis, Olga Idriss (1999) 'Life Ain't Been No Crystal Stair. The Rhetoric of Autobiography in Black Female Slave Narratives' in Conyers, James L. (ed.) *Black Lives: Essays in African American Biography*. Armonk, New York: M.E. Sharpe, pp. 151–59.

de Certeau, Michel (1989) *The Practice of Everyday Life*. Berkeley: Los Angeles.

Denzin, Norman (1989) *Interpretive Biography*. Beverly Hills: Sage.

Durrschmidt, Jorg (1997) 'The Delinking of Locale and Milieux' in Eade, John (ed.) *Living the Global City*. London: Routledge, pp. 56–70.

Dyck, Noel (1991) *What is the Indian 'Problem': Tutelage & Resistance in Canadian Indian Administration*. Newfoundland: ISER, Memorial University.

Dyer, Richard (1997) *White*. London: Routledge.

Eade, John (1997) 'Reconstructing Places' in Eade, John (ed.) *Living the Global City*. London: Routledge pp. 127–45.

Editorial Introduction (1993) Sociology. *Special Issue Auto/Biography in Sociology*, 27 (1): 1–4.

Elwert, Georg, Feuchtwang, Stephan and Neubert, Dieter (1999) 'Dynamics of Violence', *Sociologus*, supplement, 1: 9–31.

Erben, Michael (1999) 'Failure and two Jewish lives: A Biographical approach to Franz Kafka and Walter Benjamin', *Auto/Biography* vii (1 & 2): 13–9.

Erben, Michael (1993) 'The Problem of Other Lives: Social Perspectives on Written Biography', *Sociology* 27 (1): 15–26.

Fanon, Franz (1986 edition) *Black Skin, White Masks*. London: Pluto Press.

Fanon, Franz (1967) *Black Skin, White Masks*. New York: Grove Press.

Faris, R.E.L and Dunham, H.W. (1965) *Mental Disorders in Urban Areas: An Ecological Study of Schizophrenia and Other Psychoses*. Chicago: University of Chicago Press, originally published in 1939.

Farrar, Max (1997) 'Migrant Spaces and Settlers' Time' in Westwood, Sallie and Williams, John (eds) *Imagining Cities*. London: Routledge, pp. 104–24.

Featherstone, Mike and Lash, Scott (1995) 'Introduction' in Featherstone, Lash and Robertson (eds) *Global Modernities*. London: Routledge, pp. 1–23.

Feuchtwang, Stephan (1992) 'Policing the Streets' in Cambridge, Alrick X. and Feuchtwang, Stephan (eds) *Where You Belong*. Aldershot: Avebury, pp. 94–107.

Feuchtwang, Stephan (1975) 'The Discipline and its Sponsors', in Asad, Talal *Anthropology and the Colonial Encounter*. London: Ithaca Press, 71–102.

Findlay, A.M. (1988) 'From Settlers to Skilled Transients: the Changing Structure of British International Migration', *Geoforum*, 19 (4): 401–10.

Fishman, William J. (1975) *East End Jewish Radicals 1875–1914*. London: Duckworth.

Foucault, Michel (1977) *Discipline and Punish: the Birth of the Prison*. London: Penguin.

Frankenberg, Ruth (1993) *White Women, Race Matters: The Social Construction of Whiteness*. Minneapolis: University of Minnesota Press.

Freeman, Mark (1993) *Rewriting the Self*. London: Routledge.

Gallagher, Charles A. (1995) 'White Reconstruction in the University' *Socialist Review*, 24 (1 & 2): 165–87.

Giddens, Anthony (1990) *The Consequences of Modernity*. Stanford: Stanford University Press.

Giddens, Anthony (1987) *Social Theory and Modern Sociology*. London: Polity Press.

Gilroy, Paul (1993) *The Black Atlantic*. Cambridge, Mass: Harvard University Press.

Goffman, Irving (1986) *Asylums*. Harmondsworth: Penguin.

Goldberg, David Theo (1993) *Racist Culture*. Oxford: Blackwell.

Gordon, Paul (1986) *Racial Violence and Harassment*. London: Runnymede Trust.

Goswami, Manu (1996) '"Englishness" on the Imperial Circuit: Mutiny Tours in Colonial South Asia', *Journal of Historical Sociology* 9 (1): 54–84.

Guardian 3 September 2001

Guardian 7 August 2001

Guardian 27 March 2000

Handbook of Texas online tsha.utexas.edu/handbook/online/articles

Gunaratnam, Yasmin and Lewis, Gail (2001) 'Racialising Emotional Labour and Emotionalising Racialised Labour' *Journal of Social Work Practice 2.*

Gunder Frank, Andre (1969) *Latin America: Underdevelopement or Revolution.* New York: Monthly Review Press.

Hall, Stuart (1991a) 'The Local and the Global' in King, Anthony (ed.) *Culture, Globalization and the World System.* Binghampton: State University of New York, pp. 19–40.

Hall, Stuart (1991b) 'Old and New Identities, Old and New Ethnicities', in King, Anthony (ed.) *Culture, Globalization and the World System.* Binghampton: State University of New York, pp. 41–68.

Hale, Grace Elizabeth (1998), *Making Whiteness: the Culture of Segregation in the South 1890–1940.* New York: Pantheon Books.

Hannerz, Ulf (1998) 'Reporting from Jerusalem', *Cultural Anthropology* 13: 548–74.

Hannerz, Ulf (1997) 'Borders' *International Journal of Science,* 49 (4): 537–48.

Hartigan, John (1999) *Racial Situations: Class Predicaments of Whiteness in Detroit.* Princeton, New Jersey: Princeton University Press.

Havens, Timothy (2000) 'The Biggest Show in the World: Race and the Global Popularity of the Cosby Show', *Media, Culture and Society* 22: 371–91.

Held, David, McGrew, Anthony, Goldblatt, David and Perraton, Jonathan (1999), *GLOBAL Transformations.* London: Polity.

Herzfeld, Michael (1992) *The Social Production of Indifference*: *Exploring the Symbolic Roots of Western Bureaucracy.* New York, Oxford: Berg.

Hesse, Barnor (1999) 'Reviewing the Western Spectacle: Reflexive Globalization through the Black Diaspora', in Brah, Avtar, Hickman, Mary, and Mac an Ghaill, Maitrin (eds) *Global Futures: Migration, Environment and Globalization.* London: Macmillan, pp. 122–143.

Hesse, Barnor (1997) 'White Governmentality: Urbanism, Nationalism, Racism' in Westwood, Sallie and Williams, John (eds) *Imagining Cities.* London: Routledge, pp. 86–103.

Hirst, Paul and Thompson, Graham (1995) 'Globalization and the Future of the Nation State', *Economy and Society* 24 (3): 408–42.

Hobsbawn, Eric (1991) 'Exile: A Keynote Address', *Social Research,* 58 (1): 65–8.

Holdaway, Simon (1996) *The Racialization of British Policing.* Basingstoke: Macmillan.

Hollander, John (1991) 'It All Depends', *Social Research,* 58 (1): 31–50.

Iacovetta, Franca (1998) (ed.) 'Making "New Canadians": Social Workers, Women, and the Reshaping of Immigrant Families' in Iacovetta, Franca (ed.) *A Nation of Immigrants.* Toronto: University of Toronto Press, pp. 482–13.

Ilcan, Susan M. (1998) 'Occupying the Margins: On Spacing Gender and Gendering Space, *Space and Culture* No. 3. pp. 5–15.

Jackson, Peter (1981) 'Paradoxes of Puerto Rican Segregation in New York' in Peach, Ceri Robinson, Vaughn Smith, Susan (eds). *Ethnic Segregation in Cities.* London: Croom Helm, pp. 109–126.

James, Daniel (1979) 'Police-Black Relations: the Professional Solution' in Holdaway, Simon (ed.) *The British Police.* London: Edward Arnold, pp. 66–82.

Jary, David and Jary, Julia (1991) *Collins Dictionary of Sociology.* London: Harper Collins.

John (2000), Personal interview, unpublished.

Kachun, Mitchell (1999) 'The Shaping of a Public Biography. Richard Allen and the African Methodist Episcopal Church', in Conyers, James L. (ed.) *Black Lives: Essays in African American Biography.* Armonk, New York: M.E. Sharpe, pp. 44–63.

Kay, Diana and Miles, Robert (1992) *Refugees or Migrant Workers?* London: Routledge.

Kearns, Gerry (1997) 'The Imperial Subject: Geography and Travel in the Work of Mary Kingsley and Halford Mackinder', *Transactions of the Institute of British Geographers,* 22: 450–72.

Kenan, Randall (1999) *Walking on Water: Black American Lives at the Turn of the Twenty-first Century.* Littlebrown and Company: London.

Kettle, Martin and Hodges, Lucy (1982) *Uprising. The Police, The People and the Riots in Britain's Cities.* London: Pan Books.

King, Anthony (1997) *Globalization and the World System.* Minneapolis: University of Minnesota Press.

King, Elaine (1998) 'I've Always Felt Like a Parcel' in *Origins: Personal Stories of Crossing the Seas to Settle in Britain.* Bristol: The Kumba Project, pp. 40–41.

Kingsley, Mary (1982) *Travels in West Africa.* London: Virago.

Knowles, Caroline (2000a) *Bedlam on the Streets.* London: Routledge.

Knowles, Caroline (2000b) 'Home and Away: Maps of Personal and Territorial Expansion 1860–97', *The European Journal of Women's Studies* 7: 263–80.

Knowles, Caroline (1999) 'The Symbolic Empire and the History of Racial Inequality' in Bulmer, Martin and Solomos, John (eds) *Ethnic and Racial Studies Today.* London: Routledge.

Knowles, Caroline (1996a) 'Racism, Biography and Psychiatry', in Amit-Talai, Vered and Knowles, Caroline (eds) *Resituating Identities: the Politics of Race, Ethnicity and Culture.* Peterborough: Broadview Press, pp. 47–67.

Knowles, Caroline (1996b) *Family Boundaries: the Invention of Normality and Dangerousness.* Peterborough: Broadview Press.

Knowles, Caroline (1992) *Race, Discourse and Labourism.* London: Routledge.

Knowles, Caroline (1979) 'Labour and Anti-Semitism: An account of the political discourse surrounding the Labour Party's involvement with anti-semitism in East London 1934–6' in, Miles, Robert and Phizacklea, Annie (eds) *Racism and Political Action in Britain.* London: Routledge.

Kushner, Tony and Knox, Katherine (1999) *Refugees in an Age of Genocide.* London: Frank Cass.

League Against Imperialism (1929) Nehru's Letters. Oral History Archive, Nehru Memorial Library, Delhi.

Lechner, Frank J. (1991) 'Simmel on Social Space', *Theory, Culture and Society,* 8: 195–201.

Lefebvre, Henri (1996) *The Production of Space.* Oxford: Blackwell.

Lefebvre, Henri, (1994) *Everyday Life in the Modern World.* New Brunswick: Transaction Publishers.

Lesy, Michael (1973) *Wisconsin Death Trip.* Albuquerque: University of New Mexico Press.

Levi, Primo (2000) *The Drowned and the Saved.* London: Abacus.

Lieberman, Marian (1998) 'The Long Journey of Beginning', in *Origins: Personal Stories of Crossing the Seas to Settle in Britain.* Bristol: The Kumba Project, pp. 32–38.

Lustiger-Thaler, Henri (1996) 'Remembering Forgetfully', in Amit-Talai, Vered and Knowles, Caroline (eds) *Resituating Identities: the Politics of Race, Ethnicity and Culture.* Peterborough: Broadview Press pp. 190–217.

MacGaffey, Janet and Bazenguissa-Ganga, Remy (2000) *Congo–Paris. Transnational Traders on the Margins of the Law.* Oxford: James Currey.

Margolis, Maxine (1998) *An Invisible Minority: Brazillians in New York City.* Needham Heights, Mass.: Allyn and Bacon.

Mason, David (1994) 'On the Dangers of Disconnecting Race and Racism', *Sociology,* 28 (4): 845–58.

Mason, Jeffrey (1996) 'Street Fairs: Social Space, Social performance', *Theatre Journal* 48: 301–19.

Massey, Doreen (1999) 'Imagining Globalization: Power Geometries of Time-Space', in Brah, Avtar et al. *Global Futures.* London: Macmillan, pp. 27–44.

Massey, Doreen (1994) *Place, Space and Gender.* Cambridge: Polity.

Massey, Doreen (1993) 'Politics and Space/Time' in Keith, Michael and Pile, Steve (eds) *Place and the Politics of Identity.* London: Routledge, pp. 141–61.

Massey, Doreen (1991) 'A Global Sense of Place', *Marxism Today,* June issue, pp. 24–9.

Mauss, Marcel (1992) 'Techniques of the Body' in Crary, Jonathan and Kwinter, Sanford (eds) *Incorporations.* New York: Zone, pp. 455–77. First published in 1934.

Mauss, Marcel (1986) 'A Category of the Human Mind: The Notion of Person; the Notion of self', in Carrithers, Michael, Collins, Steven and Lukes, Steven (eds) *The Category of the Person.* Cambridge: Cambridge University Press.

Mazzoleni, Donatella (1993) 'The City and the Imaginary', in Carter, Erica, Donald, James and Squires, Judith (eds) *Space and Place: Theories of Identity and Location.* London: Lawrence and Wishart, pp. 285–302.

McBride, James (1996) *The Colour of Water: A Black Man's Tribute to his White Mother.* New York: Riverhead Books.

McClintock, Anne (1995) *Imperial Leather.* London: Routledge.

McClinton, Calvin A. (1999) 'Vinnette Carroll African American Director and Playwright', in Conyers, James L. (ed.) *Black Lives: Essays in African American Biography.* Armonk, New York: M.E. Sharpe.

McLean, Poly (1995) 'Mass Communication, Popular Culture and Racism', in Bowser, Benjamin (1995) (ed.) *Racism and Anti-Racism in World Perspective.* Thousand Oaks: Sage, pp. 83–114.

Mead, George H. (1952) *Mind, Self and Society.* Chicago: University of Chicago Press.

Mercer, Kobena (1994) *Welcome to the Jungle.* London: Routledge.

Merton, Robert K. (1988) 'Some Thoughts on the Concept of Sociological Autobiography', in Riley, M.W. (ed.) *Sociological Lives.* Newbury Park: Sage. pp. 17–34.

Miles, Robert (1999) 'Analysing the Political Economy of Migration: the Airport as an "Effective" Institution of Control', in Brah, Avtar, Hickman, Mary and Mac an Ghaill, Maitrin (eds) *Global Futures.* London: Macmillan.

Miles, Robert (1994) 'Explaining Racism in Contemporary Europe', in Rattansi, Ali and Westwood, Sallie (eds) *Racism, Modernity and Identity.* London: Polity, pp. 189–221.

Miles, Robert (1989) *Racism.* London: Routledge.

Miles, Robert and Torres, Rudi (1996) 'Does "Race" Matter? Transatlantic Perspectives on Racism after Race Relations', in Amita-Talai, V. and Knowles, C. (eds) *Resituating Identities: the Politics of Race, Ethnicity and Culture.* Peterborough: Broadview Press, pp. 24–46.

Miles, Robert and Phizacklea, Annie (1980) *Labour and Racism.* London: Routledge.

Miles, Robert and Phizacklea, Annie (1979) (eds) *Racism and Political Action in Britain.* London: Routledge.

Minh-ha, Trihn T. (1994) 'Other than myself/my other self', in Robertson, George, Marsh, Melinda, Tickner, Lisa, Bird, John, Curtis, Barry and Putnam, Tim (eds) *Travellers' Tales: Narratives of Home & Displacement.* London: Routledge.

Modood, Tariq (1994) 'Political Blackness and British Asians', in *Sociology,* 28 (4): 859–76.

Neeman, Rina (1994) 'Invented Ethnicity as Collective and Personal text: An Association of Rumanian Israelis', *Anthropological Quarterly* 67 (3): 135–49.

Neill, Alan W. (1923) *Official report of Debates in the House of Commons,* Ottawa: King's Publisher, Vol. 5 pp. 4643–49.

New Statesman and Nation 3 November 1934: 615.

New Statesman and Nation 16 June 1934: 904–5.

Nhui, Mai (1998) 'Freedom', in *Origins: Personal Stories of Crossing the Seas to Settlle in Britain.* Bristol: The Kumba Project, pp. 24–29.

Nightingale, Carl H. (1999) 'How Lynchings Became High-Tech, and Other tales from the Modern South', Reviews in American History 27: 140–48.

Ohio Historical Society Website, ohiohistory.org.africanam.

Ongley, Patrick (1995) 'Post-1945 International Migration: New Zealand, Australia and Canada Compared'. *International Migration Review* xxix (3): pp. 765–93.

Park, Robert E. (1967) 'The City: Suggestions for the Investigation of Human Behaviour in an Urban Environment', in Park, Robert E., Burgess, Morris and McKenzie, Roderick D. (eds) *The City.* Chicago: University of Chicago Press, originally published 1925, pp. 1–46.

Patterson, Brent O. (1991) *Popular Narratives and Ethnic Identity.* Ithaca: Cornell University Press.

Peach, Ceri (1975) (ed.) *Urban Social Segregation.* London: Longman.

Peach, Ceri, Robinson, Vaughn and Smith, Susan (1981) *Ethnic Segregation in Cities.* London: Croom Helm.

Pile, Steve and Thrift, Nigel (1995) 'Introduction', in Pile, Steve and Thrift, Nigel (eds) *Mapping the Subject.* London: Routledge, pp. 1–12.

Pinney, Chris (2001) 'Creole Europe', paper presented at the Visual Strategies Conference, *The Beautiful and the Damned*, National Portrait Gallery, London, October 5 and 6, 2001.

Portelli, Alessandro (1991) *The Death of Luigi Trastulli and Other Stories*. Suny: New York University.

Pred, Alan (1997) 'Somebody Else, Somewhere Else: Racisms, Racialized Spaces and the Popular Geographical Imagination in Sweden' *Antipode* 29 (4): 383–416.

Rapport, Nigel (1999) 'Life with a hole, howl, hill, hull in it: Philip Larkin at life's crossroads', *Auto/biography*, vii (1 & 2): 3–12.

Rapport, Nigel (1995) 'Migrant Selves and Stereotypes. Personal Context in a Postmodern World' in Pile, Steve and Thrift, Nigel (eds) *Mapping the Subject*. London: Routledge, pp. 267–282.

Reed, Kate (2000) 'Dealing with Difference: Researching Health Beliefs and Behaviours of British Asian Mothers', *Sociological Research on Line* 4 (4).

Rex, John (1981) 'Urban Segregation and Inner City Policy in Great Britain' in Peach, Ceri, Robinson, Vaughn Smith, Susan (eds) *Ethnic Segregation in Cities*. London: Croom Helm. pp. 25–44.

Rex, John and Moore, Robert (1967) *Race, Community and Conflict: A Study of Sparkbrook*. London: Oxford University Press for the Institute of Race Relations.

Rice, Alan (1996) '"Ethnic Memory". A Review of Amritjit Singh, Joseph T. Skerrett Jn, and Robert E. Hoganl (eds) Memory and Cultural Politics' in *New Approaches to American Ethnic Literatures*. Boston: Northeastern University Press, pp. 156–59.

Richardson, Janet (2000) (ed.) *David MacPherson CIE The Raj: a Time Remembered. Recollections of a Life in the Indian Civil Service*. Edinburgh: The Portland Press.

Richmond, Anthony (1992) 'Immigration and Structural Change: The Canadian Experience' *International Migration Review* xxiv (4): 1200–1221.

Riggs, Fred W. (1998) 'The Modernity of Ethnic Identity and Conflict', *International Political Science Review* 19 (3): 269–88.

Robertson, Roland (1995) 'Glocalization: Time-Space and Homogeneity-Heterogeneity', in Featherstone, Michael, Lash, Scott and Robertson, Roland (eds) *Global Modernities*. London: Sage.

Roderick, Ian (1998) 'Habitable Spaces', *Space and Culture* No. 3. pp. 1–4.

Roediger, David (1994) *Towards the Abolition of Whiteness*. London: Verso.

Roediger, David (1992) *The Wages of Whiteness: Race and the Making of the American Working Class*. London: Verso.

Roosens, Eugeen (1994) 'The primordial nature of origins in migrant ethnicity', Vermeulen, Hans and Govers, Cora (eds) *The Anthropology of Ethnicity. Beyond Ethnic Groups and Boundaries*. Amsterdam: Het Spinhuis pp. 81–104.

Roosens, Eugeen (1989) *Creating Ethnicity*. Newbury Park: Sage.

Rose, Harold (1981), 'The Black Professional and Residential Segregation in the American City' in Peach, Ceri, Robinson, Vaughn and Smith, Susan (eds) *Ethnic Segregation in Cities*. London: Croom Helm pp. 127–48.

Roseman, Mark (2000) *The Past in Hiding*. London: Penguin.

Rutherford, Jonathan (1997) *Forever England. Reflections on Masculinity and Empire*. London: Lawrence and Wishart.

Rykwert, Joseph (1991) 'House and Home', *Social Research*, 58 (1): 51–64.

Sack, Robert David (1980) *Conceptions of Space in Social Thought: A Geographic Perspective*. London: Macmillan.

Said, Edward (1999) *Out of Place*. London: Granta.

Said, Edward (1994) *Culture and Imperialism*. London: Vintage.

Samuel, T.J. (1988) 'Family Class Immigrants to Canada. 1981–1984', *International Migration* xxvi (2): 171–299.

Sandoval, Chela (1997) 'Theorizing White Consciousness for a Post Empire World: Barthes, Fanon and the Rhetoric of Love', in Frankenberg, Ruth (ed.) *Displacing Whiteness*. Durham, North Carolina: Duke University Press, pp. 86–106.

Sassen, Saskia (1991) *The Global City*. Princeton: Princeton University Press.

Sassen, Saskia (1990) 'U.S. Immigration Policy Towards Mexico in a Global Economy', *Journal of International Affairs* 43 (2): 369–383.

Schama, Simon (1991) 'Homelands', *Social Research,* 58 (1): 11–30.

Scheper-Hughes, Nancy (2000) 'The Global Traffic in Human Organs', *Current Anthropology,* 41 (2): 191–224.

Schueller, Malini Johar (1999) 'Performing Whiteness, Performing Blackness: Dorr's Cultural Capital and the Critique of Slavery', *Criticism* 41 (2): 233–56.

Shotter, John (1997) 'The Social Construction of our Inner Selves', *Journal of Constructionist Psychology,* 10: 7–24.

Smith, Michael Peter and Torallo, Bernadette (1993) 'The Post-modern City and the Social Construction of Ethnicity in California' in Cross, Malcolm and Keith, Michael (eds) *Racism, the City and the State.* London:Routledge, pp. 61–76.

Smith, Paul (1988) *Discerning the Subject.* Minneapolis: University of Minnesota Press.

Smith, Susan J. (1993) 'Residential segregation and the Politics of Racialization', in Cross, Malcolm and Keith, Michael (eds) *Racism, the City and the State.* London: Routledge, pp. 128–137.

Soja, Edward (1989) *Postmodern Geographies. The Reassertion of Space in Critical Social Policy.* London: Verso.

Stewart, Kathleen (1996) *A Space on the Side of the Road: Cultural Poetics in an 'Other' America.* Princeton: Princeton University Press.

Sunday Times 24 June 2001.

Tatla, Darshan Singh (1993) 'This is Our Home Now: Reminiscences of a Punjabi Migrant in Coventry. An Interview with Anant Ram' *Oral History* 21 (1): 68–74.

Taylor, Charles (1989) *Sources of the Self.* Cambridge: Cambridge University Press.

Thomson, Colin A. (1979) *Blacks in Deep Snow. Black Pioneers in Canada.* Toronto: J.M. Dent and Sons Ltd.

Turner, Bryan (1994) *Orientalism, Postmodernism and Globalization.* London: Routledge.

Urry, John (1995) *Consuming Places.* London: Routledge.

Valdez, Norberto and Janice (1998) 'The Pot that Called the Kettle White: Changing Racial Identities and U.S. Social Constructions of Race', *Identities,* 5 (3): 379–413.

Van Tong, Mai (1998) 'Life After Vietnam', in *Origins: Personal Stories of Crossing the Seas to Settle in Britain.* Bristol: The Kumba Project, pp. 56–65.

Verdery, Katherine (1994) 'Ethnicity, nationalism and state-making', Vermeulen, Hans and Govers, Cora (eds) (1994) *The Anthropology of Ethnicity. Beyond Ethnic Groups and Boundaries.* Amsterdam: Het Spinhuis pp. 33–58.

Wanderer, Philip (1994) 'Introduction to the Transaction Edition', Lefebvre, Henri, *Everyday Life in the Modern World.* New Brunswick: Transaction Publishers. pp. vii–xxiii.

Ward, Peter W. (1990) *White Canada for Ever.* Montreal and Kingston: McGill-Queen's University Press.

Wengraf, Tom (2000) *Short Guide to Biographical – Narrative Interviewing and Analysis by the SQUIN – BNIM Method.* Unpublished.

Williams, Colin and Smith, Anthony (1983) 'The National Construction of Social Space' *Progress in Human Geography* 7 (4): 502–18.

Williams, Dorothy (1989) *Blacks In Montreal 1628–1989: An Urban Ethnography.* Cowansville, Quebec: Les Editions Yvon Blais.

Wilson, William Julius (1999) 'When Work Disappears: new implications for race and urban poverty in the global economy', *Ethnic and Racial Studies,* 22 (3): 479–499.

Wilton, Robert D. (1998) 'The Constitution of Difference: Space and the Psyche in Landscapes of Exclusion', *Geoforum* 29 (2): 137–185.

Winant, Howard (2000) 'The Theoretical Status of the Concept Race' in Back, Les and Solomos, John *Theories of Race and Racism,* London: Routledge.

Winant, Howard (1994a) *Racial Conditions.* Minneapolis: University of Minnesota Press.

Winant, Howard (1994b) 'Racial Formation and Hegemony: Global and Local Developments' in Rattansi, Ali and Westwood, Sallie (eds) *Racism, Modernity and Identity.* London: Polity Press, pp. 266–289.

Wong, Bernard (1998) *Ethnicity and Entrepreneurship.* Needham Heights, Mass: Allyn & Bacon.

Wong, David W.S. (1993) 'Spatial Indices of segregation', *Urban Studies* 30 (3). 559–572.

Wright Mills, C. (1970) *The Sociological Imagination.* London, Oxford: Oxford University Press.

Yi, Kris and Shorter-Gooden, Kumea (1999) 'Ethnic Identity Formation: from Stage Theory to a Constructivist Narrative Model', *Psychotherapy* 36 (1): 16–26.

Zack-Williams, Alfred (1999) 'Sierra Leone: the political economy of civil war, 1991–98', Third World Quarterly 20 (1): 143–62.

Zinn, Dorothy Louise (1994) 'The Senegalese Immigrants in Bari: What Happens When Africa Peers Back' in Benmayor, Rina and Scotness, Andor (1994) *Migration and Identity.* Oxford: Oxford University Press, pp. 53–68.

Zizek, Slavoj (1996) *The Indivisible Remainder.* London: Verso.

Zlotnik, Hania (1999) 'Trend in International Migration since 1965: What Existing Data Reveal', *International Migration* 37 (1): 21–61.

Index